COURSE CHANGE
The Whaleship *Stonington* in the
Mexican-American War

PETER J. EMANUEL, JR.

Essex, Connecticut

An imprint of Globe Pequot, the trade division of
The Rowman & Littlefield Publishing Group, Inc.
4501 Forbes Blvd., Ste. 200
Lanham, MD 20706
www.rowman.com

Distributed by NATIONAL BOOK NETWORK

British Library Cataloguing in Publication Information available

Library of Congress Cataloging-in-Publication Data

Names: Emanuel, Peter J., Jr., author.
Title: Course change : the whaleship Stonington in the Mexican-American War / Peter J. Emanuel Jr.
Other titles: Whaleship Stonington in the Mexican-American War
Description: Essex, Connecticut : Lyons Press, 2024. | Includes bibliographical references and index.
Identifiers: LCCN 2023033859 (print) | LCCN 2023033860 (ebook) | ISBN 9781493074617 (cloth) | ISBN 9781493074624 (epub)
Subjects: LCSH: Stonington (Whaleship) | Mexican War, 1846-1848—California—San Diego. | Seafaring life—California—History—19th century. | Whaling ships—United States—History. | San Diego (Calif.)—History, Naval—19th century. | Mexican War, 1846-1848—Naval operations, American.
Classification: LCC E405.2 .E436 2024 (print) | LCC E405.2 (ebook) | DDC 979.4/98503—dc23/eng/20230912
LC record available at https://lccn.loc.gov/2023033859
LC ebook record available at https://lccn.loc.gov/2023033860

∞™ The paper used in this publication meets the minimum requirements of American National Standard for Information Sciences—Permanence of Paper for Printed Library Materials, ANSI/NISO Z39.48-1992.

for Patti, my navigator

CONTENTS

Contents

FORE WORDS

This book began as a short article that I wrote in the spring of 2012 as part of an application for a summer internship at Mystic Seaport Museum in Mystic, Connecticut. The Seaport was looking for history teachers in the local area that would be willing to research and develop stories about items in its vast collection, with the intent of invigorating its website. Among the items in the application's list of choices for research was the logbook of the *Stonington*, a whaleship that had been owned by the Williams & Barns whaling firm. The Williams in this case was none other than Thomas W. Williams II, the man after whom the school at which I taught—The Williams School in New London, Connecticut—had been named. I thought this would be an interesting tie-in to the school, so I decided to use it for my application.

The first section of the logbook was, as I had expected, a series of entries about weather and whaling activities. Suddenly, the focus shifted, and I found myself reading about interactions between the ship and the people of San Diego, California. The accounts continued in that manner until I realized that this was no ordinary logbook. This was a daily record of the *Stonington*'s direct involvement in the Mexican-American War of 1846–1848, an involvement that lasted for four months. I had found a story within a story, and I knew I had to tell it.

It wasn't until I retired in 2020 after twenty-nine years of teaching that I was able to devote substantial and continuous time to writing this book. While doing further research, I discovered many interesting facts about the people with whom the *Stonington* came into contact while serving in the Mexican-American War, and about the war itself. I knew, however, that I needed to maintain my focus on telling the story of the

Stonington and not go off on tangents that would interrupt the flow of the narrative. Instead, I have included some biographical sketches at the end of the book. I leave it to the reader to investigate further the background, conduct, and aftermath of the Mexican-American War, a very significant and controversial conflict that would ultimately change the course of history for the United States. When the war was finally over in 1848, the country had acquired a large swath of territory, and the debate over which portions of that territory should be slaveholding or free would consume the nation until the argument boiled over and became a full-fledged civil war only thirteen years later.

The main and guiding source for this book is the *Stonington* logbook. Throughout my research, I cross-referenced and confirmed the information within this record before including it in my book. The nature of most logbooks, including this one, is such that their writers restricted themselves to recording "just the facts" in a very terse manner. On rare occasions, they would briefly reference some pertinent dialogue. My challenge, therefore, was to expand on the information in such a way as to bring the events and characters to life for the reader while still remaining faithful to the details and historical context of the logbook.

In many cases, it was contemporary primary sources that provided the additional material. The names and physical descriptions of the *Stonington*'s crew are derived from the ship's crew list. The words that the characters speak to one another stem from the interactions, and their logical extensions, that occurred within the logbook. During my writing process, I would sit quietly and place myself among the people involved in a given scene, listening to what they were "saying," all the while maintaining a sense of their time and the language they would have used. Whenever a word or expression, such as "okay," seemed too modern for their usage, I would research it to be certain that it was contemporary to them. The story that you are about to read, therefore, is based on the historic adventures of the *Stonington*, its crew, and those with whom they came in contact during the more-than-one-year period that stretched from August 1846 to September 1847.

Krystal Kornegay Rose is the Mystic Seaport Museum representative who came to The Williams School during a faculty meeting in the spring of 2012 to tell us about the Interactive Artifact Records project at the Seaport. My acceptance into that project provided me with the opportunity to work closely with her and Laura Nadelberg, as well as with other members of the Seaport staff, including Sarah Cahill, Fred Calabretta, Paul O'Pecko, Maribeth Bielinski Quinlan, and Carol Mowrey. I am perpetually grateful to all of them for their friendly and knowledgeable assistance during my time at the Seaport, a truly world-class facility.

Katy Phillips at the San Diego History Center assisted me for three very full hours in May of 2022, pulling material from the Center's archives and recommending sources. Megan Turner Ball provided me with excellent advice about the publishing process, and she kindly critiqued my book proposal. Eugene Brissie at Lyons Press graciously took a chance on this first-time author, for which I am extremely grateful. Also at Lyons, Felicity Tucker deftly oversaw the book's production phase, Melissa Hayes offered many cogent edits after her obviously careful reading, and Jason Rossi provided helpful guidance on marketing.

My good friend and master of woodworking and yacht joinery Bill Taylor endured my barrage of questions and provided humorous, keen insights on all things nautical.

My daughters, Emily and Kaylin; my sons, Spencer and Clancy; my son-in-law, Eric; my daughter-in-law, Kara; and Nathan Towry were constant sources of encouragement and inspiration. Special thanks go to Spencer for creating the maps and illustrations that are included in the book.

Above all, I thank my wife, Patti, for keeping me on point with this project. She guides me regularly with her pragmatic approach to life. Her honest evaluations and probing questions during the research and writing phases resulted in a book that is much more coherent and focused than it would have been if I were working alone. She, of course, knows that, but I wanted to put it in print.

PART I

CHAPTER I

A Whaleship . . . for Now

"WE'RE THROWING IT ALL OVERBOARD?"

"All that work for nothing!"

"Whose ship is this, anyway?"

"He must be out of his mind!"

Frustration and disbelief were in the air after Second Officer Alanson Fournier delivered the orders from Captain George W. Hamley that the crew of the *Stonington* had to clear the storage area. This was, after all, a whaleship, meant to hold barrels of oil that had been processed from the blubber of whales, to be sold to merchants back home in New London—oil that would fuel the lamps that lit homes, oil that would lubricate the machinery that manufactured goods, oil that would make some people very wealthy. Why throw it all away, as if the dangerous and deadly work that it had taken to obtain it meant absolutely nothing? What could possibly be a worthy enough cause for such a wasteful order? They knew the answer, as reluctant as some of them may have been to accept it.[1]

The *Stonington* was a typical whaleship, one hundred feet and four inches in length, with two decks and three masts, the tallest being the center mainmast that rose to a height of nearly ninety feet above the deck, holding five tiers of square sails. The foremast held four tiers of square sails as well as three triangular sails that were also fastened to the bowsprit. The mizzenmast, closest to the stern, carried a four-sided sail and three triangular sails. Under full sail on a clear day, the *Stonington* was an impressive sight, with an array of white billowing canvas set against a bright blue sky, the dark hull gleaming in the deeper blue ocean.

Attached to the bow beneath the bowsprit was a bust of a man with a round head, straight, short hair, a high forehead, and a pointed nose. He was Richard Law, whose many credentials had earned him a great deal of respect. His father, Jonathan, was the twelfth governor of colonial Connecticut. Richard had been a delegate to the Continental Congresses, mayor of the city of New London, and chief judge of the Connecticut Superior Court. In 1789, President George Washington had nominated him, and the United States Senate had confirmed him, as the judge for the US District Court, District of Connecticut.[2]

The *Stonington* was broad, twenty-seven feet and eight inches at the beam, with a bluntly rounded bow and a squared-off stern, its black sides rising twelve feet above the water. It sat in the water at a depth of thirteen feet and ten inches, and it could carry enough cargo to displace over three hundred fifty tons. The ship was sturdy, not sleek, yet it moved through the water with surprising ease. The frame and rigging had to withstand not only the usual challenges of traveling through open seas but also the strains of hauling huge strips of blubber, most of them weighing at least a ton, up onto the deck for processing. The blubber was cut from the body of the whale that the crew had hunted, captured, killed, towed back, and tethered to the starboard side of the ship. As those strips of blubber rose away from the carcass they had encircled and up into the air, the ship leaned down toward the ocean amid the creaking sounds emitted by the ropes and pulleys under the weight of that blubber. When the crew finally maneuvered it over the gunwale and lowered it onto the deck, the release of that tremendous weight allowed the ship to roll back upright. The ship's design certainly meshed very well with its purpose.[3]

The *Stonington* had been at sea for three years, hunting whales throughout the world's vast oceans and encountering the world's remotest islands along the way. Having nearly filled its hold with thousands of gallons of oil contained in wooden casks of various sizes, it was time for the ship to begin making its way home. Twenty-four days in San Francisco after a stretch of hunting in the frigid waters of the Gulf of Alaska had given the crew of around thirty men time to get the ship ready for the lengthy voyage past South America, through the treacherous waters around Cape Horn, and then northward to its home port in Connecticut.

There had also been time in those twenty-four days for carousing and enjoying the diversions that San Francisco offered to those who had been out to sea for so long. The men of the *Stonington* took full advantage of their shore liberty, knowing that the captain intended to limit further stops on the homeward voyage and spend just enough time in selected ports to replenish food and water.[4]

CHAPTER 2

A Time in San Francisco

A WHALESHIP'S STOP AT ANY PORT PROVIDED AN OPPORTUNITY FOR THE crew to take all sorts of action. San Francisco was no exception.

George Mayors, a twenty-nine-year-old seaman from the whaling village of Sag Harbor, New York, decided that it was time to pursue a different profession. He had come aboard in April, while the *Stonington* was at the island of Tubuai in French Polynesia, as the ship steward. He supervised the cook and the meals for the crew, and also worked as the cook and servant in the main cabin for the captain and other officers.

He sought out Second Officer Alanson Fournier, a young man of twenty-three from Long Island, New York. Mayors was much more comfortable speaking to Fournier than Captain Hamley. Like most other whaleship captains, Hamley, a thirty-one-year-old experienced shipmaster from New London, Connecticut, separated himself from the crew in order to maintain his status as commander and chief disciplinarian, seeking to make the men fearful of breaking any of his rules. Fournier, on the other hand, as with most second officers, interacted with the men frequently, and his personality was such that he created an atmosphere of friendly respect.[1]

"A word, Mr. Fournier?"

"What is it, Mayors?"

"I've been thinking, sir—a dangerous activity, I know," said Mayors, "and I've come to the conclusion that I've done all the whaling that I want to do. No offense to you, sir. It's just that I've been at it for nearly half my life, and I'd like to try something different."

"I'll be sorry to see you go, Mayors," said Fournier. "You've been a fine steward, and you know your way around the rigging damn well, too. It'll be hard to find your replacement. I appreciate your honesty, however. There's many a man who wouldn't have thought twice about simply jumping ship without even a fare-thee-well before he left."

"Yes, sir," said Mayors, somewhat embarrassed by the compliment.

"The money you're owed for your work is not aboard this ship, and there's no guarantee we could get it to you once we're back in New London and have settled our affairs. Considering your experience and good service, I'll ask the captain if he'd be willing to offer you payment in oil. What say you to that?"

"I'd be much obliged, sir," answered Mayors in a grateful tone.

"If I may ask, what are you thinking of doing once you leave?"

"I'm not quite sure, sir. I might try my hand at farming. After being on the receiving end with fruits and vegetables for so long, it'd be interesting to come at them from the production side, and I hear the land around these parts is mighty good for growing."

"Lotta work, farming," said Fournier, "but knowing you, I'd say you've got a good chance of making a go of it. Who knows, maybe someday you'll be supplying the ships that come into this port."

"That'd be quite the turn, wouldn't it, sir," said Mayors with a smile.

"Certainly would. Whatever you end up doing, I hope it all goes well for you. I'll be off now to speak with the captain."

The two men shook hands, then Fournier made his way to the captain's cabin.

Hamley listened as Fournier relayed his conversation with Mayors. When he got to the part about the whale oil, Hamley stiffened. "Oil? How much oil?"

"I didn't mention any specific amount, sir," said Fournier, "knowing that you'd have to approve such a payment in the first place."

"Mighty considerate of you, Fournier," said Hamley sarcastically. After some thought, he said, "I suppose we can pay him with a small cask, given his good work, but only because it's Mayors. We can't be tossing oil out of the hold like there's no tomorrow."

"Yes, sir," said Fournier, "and thank you, sir."

And so it was that on August 29, 1846, George Mayors received his discharge papers and a small cask of that precious commodity around which his life had centered for over a decade. He made his way to shore aboard one of the *Stonington's* whaleboats with several of his now-former crewmates, who decided they weren't going to let him go easily.

"What's the matter, George, body gone soft?"

"Finally realized you smell too bad for even the likes of us greasy whalers?"

"What're you going to lubricate with that oil, George?"

The boat came to rest on the sandy shore, and George Mayors waved good-bye and called out the traditional "Greasy luck!" to his companions as he made his way into town and the next phase of his life.

The time spent in San Francisco, known to the Californios as Yerba Buena, was tumultuous for Captain Hamley. His intent on stopping there was to perform some basic maintenance on the ship and restock supplies in order to be prepared for more whaling during the long voyage home. The first few days went according to plan, with some of the crew employed in cleaning and painting the ship, while others went ashore to cut wood and hunt deer. Getting beyond houses and other buildings and into undeveloped land was easier to do at that time. Boats from the *Stonington* came ashore at what would eventually be named Montgomery Street, which later would be just over six blocks inland due to fill that was put in place to satisfy the demand for more land. The crew would cross the sandy beach and walk uphill past widely spaced houses and other buildings of one or two stories until, after about one hundred fifty feet, they would be in open land covered in nothing but low brush and moderately tall trees. They would then begin their work.[2]

The situation was markedly different when, just five days into their stop, the crew received permission from Captain Hamley to go ashore for liberty. Sunday, August 30, 1846, was a beautifully warm day—fair weather, clear skies—perfect conditions for being outdoors. The attractions for the majority of the crew, however, were indoors—grog shops and brothels.

Most of the men maintained a certain amount of self-control while satisfying their desires for drink and sexual gratification, but this was not the case for Henry Thompson, William Wallace, and John Williams. Within moments of walking into the first establishment in their path, the trouble began. The *Stonington* was not the only ship in the port, nor the only one whose crew was on liberty, but these three men behaved as if that were the case.

"Out of my way," barked Williams as he shoved toward the bar, "I've got drinking to do!"

"Keep the lane clear for the both of us!" shouted Wallace, bumping past the men that had started to close the gap behind Williams.

Thompson, the ship's blacksmith, forged his own path to the bar, thrusting his barrel-chested frame through the crowd.

By the time the three of them had reached the bar, the men they had pushed away were primed for a fight.

The trio took their bottle and glasses and went about finding themselves a table. Seeing they were all filled, the men stopped at the nearest one and ordered its three occupants to stand and give up their seats. The seated men refused, but quickly felt themselves being lifted out of their seats and onto the floor. The *Stonington* men had little chance to settle into their commandeered seats, as those they had just deposed, joined by those who had been pushed earlier, descended on them, pummeling them, carrying them to the door, and tossing them out onto the ground.

"That's what we do with the likes of you!"

"Know your place and keep it!"

Those and other cries fell on the ejected men as they attempted to right their bloodied, battered selves. As they did so, a group of men in uniform approached. It was the local police, always on the alert for trouble such as this, which was, for them, a regular occurrence. Within a matter of minutes, Thompson, Wallace, and Williams were shackled and led to the prison.

This was exactly the kind of interruption Captain Hamley wanted to avoid, as he needed every person in the crew to work steadily in order to go back to sea as soon as possible. Three men missing would slow everything down.

The next morning, Hamley sent a boat to town with enough muscle to retrieve the wayward crewmen and bail money in case it was needed.

"I ought to flog each and every one of you!" Hamley shouted as the three men made their way back onto the ship. "But you're in rough enough shape as it is, and I need you to get to work—now! Mind yourselves proper, or by God, I'll give you the lash, no matter the cost! And speaking of cost, your pay at the end of this voyage will be minus the amount of money spent to bail you out."[3]

Matters continued to be complicated for Captain Hamley as the next two weeks progressed. On Wednesday, September 2, he discharged William Wallace and William Peterson, both of whom just wanted a clean break with Hamley and the *Stonington*.

The same could not be said for two other men, Henry Thompson and Francis Bedrake, who deserted the very next day while onshore during a work detail.

Hamley was furious when the boats returned without them. "We've too much to do aboard ship, and the day is fast closing. I'm not sending you back now to find them, but I'll want every last one of you to be looking out for those two tomorrow when you're back onshore!"

So on Friday, while collecting wood and filling casks with fresh water, the men kept their eyes open for any signs of their missing shipmates. Some of them even asked around a bit as they passed through town on their way to and from their work, but to no avail.

When they returned to the ship without Thompson and Bedrake, Hamley looked at them knowingly. *These men aren't going to readily send up two of their own*, he thought.

"Fournier!" Hamley called out to his second officer.

"Aye, sir."

"My quarters."

The two men walked toward the stern of the ship and down the companionway stairs that led belowdecks, to the living area. As opposed to the sailors' bunks that were crowded into the fo'c'sle, where the bow often pounded into the sea, giving the men a rough ride, the captain's cabin was at the stern, where the ride was usually much smoother. The cabin was also quite spacious, containing a sitting room furnished with a sofa and shelves along the back wall, a desk at the front, and a separate bedroom and private head to the side.

"Fournier, I know those men ashore today were not so keen on hauling in their crewmates," Hamley began, once they had entered his quarters. "I expect a higher sense of duty from you. Tomorrow, you'll take five men with you in a boat and retrieve those two deserters. I can't afford to lose two more deckhands when there's so much to be done to be ready to head back to sea. Are we clear?"

"Aye, sir, we're clear."

"Then back up top you go."

Alanson Fournier left Hamley's cabin and headed down the hall toward the companionway that was just beyond his own quarters. The second officer's cabin was a single room, smaller than the captain's bedroom. As Fournier walked by his room, he paused, looked at the door, and pictured the space inside. He glanced back at the door to the captain's quarters for a few seconds, then continued walking.

The boat left for shore Saturday morning, with Fournier and the five men that he had selected for the retrieval of Thompson and Bedrake.

The first place they checked was the prison, Fournier thinking that maybe they had gotten into the same sort of trouble that Thompson, Wallace, and Williams had gotten into nearly a week ago. The police told Fournier that neither of the men they sought was there, nor had been there since the previous offense.

The next place they checked was the grog house, but they weren't there, either. Then Fournier thought to check the brothel. Just as they approached the building, its door opened and there in front of them was Henry Thompson with a contented grin spread across his face. He was about to tell the crewmates standing before him that they had come to the right place when he noticed Alanson Fournier among them.

"Take him," ordered Fournier, and two of the men grabbed Thompson's arms as the others blocked him from going back inside.

"Where's Bedrake?" demanded Fournier.

"Long gone, and good for him," said the blacksmith with a sneer.

Fournier had one of the men check inside, but Thompson was telling the truth.

"Bedrake isn't in there," Thompson said. "He's not even in town. He's taken his chances with another ship. Like I said, long gone."

Fournier had noticed a ship leaving port the day before. He decided to take Thompson at his word and minimize the risk of him getting away while they continued to search for Bedrake.[4]

Fournier led the group back to the boat, and as they boarded and shoved off to return to the ship, he detected resentment among the men he'd taken on this mission. He could see it in their eyes—he had coerced them into becoming enforcers against men of their own kind, setting them apart from their fellows. They didn't like it, and frankly, neither did he. If he was going to seriously pursue his desire to be a ship's captain one day, he would have to learn from this incident. He would need to figure out how to galvanize his crew in the face of adversity, not pit them against one another.

CHAPTER 3

War for California

WHILE IN SAN FRANCISCO, THE MEN OF THE *STONINGTON* LEARNED that a war had been under way between Mexico and the United States since the end of April. The root cause, as is almost always the case in wars among humans, was the acquisition of land. This time, it was the United States seeking to gain control of the western portion of North America before its European rivals, particularly Great Britain, had a chance to beat them to the prize. The British Empire may have lost its thirteen American colonies just over sixty years before, but it had not lost its desire for land in North America. The Oregon Territory, comprising what would eventually become the states of Oregon and Washington, as well as portions of Idaho and the Canadian province of British Columbia, was a huge tract of land rich in natural resources and access to the Pacific Ocean. Great Britain wanted it not only for its intrinsic value, but also as a means of reasserting its power to the upstart nation that had managed to appear victorious against the Empire yet again, this time in the War of 1812.[1]

The United States also wanted to acquire Alta California, an expanse that was currently Mexican territory, comprising what would become the states of California, Nevada, and Utah, and portions of Wyoming, Colorado, New Mexico, and Arizona. Mexico, in its quest to free itself from the colonialism that Spain had imposed on the region since the arrival of its emissary Christopher Columbus to the New World in 1492, had gained its independence from Spain in 1821 and was attempting to assert its control over the territory that Spain had previously claimed for itself.

Unfortunately for Mexico, its government was very young and unstable; its capital (Mexico City) was over a thousand miles away; and the Californios (Californians of Mexican descent) had developed a certain amount of autonomy due to decades of inattention by the Spanish government. All of those factors amounted to a situation that was challenging for Mexico and left California vulnerable.[2]

Caught in the middle of all this were the First Peoples of the land, more than one hundred non-nomadic native tribes spread throughout the territory. For over ten thousand years, the people of these tribes had enjoyed the fruits of the land and the sea, some of them simply harvesting what was available, others planting crops intentionally. Skirmishes and jostling for control of the land broke out occasionally between adjacent tribes, but there was no single tribe that attempted to dominate the entire territory. Their existence as singular groups left them susceptible to being overtaken by an entity seeking such widespread domination.

Spain became that entity when it began its establishment of outposts, known as missions, in 1769, the first of which was San Diego. In less than eighty years, it would be the United States that held such grand designs of conquest, spurred by the belief of many Americans that it was the apparent fate—the "manifest destiny," as editorial columnist John O'Sullivan put it in 1845—of the United States to be a continental nation, stretching from the Atlantic to the Pacific.

It was in this context that President James K. Polk and his supporters set out to accomplish that goal.[3]

CHAPTER 4

Back to Sea

ON WEDNESDAY, SEPTEMBER 16, 1846, CAPTAIN HAMLEY DETERMINED that the *Stonington* was ready for sea. The maintenance work was done, supplies had been restocked, and new crewmen had been recruited. He planned to leave San Francisco the next morning, but Thursday began with strong gales and thick fog, so he decided to wait one more day. Friday the 18th was clearer, with diminished winds. Hamley gave the order to get under way, initiating a flurry of activity.

While some of the men headed for their positions on deck, others climbed the ratlines and made their way up into the rigging. In addition to the noises coming from the various parts of the ship's equipment, a distinct sound was coming from the men—they were singing! Each task required coordinated precision, and the rhythm of the songs provided beats on which the men would pull a rope or push a bar at the same time:

> *When* I was a *little* boy, *so* me father *told* me, tell me
> *Way*, haul a-*way*, we'll *haul* away *Joe*-uh!
> That *if* I did not *kiss* the girls, me *lips* would all grow *moldy*, tell me
> *Way*, haul a-*way*, we'll *haul* away *Joe*-uh!

In addition to making the work more enjoyable, the singing drew the men together, developing a sense of camaraderie among them. They had begun the voyage, for the most part, as strangers, and in some cases, appeared strange to each other. Most were from the United States, places such as Connecticut, Rhode Island, Massachusetts, New York, and Pennsylvania, and among them were Whites, Blacks, and Indigenous people. Others hailed from Nova Scotia, England, the Azores, Cape Verde, and the Sandwich Islands (later known as Hawai'i). Some wanted to see the world they didn't know; some wanted to get away from the world they did know. No matter their place of origin or their background, however, what mattered most was their ability to work together in order to keep the ship running smoothly and safely. There was little room for focusing on differences. Ultimately, their lives depended on each other.[1]

"Mr. Fournier, who the devil is at the helm?" shouted Captain Hamley from the bow. The *Stonington* had only just left the bay of San Francisco when it began moving erratically. "My orders were to head southwest out to sea, not zigzag like a drunken lout back toward land. Put us right before we find ourselves on a pile of jagged, nasty, hellfire rocks!"

"Aye, sir, I'll take care of it," Fournier quickly responded from his position amidships.

"See that you do! There's more whaling ahead of us yet!" bellowed Hamley impatiently.

Fournier made his way toward the stern and found Mark Comstock, a twenty-eight-year-old experienced whaler from Massachusetts, at the helm.

"Your course is a sloppy one, Comstock. Captain wants you to straighten us out and take us to open water."

"I'm trying, sir, I'm trying, but there's something off with the tiller."

"Step aside and let me get the feel of it."

As soon as Fournier grabbed ahold of the wheel, he could tell that something was loose.

"Take a look at the rudder head, Comstock, and tell me what you see," said Fournier, as he did his best to keep the wheel from wobbling side to side.

Comstock crouched down on the deck to inspect the linkage behind the wheel. He could see that one iron band, fastened by iron bolts to the tiller and the rudder post into which the tiller was inserted, was bulging outward somewhat instead of laying flat against the wooden surfaces of the post and tiller. Another iron band, this one connecting the rudder post to the sternpost, was also bulging outward in spots. This was perhaps the most critical point on the ship, where the forces of wind and sea converged on the mechanism that all too often worked against those forces in order to drive the ship in the opposite direction from which the wind and sea were pushing it.

The rudder itself, most of which was below the water, was a long wooden blade that weighed over a ton. It was attached to the rudder post, which was attached to the sternpost. As the helmsman turned the ship's wheel, the tiller to which it was mounted would turn left or right. The rudder, to which the tiller was ultimately connected, would turn in one direction or the other, causing the ship to turn as well. Currents running against the desired direction of the ship put enormous strain on the steering mechanism. Weakness at any of its connection points could result in losing the ability to maneuver, and so it was vital to maintain it properly.

"Do your best with what you've got, Comstock. I'll let the captain know the source of the trouble. Your head's tight, all right. It's the rudder head that's sprung," said Fournier with a bit of a grin.

"I'm thankful to you for that, sir," Comstock replied, a look of relief on his face. "I've seen the captain's anger play out, and I'd rather not be on the receiving end, 'specially if the fault ain't with me."

Fournier nodded knowingly before making his way back to Hamley.

"What have you to report, Fournier?"

"It's the rudder head, Captain. It's sprung, plain to see. Comstock's doing his best at the helm to keep the course steady."

"Damn it all!" shouted Hamley. "We're finally out of the harbor and headed to sea. I'll not turn back to that hellhole San Francisco. Far too much trouble there, and sure to be more should we return so soon. Set a course for Monterey. We'll see if Thompson is up to the task when we get there."

"Aye, sir, Monterey it is."[2]

Fournier headed to his charts to plot the new course. Monterey was just under one hundred miles southeast of their present position. Not a terrible distance, but certainly much farther than San Francisco. He questioned Hamley's decision to be at sea any longer than necessary, given the situation with the rudder. Why take the chance? Why risk the ship as well as the crew?

He checked his thoughts. He wasn't the captain; he was second officer, and he had orders to follow. He finished plotting the course and then called the heading to Comstock.

Fournier had just given the order to Comstock when the cry came from the lookout stationed near the top of the mainmast. "Thar she blows!" A pod of humpback whales was swimming less than a mile away from the ship.

Captain Hamley quickly assessed the situation and briskly shouted, "Lower away boats!"

Those were the words every whaler wanted to hear, the words that let them know they were about to do the thrillingly dangerous task they had signed on to do: go out and catch a whale.

Groups of six men headed to each of the four boats that hung at the sides of the ship. The boats themselves were about thirty feet long, and the men made sure that each boat had the equipment they would need for the hunt, including weapons and rope.

Two men in each group then lowered their boat so they could climb in and finish lowering it to the water. The remaining four men climbed down the side of the ship and into their boat. All six men put their oars in position, five on the sides for rowing, one in the stern for steering, maneuvering the boat away from the ship and out toward the whales.

The very fair weather and mild winds made it easy for the men to move their boats without any trouble. The late afternoon sun in the clear blue sky cast a wide swath of bright light across the surface of the ocean, and the water flickered as ripples passed across its surface. As the oarsmen rowed, the boatheaders steered the boats toward the area where they had last seen the telltale spouts and arching backs of the whales.

They were now within a few hundred feet from the whales, close enough that they needed to move the oars quietly and speak in hushed tones in order to avoid gallying, or scaring, the whales, causing them to swim away and making the hunt much more difficult.

One boat drew nearer than the others, and Edwin Arthur, a young harpooner in his late teens, from Connecticut, gently lowered his oar into the boat, picked up a harpoon, stood tall, braced himself in the bow, and waited for his moment.

Within seconds, the broad back of a whale rose up above the water, a mere dozen feet or so from the boat, and Arthur threw his weapon as hard as he could into the whale. The line attached to the harpoon began paying out as the shocked and pained whale began swimming rapidly to escape its predators, who had already stowed their oars in preparation for the "Nantucket sleigh ride" that the whale was about to give them.

The rough, bouncing tow did not last very long, however, as the stricken creature sounded heavily. The whale's deep dive caused the line to tighten, and the bow of the boat was close to going under when, before the crew could pay out more line, it slackened on its own. They knew in an instant that the harpoon had popped out of the whale.

In the meantime, the other whales, now sufficiently gallied, had swum or sounded far enough away to make chasing them impractical.

The hunt was over.

The boats returned to the ship, and the voyage to Monterey resumed.[3]

CHAPTER 5

The Greenhand

ON TUESDAY, SEPTEMBER 22, TWO DAYS AFTER THE WHALE HUNT, CAP-
tain Hamley called Alanson Fournier into his cabin.

"Mr. Fournier, we've made damn little progress toward Monterey
on account of that blasted rudder head. Our next best chance of a place
that would have what we need for repairs is San Diego, so I've decided
to take us there. Set your course for San Diego and give the order to the
helmsman."

Fournier hesitated to respond as quickly as he usually did. Once
again, the captain seemed to be putting the crew at risk by staying longer
in the open waters of the Pacific in a ship with a damaged steering system. Was it worth the gamble?

"I gave you an order," said Hamley impatiently, breaking the uncus-
tomary silence.

Fournier swallowed his objections and managed to squeeze out an
"Aye, sir, I'll see to that" from his throat before making his way out of
Hamley's cabin and toward his own.[1]

The *Stonington* continued sailing toward the southeast through fair
weather and, at times, strong winds.

On September 24, Santa Cruz came into view. It was one of the
Channel Islands, an archipelago stretching one hundred fifty miles along
the coast from Santa Barbara to San Diego.

The next day, as the ship neared Santa Catalina Island, about one
hundred miles northwest of San Diego, Fournier, who was standing

amidships near the main hatch, heard a commotion of voices at the fo'c'sle companionway.

Making his way forward, he could see a group of five men with their backs toward him, facing one man standing at the top of the stairway. Fournier was close enough now that he could catch some of what the men were saying, even though they were all talking at once.

"Who, you say?"

"Whereabouts, exactly?"

"Since when?"

"What in hell for?"

"Why this ship?"

The man at the top of the stairs had little chance to respond to the flurry of questions until Fournier called out, "Hey-oh, hey-oh! What goes on here?"

As the group turned to him, he saw the face of the man they were peppering with questions and understood immediately why there were so many. This was a man that none of them had seen before.

"He says he's been—".

Fournier cut the crewman off mid-sentence. "Quiet down, now, quiet down! I'll be asking the questions." Turning to face the stranger, he said, "I'm Alanson Fournier, second officer aboard this ship, and I expect some clear answers from you. What's your name?"

"J-J-James Rice, sir," the young man responded nervously.

"Where've you come from, James Rice?"

"I was down in the hold by the—"

"No, man, where'd you come from to get on this ship?"

"I was in San Francisco, aboard another whaleship, sir, the *Trescott*."

"Why the jump from one whaleship to another?"

"Well, sir, the *Trescott*'s a Mallory ship, out of Mystic, and Mr. Mallory, he's got some high expectations for his business, and the captain's determined to meet the old man's expectations and fill the hold chock-full before heading 'round the Horn. Me, sir, I've got a girl waiting for me back home, and after asking around town in 'Cisco, I learned that your ship has been out a few years more than the *Trescott*, and that you're headed back to New London, so I figured I've got a better chance of shortening my time by riding with you, sir."

"You'll not be riding, Rice, you'll be working, let's be clear on that! What's your experience?"

"This is my first time at sea, sir."

"Well, well, now. From out of its belly, this ship has birthed a greenhand!"

The men reacted with a mixture of chuckles and groans, knowing how amusing yet difficult it could be to have a sailor on board that was unfamiliar with the ways of a ship.

"We could toss you over now, Rice . . ."

"No sir, please!"

" . . . or we could take you on as a replacement for that good-for-nothing Bedrake. Are you ready to show us you're not a worthless deserter like him, that you're up to the work?"

"I'm ready, sir, yes I am."

"That's good to hear, Rice. I'll be keeping watch on you, but my duties will keep me from being with you as much as might be needed."

Fournier looked around the group and stopped at Peter McDonnald.

"McDonnald, you look to be almost twice Rice's age. Do you think you could pack twice as much knowledge into his head as he has now before we get to the Horn, where we'll need him to be in top form?"[2]

McDonnald was a veteran of the crew, a sandy-haired, solidly built sailor from New York with an easy way about him. He knew the importance of having a tightly knit, well-functioning crew aboard a ship as large and complex as the *Stonington*, and his even temperament and steady focus, as well as his wry sense of humor, would be just what Rice needed.

"I believe I can handle him, sir. I may have to bounce him off the deck from up in the rigging a few times to get his attention, but I'll get him shipshape."

"All right, then," said Fournier. "I'll be off to the captain to let him know we've just acquired a new hand."

McDonnald and the rest of the crew didn't have long to wait in order to see what Rice could do. No sooner had the discussion ended than they heard the call from the lookout, "Whales ho!" A great many humpbacks were swimming in the waters between San Nicolas and San Clemente, two more of the Channel Islands.

"Follow me," McDonnald called to Rice, and they headed for a boat on the larboard side.

After the boat was in the water, McDonnald watched Rice as they clambered down the side of the ship. *He's got his legs, all right*, thought McDonnald. *Let's see what he can do in a boat.*

The six men, including McDonnald and Rice, set their oars and began heading for the whales along with the other boats.

He's a good strong back, McDonnald thought as he observed Rice's movement with the oar.

The boats got near enough that it was time to be quiet in order to avoid gallying the whales.

"Soft row, now, men," the boatheader ordered in a hushed tone.

James Rice misunderstood the command, thinking that it meant to slow down rather than row quieter. The change that he made in his stroke caused his oar to hit the oar of the man behind him. The loud *thwack* was all it took for the whales to sense danger and take off.

"Stern all!" cried some of the boatheaders, their crews rowing their boats backward in order to avoid being hit by the whales' flukes as they whipped their tails up and down to propel themselves forward and away.

Rice looked across the boat to McDonnald, who was looking at him with his mouth set and one eyebrow raised. The first words were from Joseph Frank, the boatheader from the Azores. "That be a mistake you not make again, yes?" he said with a thick Portuguese accent.

"No, sir. Er, I mean, yes, sir."

"I not be sir, I be Joseph," he continued in a deliberate manner as the men rowed and he steered them back to the ship along with the other boats. "I need you pay attention to orders in boat, know my words. Soft not mean slow; soft mean quiet. Like in music. You want guitar play quiet, you say soft. You want fast, slow, you say those words. You know my words now?"

"Yes, s—I mean, yes, Joseph."

"Good. All we need. We go back now."

CHAPTER 6

Harsh Discipline

THE *STONINGTON* CONTINUED TO MANEUVER BETWEEN THE CHANNEL
Islands despite the difficulty caused by the faulty rudder head. Captain
Hamley displayed his sailing skill by having the crew steer by the wind,
adjusting the sails in order to maintain a steady course for San Diego.
Alanson Fournier had observed Hamley throughout the voyage and
admired him for his ability to keep the ship going in a nearly straight
line for days, even in rough weather. He questioned, however, the apparent stubbornness of his captain in continuing to sail even though it was
within his power to stop and fix the equipment problem.

There were other aspects of Hamley's manner of command that did
not sit well with Fournier. Such was the case on the morning of September 26, when Alexander Anthony got on the wrong side of the captain.

Hamley was on deck, giving direct orders to the men in the rigging,
among whom was Anthony. He had come aboard two days before the
ship left San Francisco, and Hamley had given him the position of steward, replacing the discharged George Mayors, on a trial basis.

Anthony had willingly agreed to take the position, knowing that it
would give him a certain amount of authority as well as limit the amount
of regular ship's duty he would have to do. Due to the sprung rudder head,
however, working conditions had changed, and all hands were expected
to contribute to the actual sailing of the ship when needed. This did not
please the thirty-four-year-old Anthony, originally from Westerly, Rhode
Island, and, at five-foot-three, one of the shortest men on the crew. His
mouth was quick, and his temper could be as short as the man himself.

"Hired me as a steward, did he?" Anthony began grumbling, loud enough that the man working with him on the yard of the mainsail could hear him. "Serve him his dinner, do I? Sure, I can serve from right here." His voice had gotten louder, and the men on the yard of the topsail above him could hear him now. "Ya like clams? Comin' right up—or should I say down?"

Anthony began clearing his throat with an exaggerated grating sound, collecting a wad of mucus that he moved to the front of his mouth. Leaning backward to avoid hitting the sail billowing below him, he took a deep breath and then spat toward where Hamley was standing on the deck. The spit landed with a splat, barely missing the captain.

Hamley looked around, then up, and spotted Anthony.

"Doin' my duty, Captain, servin' you up some dinner. How about a nice steak to go with that clam? I can getcha a nice rump cut," he shouted, loud enough that he was drawing the attention of even more of the crew. "Right here!" he cried, and then he patted his right buttock with his right hand. Some of the crew were now starting to laugh.

Hamley was not amused. "That's enough!" he shouted to Anthony.

"You sure it's enough, Captain? Maybe you oughta have a closer look." And with that, Anthony grabbed the waist of his pants with one hand and pulled them down just far enough to expose his bare backside to Hamley.

Even more laughter now erupted from the crew, and Hamley knew he had to squelch this situation fast in order to maintain his control and authority.

"That's all of the saucy behav—" he began, but Anthony cut him off.

"Oh, you want sauce with that steak? I got some right here," he called out, as he put his hand to his crotch.

"Seize him!" the captain shouted furiously to two of his officers standing nearby.

They quickly climbed up the ratlines and before Anthony had a chance to get away from them, they grabbed ahold of him and brought him down to the deck.

"Set him up tight," growled Hamley, and they tied each of Anthony's hands to the lanyards of the ratlines, just below the deadeyes. Then they pulled his shirt down to bare his back. "Let this be a lesson to you,

Anthony," Hamley snarled menacingly, and then, raising his voice so that all could hear, he hollered, "I will not tolerate impudent behavior from any man aboard this ship, toward me or any of my officers. This is the response you'll get if you dare to act as this man has!"

With that, Hamley raised his right arm high in the air so that all could see the tarred piece of rope that he held in his hand. Everyone on board, from the men up in the rigging to those down on the deck, felt their bodies tense as Hamley cocked his arm and then slammed the rope on Anthony's back. Anthony flinched in pain but did not make a sound. He had resolved before the flogging began that he would not give Hamley the satisfaction of hearing him cry out.

Hamley continued until he had delivered a dozen blows to Anthony's back. As he did so, Alanson Fournier glanced around at the faces of the crew nearby, and he could sense in their eyes the same sort of resentment that he'd observed when he had taken a detail to shore in San Francisco to retrieve deserters. This was worse, though, and it made him wonder if such a hardening attitude might eventually lead to mutiny.

He also made careful note of the reactions of George Hopkins and William Fisher, two Black members of the crew standing nearby. What was going through their minds, he wondered, as they watched the master of the ship whipping one of their fellow workers. They were free men, but too many such as them in too many states were not.[1]

Fournier was an abolitionist. He agreed with the immediatism as put forth by the Tappan brothers, Lewis and Arthur, who had been born in Massachusetts but had eventually moved to New York City and established themselves as two of the most prominent abolitionists in the country. They supported freeing all of the enslaved people in the United States immediately.

Fournier was also well aware of the *Amistad* case that the US Supreme Court had decided in 1841, freeing fifty-three captives that slave traders had brought illegally from Africa to Cuba. The case had special meaning for Fournier, as the US Navy had seized the *Amistad* at Montauk Point on Long Island, just over thirty miles from his home in Greenport, Long Island. The captives had commandeered the ship after being transferred from the *Teçora*, the slave ship that had brought them across the Atlantic, and were attempting to sail back to Africa. Fournier felt great sympathy for them and their plight.[2]

"Take him down," growled Hamley to the two officers that had tied Anthony to the lanyards. "Bring him to his quarters and see to his stripes. He's got steward work to do."

Anthony's back was crisscrossed with welts and bloody gashes, and he had dropped to the deck after being untied. As the officers took him down below, Hamley shouted to the crew, "Back to your work, all of you—and mind what you've just seen and what I've said!"

Hamley made his way to his cabin, stopping at Anthony's bunk in steerage. He saw one of the officers applying a salve to Anthony's back. It was typically the captain that tended to the sick and injured aboard a whaling ship, but this was not a typical case.

"I've a mind to send you up to the fo'c'sle, Anthony, and find someone to take your place, but that's more trouble than I want right now. Besides, I'm thinking it'll be better to have you close by where I can keep a watch on you," he said with a menacing smirk, then he proceeded to his cabin.

Alexander Anthony thanked the officers for tending to him. He winced as they helped him put on his shirt, and then he began preparing the meal for the captain and the officers, anticipating, with good reason, an awkward situation when it came time to serve them.

The weather on Sunday, September 27, was calm, but there was a thick fog that persisted throughout the day, making navigation even more difficult for a ship with a faulty rudder.

The fog lifted the next day, providing a glimpse of the mainland, about twenty miles to the east. The lookouts shouted, "Land ho!" and then surprisingly quickly afterward came the "Whales ho!" call. The captain ordered the boats to be lowered, and the chase was on.

Although they came up empty-handed once again, they consoled themselves with thoughts of more opportunities once their rudder was repaired.

Unbeknownst to them, this would be the last whale hunt they would have for quite some time. They were about to begin an experience that would set the *Stonington* apart from all other whaleships in history.[3]

CHAPTER 7

On to San Diego

"BE MINDFUL OF THAT COASTLINE, MR. FOURNIER," CAPTAIN HAMLEY called to his second officer. "Don't let the first mouth fool you. They don't call it False Bay for nothing."

Fournier looked over the larboard bow and saw a strip of smooth, white sand lining the coast. Toward its southern end there was an opening large enough for a ship like the *Stonington* to enter, but once inside, the passage became constricted and shallow, leading to some very difficult maneuvering in order to get back out.

"The cliffs farther south may look inhospitable, but around their point is the true harbor. Steer your course accordingly," Hamley instructed.

Fournier looked beyond the mouth of False Bay and saw that the coastline changed dramatically. Within a few thousand feet of the inlet, the flat beach gave way to gradually rising sand cliffs that eventually reached a height of over four hundred feet. In some places, the waves crashed against grayish-black rocky ledges along the bottom of the cliffs. In other areas, the waves pounded directly on the sand, which varied in color from nearly white to a dull orange.

As he watched the forceful action of the water, Fournier marveled at the fact that the cliffs were still standing, especially because he could see some scooped-out indentations that showed a great extent of erosion. *How long will they last?* he wondered.

"You're doing a fine job with that rudder, Comstock," said Fournier to the helmsman. "I see steadiness runs in the family." He was speaking to Samuel Comstock, who at the age of thirty was just a year younger than his brother Mark, the man who'd been at the helm when Fournier first discovered that the rudder head was sprung.

"Those cliffs may be made of sand," said Samuel, "but there's plenty of rock about their base that would chew the hull of this ship if given half the chance. I've no intention of providing them with even a hint of a meal, sir, no matter how much this wheel wants to buck at my grip."

As the *Stonington* made its way southward, the cliffs rounded to an end, on the other side of which was a clear, wide channel. The ship was now on the eastern side of Point Loma, and where before there had been a gradual slope in most places from the water's edge to the land's summit, now the cliffs rose straight up to their towering heights, creating a massive wall of dense golden sand topped by purplish-black rock and sparse, green scrub brush. The tall cliffs continued for about five thousand feet, and then they began to subside until they became a beach that stretched around a promontory of nearly twenty acres. This was La Playa, the place where, for the past several decades, merchant ships had come to trade their goods, and whaling ships had come for supplies and a brief respite.

The ship had reached the tip of Point Loma and was about to make its way into San Diego harbor. It had been a difficult ride from San Francisco, but now, thought Fournier, they could finally take care of that troublesome rudder head and get back to smooth sailing.

Captain Hamley sent a boat to check the depth of the channel that led to La Playa, about two and a half miles to the north. After getting word from the boat that the depth was sufficient, Hamley brought the *Stonington* into the harbor and anchored it in hard ground at a depth of nine fathoms. It was one p.m., Tuesday, September 29, 1846. Hamley was just as anxious as Fournier to get the rudder repaired.

"Fournier, you and a detail take a boat to shore and inquire in the town about fixing that rudder. Tell them we want it done quickly. I don't want to spend any more time than necessary anchored here. We've got whaling to do."

"Aye, sir, we'll be off right away."[1]

Fournier rapidly gathered five men, and within minutes, they had lowered the boat and begun rowing, with Fournier at the steering oar.

After a short ride to shore, two of the men stayed with the boat while Fournier and the other three made their way to the main road, the La Playa Trail, walking about five miles to the town of San Diego.

The Trail was well worn, having been used for thousands of years by the Indigenous Kumeyaay people as a way to reach the coastline of the bay. When Spaniards began settling the territory in the mid-eighteenth century, they had increased the Trail's length in order to reach the land where they would eventually establish the town of San Diego and their very first mission in California.

Fournier and his men walked on the hard-packed dirt, with views of the water to their right and scrubland to their left. After staying level for most of the way, the Trail began to rise gently before dipping down into a ravine that ran alongside the San Diego River. Here was the town, and on a hill farther ahead stood the remains of the Presidio, the fort that the Spanish had built to protect the town.

Fournier was looking forward to finding someone who could help with the rudder repair.

What he found was a town in turmoil due to the progress of the war between the United States and Mexico.[2]

PART II

Chapter 8

The Struggle for Control

US PRESIDENT JAMES K. POLK HAD DESIGNS ON CALIFORNIA AS SOON AS he took office in March of 1845. By whatever means necessary, his goal was to obtain California from Mexico and annex it to the United States. He and his cabinet had become increasingly concerned after learning in early October of that year about overtures that Great Britain had made toward Mexico regarding a potential acquisition of the territory.

On the evening of October 30, Polk met with Lieutenant Archibald H. Gillespie of the US Marines to explain the mission for which he had been recommended by George Bancroft, secretary of the navy. Gillespie was to bring confidential messages to Thomas O. Larkin, the US consul in Monterey, and to John C. Frémont, a captain in the Army Corps of Topographical Engineers on assignment in California, who, through his exploits during exploratory expeditions in the West, had gained fame and was known as "The Pathfinder." Frémont also had strong connections in Washington through his marriage to Jessie Benton, the daughter of Thomas Hart Benton, a most powerful and influential member of the US Senate and, like Polk, heavily in favor of expanding the United States.[1]

Gillespie traveled incognito as a merchant in order to safeguard his mission, sailing on November 16, 1845, from New York to Vera Cruz. He proceeded overland across Mexico to Mazatlán, where he boarded the USS *Cyane* that took him to Honolulu and then to Monterey. Along the way, Gillespie had memorized the confidential messages to Larkin and Frémont and then, as an additional safeguard, destroyed the originals.

When Gillespie finally met with Larkin on April 17, 1846, he delivered to Larkin a transcription that he had made of the letter originally written by James Buchanan, Polk's secretary of state. Buchanan's message contained instructions to be extremely observant of the political situation in California regarding the intentions of the Mexican government, and to promote among the Californios the sentiment that the potential annexation of their homeland to the United States would be most advantageous for them.[2]

Archibald Gillespie next had to find Captain Frémont in order to deliver a packet of letters to him. He eventually caught up to him at the south end of Klamath Lake, about five hundred miles north of Monterey, in the southwest portion of the Oregon Territory, on the evening of May 8, 1846. The packet included a brief introductory note from Secretary Buchanan, a note from Frémont's wife, and a somewhat cryptic letter from his father-in-law. Gillespie delivered orally the confidential messages from the administration, among which were likely instructions from Polk, Buchanan, and Bancroft.

Frémont interpreted all of this information—including the fact that the president had sent a military courier to meet with him personally—to mean that it was now his duty to ensure that the United States would gain control of California.

After a series of bloody encounters with the nearby Klamath tribe, Frémont and his company of about fifty men began heading south into California. Along the way, they encountered a band of hard-hewn mountain men, one of whom was Ezekiel Merritt, a burly former trapper dressed in fringed buckskin who chewed tobacco constantly, drank liquor frequently, and stammered persistently. They called themselves the Osos, invoking the strength and ferocity of the grizzly bears that roamed the territory, and they were intent on preventing any attempts by the Mexican government to expel them and other American settlers from California.[3]

Comandante José Castro was well aware of the presence of Frémont and his men in the area. Castro was a Californio who had been appointed to his position after a period of turbulence between Mexico and California in Mexico's awkward attempts to establish control in its northern territory. He had confronted Frémont and a portion of his company in January, when they had defied his orders to keep their distance from settled areas. Castro was suspicious of the intentions of these well-armed men who claimed that they were simply exploring the land. Having been in California for multiple generations, Californios were becoming increasingly concerned about the number of settlers making their way west from the United States.

Ironically, they had, for the most part, lost sight of the fact that they, too, had at one time been settlers seeking to establish their homes in a land that was already populated—in their case, for thousands of years—by Indigenous peoples.[4]

CHAPTER 9

The Bear Flag Rebellion

AT THE BEGINNING OF JUNE, CASTRO RODE NORTH NEARLY TWO HUN-
dred miles from Monterey to Sonoma to meet with General Mariano
Vallejo, a fellow powerful Californio. Vallejo agreed to provide a herd
of almost two hundred horses for Castro to use in preparing to drive
Frémont and his company out of California. Castro then assigned lieutenants Francisco Arce and José Aviso to drive the herd southward to
Santa Clara.

Meanwhile, Frémont had made his way to Sutter Buttes, about two
hundred eighty miles south of Klamath Lake. On the morning of June
9, 1846, William Knight and William Ide, two settlers who lived nearby,
rode into Frémont's camp with the news about the horses. Frémont
resisted sending any of his own men to intercept the herd, but he gave
his tacit approval to the formation of a party led by Ezekiel Merritt, who,
with about a dozen men, rode off later that day.

The following morning, nearly eighty miles south of Frémont's camp,
they surprised Arce and Aviso at Murphy's Ranch and took control of
the horses. Merritt allowed the two lieutenants and the few men with
them to each have a horse on which to ride back to Castro to let him
know that if he wanted his horses, he would have to come and get them.[1]

Emboldened by their success at taking the horses, the Osos determined that they should go to Sonoma and confront General Vallejo
about his cooperation with Castro. Although they were both Californios,
Vallejo was known to be supportive of what he viewed as the inevitability
of the United States' involvement in California. He thought that it would

actually be more beneficial to be in a cooperative relationship with the increasingly powerful United States rather than the disorganized and inattentive Mexico.

Merritt saw it as his duty to reinforce the notion that Americans were here to stay. On Saturday, June 13, he rode out from Frémont's camp with just over thirty men and headed for Sonoma, about one hundred twenty miles to the southwest.

In the predawn hours of Sunday morning, Vallejo heard someone knocking on his door. He opened it and saw nearly thirty-five men, with Merritt at the front, clad in a variety of fur hats and wearing buckskins, armed with all sorts of guns and sharp-bladed weapons. Vallejo invited Merritt and two others into his well-appointed home and provided them with brandy while they explained the purpose of their visit. An interpreter and two of Vallejo's officers joined the meeting.

After what seemed to be an unnecessary amount of time, those outside began to wonder what was taking so long. They chose another of their group, John Grigsby, to go inside and see what was going on. When Grigsby did not return, William Ide entered the house and saw that the brandy had obviously taken its toll in causing the delay in negotiations. He finalized the terms, whereby Californios would not put up armed resistance to settlers, and settlers, in turn, would limit the amount of property that they took.[2]

As a precautionary measure, Merritt and a few others took Vallejo and his officers prisoner and rode back to Frémont's camp. Ide and the majority of his group stayed in Sonoma and, in their enthusiasm at having negotiated, without the official assistance or involvement of the US government, a treaty of sorts with the Californios, decided that it was fitting to declare themselves a republic. They determined that a flag would be appropriate, and the man that they selected to create it was William Todd, whose Aunt Mary was now married to a lawyer named Abraham Lincoln.

Using the crude materials available, Todd's banner was white with a red stripe at the bottom, a star in the upper left corner, and a bear to the right of the star, and below them the words "California Republic." They hoisted the flag in Sonoma's plaza that afternoon, June 14, 1846, to honor what became known as the Bear Flag Republic.[3]

CHAPTER 10

The Conflict Intensifies

COMANDANTE CASTRO WAS INCENSED UPON LEARNING OF THE AUDA-cious exploits of Merritt, Ide, and the others. He and many other Californios were determined to retain the land that they had controlled for decades. Castro issued a proclamation on June 17 to protest the actions of the men whom he associated with Captain Frémont and the US government. He then began recruiting and formed three divisions of soldiers whose mission was to fan out into the territory and drive the American insurgents back to the United States.

A series of skirmishes occurred from the end of June to the beginning of July in the area to the north and south of Sonoma. The combined forces of the Osos and Frémont's battalion were victorious in enough of those fights that the Californios returned to their bases of operations in order to regroup. The Americans gathered in Sonoma in time to celebrate Independence Day on July 4. They decided to formalize their newly created California Republic by having a committee compose their own declaration of independence. One of the three committee members was John Bidwell, a member of Frémont's battalion, who in 1841 was among the nearly seventy people in the first group of settlers to travel across the Rocky Mountains and into California.[1]

Three days earlier, on July 1, John D. Sloat, commodore of the US Pacific Squadron, arrived at Monterey aboard the flagship *Savannah*, joining two other squadron ships that had been there for a month or so. In mid-May, Sloat had learned of the incident between US and Mexican forces that had occurred on April 25. President Polk had sent General

Zachary Taylor and his troops into disputed territory along the border with Mexico. The skirmish that ensued became the first action of a war that the United States would declare officially on May 13.

Sloat acted according to orders that he had received previously from George Bancroft and prepared to take command of Monterey, the capital city. Consul Thomas Larkin had been conducting negotiations with the Californios that he hoped would lead eventually to peaceful annexation, but Sloat insisted that he had to take action immediately, based on three factors: combat was already under way in Mexico and California; a British warship was nearby; and a group of insurgents had declared a republic of their own. On the morning of July 7, Sloat sent Captain William Mervine ashore with a letter for Comandante Castro detailing the terms of surrender. A few hours later, two hundred fifty men from the squadron landed at the custom house with strict instructions to conduct themselves in an orderly manner and to treat the inhabitants of Monterey with dignity and respect. A proclamation from Sloat was read aloud, and the US flag was raised at the custom house.[2]

Castro responded to Sloat's letter on July 9, writing from his headquarters at San Juan Bautista, about thirty-five miles northwest of Monterey. He refused to surrender and insisted that he would defend his country. Two days later, he wrote to Governor Pío Pico, who was in Santa Barbara. Pico, like Castro, was a Californio, and both men had been named to their positions in March of 1845. Castro had only about one hundred soldiers, and he asked Pico to recruit as many as he could. They met at Santa Margarita, and, with fewer than two hundred men altogether, they began the long march to Los Angeles to confront the US forces that were heading for that same place.

During that time, Robert F. Stockton, a haughty and ambitious navy officer, had replaced the ailing Sloat as commodore of the Pacific Squadron. Aboard his ship *Congress*, now the squadron's flagship and making its way to Los Angeles, were nearly four hundred eighty men and a stockpile of arms and ammunition. Also headed for Los Angeles was John C. Frémont, whom Stockton had recently promoted to the rank of major, and his battalion. Frémont was coming from San Diego, where he and his men had participated in the US occupation of that town.[3]

By the time the opposing forces were gathered in and around Los Angeles, it became apparent to General Castro that he was greatly outnumbered. He made an attempt to negotiate with Commodore Stockton, who, like Sloat before him, demanded Castro's surrender before any negotiations could begin. Castro again refused such conditions, reluctantly disbanded his army, issued a proclamation decrying the US invasion of California, and announced that he would be leaving for Mexico. Governor Pico issued a similar proclamation and announcement, and during the night of Monday, August 10, he and Castro left California separately and headed for Mexico.

Pico had met earlier that evening with the legislative assembly to explain the gravity of the situation and to announce his departure. The assembly, in a somber mood, voted to dissolve itself. Los Angeles was now open for the taking.

Stockton had already begun leading his men toward the town, and they arrived two days later and established control. On the following Monday, August 17, Stockton issued a proclamation in which he affirmed that, with the addition of Los Angeles to the group of major towns occupied by US forces, California was now a part of the United States, and he instituted martial law until a new government for the town was established. For now, it seemed as though the US command of the territory was stable, but it would not remain that way for long.[4]

PART III

CHAPTER 11

Requests

WHEN THE *STONINGTON* ARRIVED AT SAN DIEGO ON THAT BRIGHT, sunny, late September day of 1846 and came to anchor in the harbor, Captain Hamley was looking forward to getting the rudder head repaired and returning to sea as quickly as possible. Second Officer Fournier and his landing party were expecting to find what they needed in town so they could return to the ship and soon be under way. Unbeknownst to all, the *Stonington* was about to make its longest stop in the entire voyage, a stop that would set it apart from any other whaleship in history.

"Good day to you, sir," said Fournier to the first person he and his men encountered as they entered the town. "Tell me, please, where I might find a person in this town who knows a thing or two about repairing a ship's rudder."

The man looked at Fournier with a perplexed expression. "You might find him preparin' to get out of town, like the rest of us."

"Get out of town? Why?" asked Fournier.

"Californios comin' to take it back."

"Take what back?"

"The town, man, the town!"

"Take it back from whom?"

"From us! Major Frémont and his men come in the end of July with Gillespie and his crew and raise the Stars and Stripes and say the town is ours now. Frémont goes, Gillespie stays, Frémont comes back, then they both go up to San Pedro, figurin' we're good on our own, here. Gillespie makes a mess o' things in Los Angeles, the Californios get fightin' mad and take it back. Now they're on their way here to take *this* back. That's alls I can tell ya. I gotta get goin'—don't know where, don't seem to be no place to get *to*, but I know I gotta get out before them Californios get here. I suggest you fellas do the same. Good luck to ya."

With that, the man turned and hurried on his way.

Fournier turned to his men, thought for a moment, then said, "We'd best get back to the ship and let the captain know the situation here, see what he wants to do."

The group marched to their boat and made their way to the ship. Having reboarded, Fournier went straight to the captain and was in the midst of explaining to him the situation onshore when one of the crew called out that a boat from shore was approaching.

Hamley and Fournier went to the starboard rail.

"I'm the captain of this ship," Hamley called down to the men in the boat. "Who are you, and what's the nature of your business?"

"We come with a message from the chief of San Diego," answered one of them. "He demands that you send ten men ashore to guard our town against the enemy for as long as your ship lays in our port."

"Demands, does he?" replied Hamley. "You tell your chief that I'm aware of his situation and that I'll take his 'request' into consideration."

"Much obliged, Captain. We need all the help we can get."

As the men rowed back to shore, Hamley turned to Fournier. "I'll need to think on this, Fournier. I'll be in my cabin."

"Aye, sir."

As Hamley headed for the companionway and his quarters, Fournier was not sure what Hamley's decision would be. He wondered what his own decision might be in this situation. Would he send men into a town in peril? Would he keep a ship in port longer than planned in order to help others? The day may come, he thought, when he would need to be ready to make such decisions.[1]

The next day, Wednesday, September 30, began with very fair weather, and Captain Hamley planned to make the best of it. He had considered the request for protection that the men from town had delivered the day before, and he had decided to take the *Stonington* to sea rather than make a prolonged stay in San Diego.

The crew was busily preparing the ship to get under way when they heard Alanson Fournier call out, "Captain, a boat approaches."

As Fournier waited for Hamley to make his way to the rail, he looked carefully at the men in the boat. He could see there was a passenger dressed differently than the men clad in work clothes that were rowing the boat. The passenger was wearing a collared black jacket and matching black trousers with a white, starched-collared shirt and white bowtie that gleamed in the sunlight in contrast to his dark jacket and the dark hair on his head.

The boat drew near the ship, and the passenger rose to his feet in a steady stance that suggested he had a good amount of experience at sea. At six-foot-four, he towered over the others in the boat.

"Good day, sirs," he called up with a booming voice to Hamley, who had by then joined Fournier at the rail. "I am Henry Delano Fitch, chief officer of this town. Might I be addressing the captain of this ship?"

"You are, indeed, sir. I am George W. Hamley. What brings you here?"

"An urgent matter, Captain Hamley. Permission to come aboard, sir?"

"Granted. Give him some steps, men."

Some crew members put a rope ladder over the side, and Fitch clambered up onto the deck of the *Stonington*.

"You make your way easily for a townsman and dressed as you are, Mr. Fitch," Hamley noted.

"Born in Nantucket to a sea captain, sir. Sixteen when I started my own time on the water. In my blood, as it were. But I'm not here to tell my story. People in town elected me *alcalde*, and I'm here for them."

"I gathered as much, Mr. Fitch, seeing as we received your message—or should I say, your demands—just yesterday."

"Yes," said Fitch, "and by the look of your rigging, I can fair well measure your response. I could tell it from shore. That's why I've come to you personally. I tell you, sir, we are in desperate circumstances. An enemy force is approaching. If you leave this port, we have no other place of retreat for the safety of ourselves, our families, and our property."

"If we stay, Mr. Fitch, then I'll be putting my own men in danger as well. As I told your messengers yesterday, I'm giving the matter my consideration."

"We need more than your consideration, sir. We need your protection," replied Fitch, with a determined set to his chin.

"You'll have your answer by this evening, Mr. Fitch."

"We've likely not more time than that, Captain Hamley."

With that, the *alcalde* of San Diego returned to his boat and then to shore to await Hamley's response, and the captain of the *Stonington* went to his quarters to ponder Fitch's request.[2]

CHAPTER 12

Californio Resurgence

HENRY D. FITCH'S CONCERNS WERE WELL FOUNDED. IN JUST A MATTER of a few days at the end of September and the beginning of October, the situation in San Diego had grown urgent. As a result of Lieutenant Archibald Gillespie's heavy-handed administration of martial law in Los Angeles, Californios under the leadership of Serbulo Varela had organized a revolt against the US forces that were occupying the town. Word of the revolt had spread, prompting Fitch to send a request to Gillespie for protection for San Diego. Aware that the growing revolt might reach farther south, Gillespie had ordered Ezekiel Merritt to take a dozen men to San Diego. John Bidwell, whom Major John C. Frémont had appointed as *alcalde* of San Luis Rey in August, was alert to the growing danger and decided to ride the approximately forty miles to San Diego, where he joined Merritt's force.[1]

Serbulo Varela began his assault on Archibald Gillespie on Wednesday, September 23. The two sides were initially fairly equal, numbering about two dozen men each. Enthusiasm among Californios for Varela's actions grew, however, and within days his force had grown to over three hundred. Some Californios that sympathized with the United States had joined Gillespie, raising his force to a bit less than sixty. José Flores, a professional soldier whom Varela's expanded Californio force had elected as their commander, took advantage of his superior numbers and sent to Gillespie a demand for unconditional surrender. After a few days of refusals and negotiations, Gillespie acknowledged the reality of the situation and signed the terms of surrender on Tuesday, September 29.

The prideful Gillespie, however, did not intend to abide by those terms. He sent to Commodore Stockton for assistance, and Stockton dispatched the USS *Savannah* from Monterey. The ship, just over two hundred feet in length and now commanded by Captain William Mervine, arrived at San Pedro on Tuesday evening, October 6, carrying a force of about three hundred, as well as rifles and ammunition.

Mervine's dismissiveness of the Californios' capabilities had led him to send his forces ashore with sparse ammunition and no artillery. For the next two days, they attempted to retake Los Angeles, but encountered persistent ambushes by the Californios, who, though they were less in number by about one hundred, were able to repel the larger US force with their clever guerrilla tactics that included the use of a four-pounder cannon. The Californios had found the cannon in an old woman's yard while they were gathering arms that their compatriots had hidden or buried in the countryside when Gillespie's forces had first taken over Los Angeles. They mounted the gun on a crude frame that they then towed with horses to various positions along the route that the US forces were taking in their march to Los Angeles. The effectiveness of the Californios' tactics in what became known as the Battle of the Old Woman's Gun eventually forced the ill-equipped US marines and sailors to retreat, re-embark, and sail to Monterey.[2]

Buoyed by his victory over Gillespie and Mervine, Flores sent fifty men, led by Francisco Rico, and later, Serbulo Varela, to retake San Diego. Fitch, Merritt, and Bidwell were well aware of the situation in Los Angeles at the end of September and had expected that an enemy force of some significant size would eventually be heading their way in early October.

Fitch and Merritt began making demands on the readily available whaleship in San Diego harbor, demands that would gradually increase.[3]

CHAPTER 13

Shifts in Authority

Peter McDonnald and James Rice had been in the rigging just above where Hamley and Fitch were speaking. As Fitch made his departure, Rice turned to McDonnald and said, "I know a bit about needing the safety of a ship. I hope the captain finds it in himself to give those people some help. You think he will?"

"I'm not so sure," McDonnald replied. "He can be right hard—you've seen it—and he's got the job of getting this ship back to its owners. Those people do need help, though, and right now we're the only ones that can give it to them. I know what I'd do, and I'm pretty sure you'd do the same. But we're not the captain, are we? Don't know where he'll drop anchor on this. We'll know soon enough."

Around eight p.m., as Henry Fitch was contemplating what action to take if Captain Hamley refused to offer any assistance, he heard the sound of horses approaching. Thinking that it might be the Californios arriving, he peered carefully through one of the windows of his home and saw that it was a group of about a dozen men wearing buckskin clothes and a variety of fur hats, armed with an assortment of guns and blades.

He went out to the plaza to see who they were and what they wanted.

The burly man on the lead horse spat a wad of tobacco juice on the ground, turned to face Fitch, and asked with a pronounced stutter, "Who's in ch-ch-charge here?"

"I am the *alcalde*, sir, Henry D. Fitch. Who are you?"

"N-n-name is Zeke Merritt, and I'm t-t-taking command of this t-t-town by order of L-L-Lieutenant Gillespie."

"So, you're the protection I requested from Gillespie," responded Fitch somewhat skeptically.

Further conversation with Merritt assured Fitch that the men had indeed been sent by Lieutenant Gillespie, and Fitch went on to explain the situation regarding Captain Hamley and the whaleship in the harbor.

"L-l-let's go pay Captain Hamley a visit, men, help him make up his mind."[1]

Merritt and company rode on the trail through the dark down to La Playa, where he and a few of his men found an available boat and rowed out to the *Stonington*.

The crew members on watch aboard the ship heard the boat coming before they could see it clearly. As it drew nearer, they saw that this was a rough bunch of men.

"Sir, I think you'd best have a look here," one of them called quietly to Alanson Fournier, who was the officer on deck.

With one look at the men in the approaching boat, Fournier understood their concern and went below to alert the captain. The two of them soon emerged from the companionway and made their way to the starboard rail.

Hamley watched the boat for a moment, then turned to Fournier and the crewmen and said in a low tone, "Stay alert, men."

Looking at the men gathered on the ship above him, Merritt called out, "You up there! L-l-lower a ladder. I n-n-need to meet with your captain."

The crewmen looked at Hamley questioningly. He turned the palm of his left hand toward them to signal "Wait," then called down, "I'm the captain. Who are you and why do you need to meet with me?"

"I'm Captain Merritt, with orders for you from the gov'ment. Now send down that l-l-ladder!"

Hamley hesitated for a moment, then said, "I'll give you the ladder, Captain Merritt, but only you can come up. Your men will need to wait in the boat."

Merritt replied confidently, "L-l-lower away!" He spat some tobacco juice into the water as he waited impatiently. His strength was obvious as he climbed quickly to the deck and faced Captain Hamley.

"Captain Hamley, in the n-n-name of the gov'ment of the United States, I order you to give assistance to the good people of this t-t-town. Get fifteen men and whatever weapons you got and follow me to shore."

"Captain Merritt," began Hamley, "I'm not so sure—"

"I ain't got t-t-time nor patience for argument, Captain. There's people that n-n-need our help. Get yer men and t-t-take 'em to shore!"

Merritt turned to go back to his boat. As he did, he could see there were more men gathered on deck than when he'd first come aboard. He stood at the rail for a moment, checked the wind direction, and after spitting more tobacco juice into the water, looked at the crewmen and said, "I 'spect I'll be seein' you in t-t-town. You look t-t-tough enough for a good fight."

With that, he climbed over the rail and down to his boat.[2]

The Comstock brothers, Joseph Miller, Peter McDonnald, and James Rice were among the crew on deck that had heard most of what Merritt had said to Hamley. They knew what it meant to be in a challenging situation. Some of them began calling out to Hamley.

"I'll go, Captain."

"Aye, count me in."

"I'm willing as well."

Hamley stood silently as he mulled over Merritt's orders and the reaction of those crewmen. If he were to refuse, he would be defying the US government. He would also appear to be less brave than the men who were willing to join the fight. He was facing a true dilemma—should he relinquish some of his authority to Merritt in order to maintain his authority over the crew? His thoughts rolled over each other in his mind, colliding and eventually settling. After a long moment, he spoke to the waiting crew. "All right, men," he said in a deliberate tone, "get two boats ready. I'll be joining you in one of them. Bring cutting spades and lances and any other arms that might be useful. Fournier, you stay aboard and keep the ship ready for whatever may happen."

"Aye, Captain," said the men as they prepared for departure, "we'll show this town what the men of the *Stonington* are made of."

For some, like James Holden of Nova Scotia and John Dias of Cape Verde, it was yet another adventure among the many that they had experienced during their time as whalers. For others, like New Englanders Nelson Davis and Gardner Jaques, it was an opportunity to demonstrate their patriotism. For Black men such as William Fisher of Philadelphia, Pennsylvania, and John Jennings of Norwich, Connecticut, it was a chance to show that they, too, were willing to defend their country.[3]

The two boats, with eight men in each, went to shore. Merritt and his men were not there, but the tracks of their horses were plainly visible.

"Larkins, you guard these boats," Hamley said to eighteen-year-old Martin Larkins from New York. "The rest of you, gather your weapons and follow me."

The group made their way along the trail to town, and Merritt greeted them upon their arrival.

"Wise choice, Hamley," he said. "You wouldn'a wanted t-t-to make me come back and getcha." He spat tobacco juice on the ground for emphasis. "You men can put up here for the n-n-night," he said, gesturing to an adobe house behind him. "Hamley, you'll come with me so's I can keep an eye on you."

The two men walked down the road to another, larger house where Merritt and some of his men were staying, and they remained there for the rest of the night.

When the sun rose the next morning, October 1, it was a beautiful day in San Diego. The weather was fair and the wind was mild. Perhaps the pleasant conditions had a soothing effect on Ezekiel Merritt, or maybe the compliance shown by the men of the *Stonington* had gained his favor. Whatever the reason, he allowed Captain Hamley and his boat's crew to return to their ship. The other seven men would remain in town to augment his forces, and possibly as a guarantee that Hamley would not leave the harbor without them.[4]

Hamley and his crew arrived back at the ship at eight o'clock that morning. Within three hours, another boat was heading to the ship, but it was not, as some thought it might be, the remainder of the crew that had gone to town. As had been the case the day before, there was a passenger in the boat wearing a dark suit. He bore a strong resemblance to the earlier passenger, Henry D. Fitch, including his long side whiskers, and some aboard the ship thought that it was indeed Fitch. As the boat drew closer, however, they could see that it was a different man.

Alanson Fournier was at the rail when the passenger called up to the ship.

"I am Pedro Carrillo, the customs collector for the port of San Diego. I need to see your ship's papers and speak with your captain. Please lower a ladder for me to come aboard."

Fournier complied with the request and went to alert the captain.

As he and Hamley watched Carrillo climbing the ladder, Fournier said, "We seem to have become a popular attraction for this town," to which Hamley muttered an unenthusiastic "Mmm-hmm."

The captain greeted Carrillo and showed him the papers. "I will need to take those to my office in order to process your ship properly, and I will need you to accompany me," Carrillo informed the captain.

"You may take the papers with you, sir, but I will remain with my ship," asserted Hamley.

"But, Captain—"

"There is no 'but' about this, sir. You go, I stay. Good day, sir."

Hamley turned and strode determinedly back to his quarters, leaving Carrillo with no option but to return reluctantly to shore.

The day got busier at one p.m. when yet another boat arrived from shore.

A messenger came aboard with orders from Captain Merritt: Hamley was to get the ship ready for sea. Merritt and his forces, including the crewmen that had stayed ashore, would be joining him, as would any of the town's citizens that wanted to be out of harm's way when the Californios arrived. They would bring their food and belongings, and Merritt's forces would bring their weapons and ammunition. Merritt's plan was to sail along the coast until they met with other US forces.

Captain Hamley paused to let the meaning of those orders sink in.

Bringing some of the crew into town to provide additional protection was admittedly a serious duty, but now the US government was commandeering the *Stonington* and its entire crew to become a part of its Pacific fleet. How long would this change of mission last? How dangerous would the conditions become for the ship and the men? Would the crew rise up in mutiny if he acquiesced to the government's demands?

He wanted time to think this over, but time was, he knew, in short supply. Remembering the old proverb "Two heads are better than one," Hamley called across the deck. "Mr. Fournier, a word with you in my quarters."[5]

When the two men entered the captain's cabin, Hamley closed the door.

"Have a seat, Mr. Fournier. I've something to discuss with you that will affect the future of this ship and all those aboard."

Fournier sat facing the captain, who was seated on the cushioned bench that ran below the stern windows. He could see by the troubled look on Hamley's face that this was a serious matter, and his own brow furrowed as he listened intently to the captain's explanation of the situation and the questions that had arisen in his mind.

When he had finished, Hamley looked earnestly at his second officer. "Fournier, you're a level-headed sort," he said, "and I admire your approach to problems. Tell me—what would *you* do in this situation?"

Fournier looked directly at Hamley. "I appreciate your words about me, sir, and I also appreciate the situation that we're facing. The solution, I believe, is to consider the consequences of the choices and find the one that does the most good while doing the least harm. We can't say for certain what will happen to the ship and its crew if we follow the government's orders. We don't know the strength of the enemy and what they might do, but I'd venture to say that we do know the strength and bravery of our crew. What we know for certain is that if we don't give these people the help they need, there's a hard fate awaiting them."

Hamley rose from his seat and stood looking out the windows of his cabin at the waters of San Diego harbor. The silence seemed interminable. Fournier wondered if he had perhaps overstepped his boundaries by speaking so freely.

Then Hamley turned to face his second officer.

"You've said it well, Mr. Fournier. You may tell the crew to heave short, hoist the topsails, and get the ship ready to go to sea in service of the US government."

"Aye, Captain."

As Fournier stood and made his way up top, the relief he felt at the captain's decision was clouded by uncertainty as to how the crew might react to the change of duty he was about to explain to them. He stood in front of the skylight between the main- and mizzenmasts, collected himself, and called out, "All hands on deck!"

The men passed the word along to those who were belowdecks, and eventually the entire crew of nearly thirty men was assembled in front of Fournier.

"Men," he began in a calm and even tone, "we have orders to go to sea, orders that are from the government of the United States. Some of you have gone into town, and others have heard what our visitors on board have said. By now, most of you know that our countrymen in San Diego are in a tough spot. At this point, we are their only hope for escape, and we're going to give them safe haven.

"We'll be taking them and their goods aboard. Captain Merritt and his men will be joining us, too. It'll get a bit crowded on this ship, but I'm confident you know your jobs well enough to weather the distractions. I'll do my best to keep the townsfolk out of your way. Captain Merritt and his men will be on the lookout for United States forces to meet with as we make our way along the coast. With good fortune on our side, we'll give these people the help they need, and in due time, we'll be back on course for more whaling, and then home. All right then, let's heave short, hoist the topsails, and get this ship ready for sea!"

The men stood silently for a moment, some of them stunned by what they had just heard, others trying to determine what this change of duty would mean for them. They began talking among themselves, commenting and questioning, until their sound grew to a deep, resonant buzz. Then a strong and clear voice rose above all others. It was Peter McDonnald.

"You heard the man. We've got a job to do. We're going to help these people just the same as we'd want them to help us. Let's get to work!"

Any remaining reluctance fell away, and with shouts of, "All right, then," "Into the rigging," and "Man the windlass," the crew sprang into action.

By now it was three p.m., and goods and ammunition had begun arriving from shore. Bundles of blankets, crates of food, and boxes of musket balls were some of the items that the crew began hauling on board. They were bulky but not particularly heavy. Soon, however, loads arrived that had to be lifted on board using the same devices that the whalers had used to hoist blubber onto the deck.

"These bundles are getting heavier and heavier. What in hell are they sending us now?" said Mark Comstock to his brother Samuel as they maneuvered a large sack onto the starboard deck. Samuel pulled open the mouth of the sack just enough to peer inside.

"It's what I guessed, by the lumpy shape—cannonballs!"

"I suppose we know what's on the next boat," Mark replied, receiving a nod from his brother.

Just as suspected, the Comstocks looked down and saw a small brass cannon nestled in the boat that had just pulled up to the side of the ship. That afternoon, on the first day of October, 1846, the *Stonington* had begun its transformation from a civilian whaleship to a naval warship.[6]

CHAPTER 14

Ready for Duty

THE ORDERS THAT ARRIVED FROM SHORE THE NEXT MORNING WERE startling yet not completely unexpected—"Clear out between decks and make preparations for taking goods and passengers on board." That meant hoisting out of the hold the casks of whale oil that the men of the *Stonington* had collected during their voyage of some three years. In all, the casks of various sizes amounted to about 7,850 gallons of the precious commodity. At $1.50 per gallon in 1846, that was $11,775 ($467,469 in 2023). The crew would have to heave the barrels overboard and out to sea rather than put them onshore, where they would be available for the Californios to take and use for their own purposes, possibly to even finance their war efforts. This would amount to a total financial loss for the Williams & Barns firm that owned the ship. Captain Hamley knew they would hold him responsible, but he hoped they would understand that it had been an order from the US government, as well as a humanitarian effort.

The captain may not have realized that their acceptance of his explanation would depend on their views about this war and the expansionism that was at its basis. Thomas Williams II and Acors Barns were from a part of the country that was generally suspicious of efforts by the US government to acquire more territory, fearing that some forces in the country would take advantage of the gains in order to spread the system of slavery into those lands. The ship's owners may also have been among those that objected to the war because they believed that President Polk had instigated it by sending troops, under the command of General

Zachary Taylor, into Mexican land that was beyond the southern border of Texas. Be that as it may, the orders stood, and Hamley had to communicate them to the crew.

Once again, he called upon Alanson Fournier, his second in command, to deliver some jarring news to the men of the *Stonington*. Upon hearing the orders, most of the men understood that this was yet another step they had to take in order to save the desperate people of San Diego. However, some expressed their doubts, with comments like "Where else can we fit all the people?," "There's no room for them in our bunks," and "We can't have the whole town on deck with us!"

A relative few saw it as a foolish waste. "All that time and hard work just gone"; "We put our lives on the line, and for what?"; "Might as well call this ship the *Stolenton!*" were among their retorts.

Whatever their opinions might have been, they had orders to follow, and willingly or not, they began hauling the precious cargo out of the hold and over the side into the waters of the harbor and eventually out to sea.[1]

The casks of whale oil floated away from the *Stonington*, carrying the crew's thoughts with them, drifting backward through time into memories of what they had done in order to get that oil. They saw in their minds oh so vividly the rowing of the whaleboats toward the whales, the valiant attempts of those massive animals to escape their hunters, the harpooning and lancing of the whales that they managed to take after a fierce battle, the towing of the lifeless creatures back to the ship where they would butcher them and then toss their carved-up blubber into the heated trypots that melted the flesh into oil. It was dangerous, gruesome, savage work that had seared itself forever into their beings, and they felt as though a part of their own selves was floating away with those casks. They now had to turn their attention to a different conflict, one that pitted human against human and carried great controversy, as would eventually the whaling that they had done.[2]

CHAPTER 15

Stay and Fight

"How much longer with the loading, Mr. Fournier? It's likely that we'll need to be under way soon, and on short notice at that," said Captain Hamley. It was still October 2, but now about four o'clock in the afternoon. "We've most of the weaponry on board, sir, excepting four brass pieces that remain onshore. We'll get them tomorrow unless we're obliged to leave sooner. For now, we're bringing the townsfolk aboard and getting them settled," replied Fournier.

It was well into the night by the time nearly forty San Diegan men had made their way onto the *Stonington*. Among them were settlers from the United States as well as Californios who aligned themselves with the Americans. Those that had families had already said good-bye to their loved ones, who were taking refuge at the large, U-shaped home of José Antonio Estudillo and his wife, María Victoria Dominguez de Estudillo, highly respected citizens of San Diego who were sympathetic to the Americans. The men made themselves as comfortable as possible in the crowded hold of the ship, commenting on the strange, pungent odor that hung in the air, eventually realizing that it was the lingering traces of the whale oil that had been jettisoned during the day.

The following morning, after a restless night, those that had been able to get a little sleep awoke to a flurry of noise above them.[1]

"Now that we've got those brass pieces aboard, Mr. Fournier, let's heave short and get under way," called Hamley.

"Aye, Captain. You heard him, men. Haul anchor and set sail!" shouted Fournier to the crew. Chains rattled, ropes tautened, wood creaked, and canvas snapped tight as the *Stonington* began to leave the harbor. Within moments, however, the ship swerved in the wrong direction and headed toward shore, in danger of grounding.

"Drop anchor, furl the sails!" cried Hamley to the crew. "Blasted rudder head!" he snarled to himself. Not entirely to himself, however, as Fournier, who was within earshot, glanced simultaneously down and toward Hamley. Some of the crew that were nearby caught Fournier's look and sensed that he was not in total agreement with the captain's previous decisions. He was, they were beginning to see, his own man, capable of making decisions that would benefit the group rather than satisfy his own concerns.

Without the necessary repairs, it was difficult to maneuver the ship, particularly in constricted areas such as a harbor. Hamley kept it anchored for the rest of the day. Many of the crew wondered why he would do so, knowing all the while that with the Californios fast approaching San Diego, he would have to move it into a much less vulnerable position. They thought back to the look they had seen from Fournier when Hamley was cursing the rudder head, and they waited.[2]

The passengers from town spent another tense night in the hold. Everyone tried to find a comfortable position that would allow them to have at least a few moments of restful sleep. It had been a stressful two days, and they were beginning to wonder if they had made the right decision to leave their cozy homes and crowd themselves into this smelly ship that afforded them little privacy for their basic functions. Limited though it may have been, their freedom of movement on land now seemed greater than the constrictions they faced on a ship that was stuck in place due to its inability to sail properly.

Sunday morning, October 4, began as another fine-weather day, but the news that arrived with a messenger from shore clouded the outlook.

"The Californios are here and they've taken the town," called the messenger that had rowed out to the ship. "They've hauled down the

Stars and Stripes and raised their own flag in the plaza. They'll likely be down to destroy the storehouses on the beach before long." Merchants had been using the storehouses for decades to hold the cattle hides and tallow that were the basis of the trade that flourished in San Diego's harbor.

"Much obliged, friend," responded Alanson Fournier, as the messenger began to row back to shore. "Keep yourself safe."

On his way to the captain's quarters to explain the situation to Hamley, Fournier's thoughts turned to possible solutions.[3]

"Permission to speak freely, sir?" queried Fournier after relaying the messenger's news.

"Go on," replied Hamley hesitantly.

"Seeing as there's not much time, Captain—nor too many options, given our difficulties with getting under way—perhaps we should make the best of what we've got, and what we've got now are guns. We could mount the guns on both sides so we could drop the ship up abreast of those storehouses and defend them in either direction, and we'd give the guns portholes by cutting into the bulwarks. The men working them would need plenty of space for firing and reloading, so as much as I don't like the thought of it, we'd have to remove the tryworks."

Hamley, who had been listening somewhat patiently, shot Fournier an incredulous look, eyebrows raised and mouth opened.

"I know, sir, the tryworks are the beating heart of our whaling," Fournier continued, "but we're not doing much whaling now. Our duty seems to have shifted, and it's the beating hearts of the people we've taken aboard that we need to be thinking about, as well as our own."

Hamley stared up at the ceiling of his cabin, as if his gaze were going beyond it, trying to envision the changes to the ship that his second officer had suggested. Then he bent his head downward, seeming to consider the people of San Diego that were huddled below. After a long pause, he leveled his eyes at Fournier with a resigned look that hinted at admiration. "You've made your points, Mr. Fournier," he said drily. "Organize the work details and get them started. I'll be up soon to check your progress."

"Aye, Captain, thank you, sir," replied Fournier, and he made his way up and forward to organize the crew.

Passing by the tryworks, he paused to consider the thousands of hours the men had spent at this furnace, comprising two large cast-iron kettles surrounded by bricks, which performed the ultimate whaling task of transforming blubber into oil. What he was about to order the men to do seemed almost sacrilegious, but he knew it had to be done for the protection of the souls on board.[4]

Just past the tryworks and situated behind the foremast was the companionway ladder that led down to the general sailors' quarters. Fournier was about to head down there when he saw several crewmen gathered on the deck ahead of the mast. Among them was Thomas Milnor, the ship's carpenter. He was a compactly built man of less than average height, with sandy brown hair and blue eyes that twinkled almost perpetually with a look of mischief in them. There had been a brief disciplinary incident between Milnor and Fournier one night that past April when he had refused an order while on watch. This had caused Fournier to confront him, at which point Milnor backed off without any further trouble. Later the next day, Milnor had approached Fournier and apologized for his actions.

"I accept your apology, Milnor, on the condition that you do better in the future," responded Fournier sternly.

"You have my promise, Mr. Fournier. I simply ask that you speak no more about it."

Fournier suspected that Milnor did not want word of the incident to reach the captain, whose reaction would likely be much more severe.

"The matter ends here, Milnor. Now get on with your work and do as you've promised."

Six months had passed, with no further incidents from Thomas Milnor.

Fournier approached him and stated the issue.

"Milnor, we need to cut into the bulwarks and make portholes for the guns that we'll be mounting on deck in order to defend ourselves from an attack that's likely to come from shore. Who'll be best to help you get the work done right, and quickly?"

Milnor cocked his head and looked at Fournier in silent disbelief.

"I know, Milnor. It's uncommon but necessary, given our situation. Now, who'll be best to help?"

"Miller, Desantos, and Harry, sir," said Milnor, gesturing to three men who were nearby, the first two from the Azores, the third, an Indigenous man from Rhode Island. "All three know a thing or two about tools and such."

"All right, Milnor," Fournier responded. "Take them with you and get started. The captain'll be by momentarily to see your progress."

Looking around at the others gathered before him, Fournier spotted Peter McDonnald.

"McDonnald, I want you to take the rest of these men and set about removing the tryworks," Fournier said. "As much as it pains me to say it, you'll have to toss it all overboard. We need that deck area clear, and what with the hold as it is, there's no room on the ship to store it. Move quickly now, as we'll need to get those guns in place soon."

McDonnald looked back at Fournier, stunned at first, trying to put together in his head the orders he had just heard and the picture they created.

Realizing Fournier was expecting action from him rather than an opinion, he called to James Rice and the others around him. "All right, men, you heard Mr. Fournier. Let's get to it."[5]

Disassembling the rows of bricks that enclosed the pots released the pungent odor of whale oil into the air, causing the men to reflect back to a time when they had been engaged in tasks far more challenging than the menial one they were performing at present. As they carried the bricks to the sides and dumped them over the rail, they gazed at the shore, pondering whether their current task would result in them facing conflicts of a different sort, pitting them against people rather than whales, requiring them to exhibit strengths they were not entirely sure they possessed.

The test would come soon enough.

For now, having removed the structure that surrounded and protected the trypots, they had to wrestle the two massive black iron cauldrons, each weighing hundreds of pounds, to starboard and heave them overboard through the gangway bulwark. Each trypot landed in the water with a tremendous splash that sprayed the men who had jettisoned them, as if in some sort of retribution for having deposed them from their "thrones."[6]

Meanwhile, Thomas Milnor and his crew had been hard at work on the larboard side, cutting carefully and skillfully into the oak planks that formed a protective wall that rose about four and a half feet above the deck. Using chisels, hammers, and saws, they created square openings large enough for the small cannons to fire through but not so big as to compromise the strength of the bulwark.

"It don't seem right, fellas," said Milnor to his three crewmates, "piercin' the skin of the ship this way, but I suppose it's all for the best, considerin' the fix these folks are in."

If William Harry, who was hammering at one of the chisels, had known the background of the situation, he may well have seen something else as not quite right. Here he was, an Indigenous man, on the other side of the continent from his home, making preparations to defend men fighting over land they had claimed as their own, land that Indigenous people had originally inhabited for thousands of years. Then again, if he had heard the stories of his people back in Charlestown, Rhode Island, he might have known that a tribe from Upstate New York had made their way south searching for greater food resources, challenging his people for dominance over their land. His people had called that other tribe *Pequotog*—invaders. Harry might well have reached the conclusion that people clashing over control of land seemed to be a constant facet of human existence that had no boundaries nor a foreseeable end.[7]

CHAPTER 16

Further Adjustments Required

MILNOR'S CREW FINISHED THEIR LARBOARD-SIDE WORK AND THEN went to work on the starboard. McDonnald and his group had cleared the deck between both sides, making it easier for the men who would be using the guns to load and fire them from either side.

Captain Merritt and Captain Hamley had been monitoring the men's progress. Hamley was generally pleased with the transformation that his crew had accomplished. Merritt, however, saw the vulnerability of the ship's overall position. He looked around at the whaleboats hanging from their davits, thought for a moment, then called to John Bidwell, who was also on deck at the time.

"Bidwell," he shouted above the noise, beckoning with his arm.

Bidwell made his way across the deck. A well-educated former school principal, he did not care much for Merritt and his coarse, uncouth manner. Bidwell realized, however, that he was now subordinate to Merritt, having fled his post at San Luis Rey to find protection in San Diego.

"Bidwell, t-t-take one of these boats to San Pedro. Bring four men with you. Get the l-l-latest n-n-news about this war, and send d-d-dispatches up the coast for any help we can get."

Bidwell nodded silently to Merritt, then turned to Hamley. "Captain, please select four of your strongest men to prepare one of your boats and assist me on this voyage."

"Aye, Mr. Bidwell. They'll be with you presently," Hamley replied, and then called to his second officer, "Mr. Fournier, a word."

As Fournier approached, Hamley said, "Mr. Bidwell here needs four men to take him up to San Pedro in one of our boats. It's a journey of about a hundred miles on open water, and though they'll have a sail, there'll be plenty of rowing to do, so give him some strong ones that know their way with a boat."

"Aye, Captain, I know just the men for the job. Mr. Bidwell, there's work being done starboard, so make your way larboard to the stern boat. I'll fetch the men."

Bidwell did as Fournier asked, and Fournier went to the fo'c'sle and found James Holden, Nelson Davis, Gardner Jaques, and John Dias, four of the men that had gone to town with him when the *Stonington* first arrived at San Diego.[1]

"Men," began Fournier, "I have an important mission for you that may well give all of us, including the townsfolk, a better chance at making it through this rough patch we're in. I know you well enough to say you're the right men for what I'm about to ask you to do." He then told them about their passenger and the purpose of the journey. "You need to know there'll be a certain amount of danger involved, so tell me now if you'd rather I find someone else to go in your place."

The four crewmen stood looking at Fournier for a moment, then turned to look at one another, measuring each man's resolve against their own, silently nodding as they did so. They returned their gazes to Fournier.

Gardner Jaques, a native of Halifax, Nova Scotia, was the first to speak.

"We've faced plenty of danger on this voyage, Mr. Fournier, and you've been through it with us. If you say we're the ones for the job, then so be it. We're ready to prove you right. Eh, men?"

The other three responded nearly in unison with a firm "Aye."

Fournier looked directly at each of them, nodding approvingly.

"All right, then," he said. "Get your open-water clothes, go to the galley for some food and water, and meet me at the larboard stern boat. Mr. Bidwell's waiting there for you."

The four crewmen collected their supplies, and as they made their way along the deck, they marveled at the transformation that had occurred. The empty space where the tryworks had stood, the portholes in the bulwarks, and the guns being put into place lent an even greater sense of seriousness and importance to the journey they were about to take. They held their heads a bit higher as they approached Fournier and Bidwell.

After being introduced to the crewmen, Bidwell listened as Fournier quickly explained the basic aspects of rowing, steering, and sailing the boat. Bidwell took it all in, acknowledging that he would need to be more than just a passenger. He waited as the crewmen checked the boat's gear, loaded their supplies, and began lowering the boat. He climbed in with the rest of them, the boat settled into the water, and within minutes, at around eleven a.m. on Monday, October 5, they were on their way to San Pedro with the hope of securing some help.[2]

Fournier approached Milnor and his small crew. "Milnor, your next job is to mount those guns that we took on board at the portholes that you've just created. You'll have to account for loading and recoil, so you'll need to fashion some sort of bed on which the support structure can slide. A sturdy line run through the breech loop with both ends attached to the bulwark would likely be useful to keep the whole business from sliding too far backward."

"Would you like to join my crew, Mr. Fournier, seein' as you've got such a clear notion of how to go about buildin' this rig?" said Milnor with a slight grin.

"No, Milnor," responded Fournier wryly, "I'm sure you've got a good sense of what I expect from you."

"Aye, sir, that I do," replied the ship's carpenter. "All right, fellas," he said, winking at Joe Miller, Joe Desantos, and William Harry, "let's find some wood that's up to the task!"

By the next day, Milnor and his crew had finished mounting the guns. Seeing the men on the deck, Fournier approached them.

"That's fine work you did with those guns, men."

"Yes, sir, we're pretty good at mountin'—even though we're a bit out of practice, eh, mates?" Milnor said with his *hee-hee* chuckle. His crewmates burst out laughing.

Fournier gave a knowing grin and moved on. It was time to inspect the hold.[3]

It had been four days since the inhabitants of San Diego had come aboard, and he wanted to assess their situation. The crewmen that had lived aboard the *Stonington* during the past few years had become accustomed to the spartan conditions. The men now occupying the lowest area of the ship were not so hardened, and Fournier wanted to see for himself how they were doing before making a report to the captain.

As he made his way below, the light of the fine-weather Monday became gradually dimmer, from direct sunlight on the main deck to the refracted light of deck prisms on the 'tween deck, to the limited light through the hatch gratings above the hold. He could also detect a slight change in the odor. The dominant scent was still that of whale oil, but mingled with it now were the smells of people and their bodily functions. He was surprised by the fact that the human odors had actually begun to cut through the whale odors, and were, to a small degree, neutralizing what he had come to expect as the normal smell of this part of the ship.

Where before there had been large barrels of whale oil piled on top of each other and held in place by pen-boards on both sides of the hold, now there were people spread across the planking. Most of them had placed blankets beneath themselves to provide a bit of comfort and warmth. A bucket at the stern, just behind the lower mizzenmast, served as the latrine. Fournier walked carefully in the shadowy, cavernous expanse, whose ceiling was about ten feet above, doing his best to avoid stepping on anyone or their belongings. As he made his way, he paused and introduced himself in a low tone so as not to disturb anyone who may have managed to fall asleep.

"I'm Alanson Fournier, second officer aboard this ship. How are you faring?"

The answers were varied.

"It ain't the most comfortable spot we's been in, but it's safer than where we was."

"Much obliged for your hospitality, sir."

"If you please, sir, could we have a bit more water next portion?"

"I am Californio, *señor*, but I do not agree with those who wish to drive you away. Our peoples have much to offer each other."

"How much longer before we can go back to our homes?"

Fournier listened patiently and responded calmly to each comment and question. He gave reassurances that the ship was prepared for defense, that a boat was on its way for reinforcements, that the crew of the *Stonington* and Captain Merritt and his men would do their best to keep them safe and, as soon as possible, get them back to their families and their homes.

He then made his way up to the captain's cabin to deliver his report.

"Captain Hamley, sir?" he said, when he had reached the cabin door.

"What is it, Mr. Fournier?" replied Hamley, who was seated at his table.

"I've a report to give you on the condition of the ship and the inhabitants in the hold."

"All right, Fournier, come in. Let's have it."

"Sir, the guns are mounted and ready to be armed. You saw for yourself that the portholes are cut and the deck is cleared. The inhabitants are doing as well as can be expected, sir, and are of generally good humor, but I'm not certain how long they can remain so, and how long our water supply will last."

"Frankly, Mr. Fournier, I'm not as concerned with those inhabitants as I am with the ship," replied Hamley somewhat coldly. "It's my duty to see that we make it through this experience and get back to New London in one piece." Fournier's brow furrowed as Hamley continued. "The enemy will be here any day now, and whatever news that boat may bring us from San Pedro, we've got to get this ship in position to defend against an attack from shore. That's where I expect them to make their first attempt at us. We'll need additional anchors to make a mooring abreast of the shore. When you've got them, set us abreast to present our starboard side. There's more mooring chocks available there than on our larboard side."

"Aye, sir, I'll see to it. Just one more thing, sir."

"What is it?"

"With your permission, sir, I'd like to provide a bit more water for those in the hold."

"Damn it all, Fournier, we've got our own to keep watered."

"Yes, sir, that's true, but if we do end up in a fight with the enemy, we may very well need those men to help us."

"There is that, Fournier, there is that. All right, you may increase the water rations. Mind, though, no more complaints from them, and keep our own crew watered properly, for the safety of all aboard depends on them. Now be off and tend to those anchors."

"Aye, sir, and thank you."

Fournier's step had a bit more of a spring to it as he went up the companionway stairs. He headed toward the galley to speak with the steward about the water rations, then he began the search for extra anchors.

CHAPTER 17

Battle Positions

At ten o'clock on the morning of Wednesday, October 7, two anchors from shore were delivered to the *Stonington*. The crew rigged them and then moored the ship so its starboard side faced the shore.

Captain Hamley had been on deck observing the process, and so had Captain Merritt. When the crew had finished its work, Hamley called out to them, "Well done, men. Now get some supplies to those guns so's they'll be set for loading and firing." Hamley then walked over to Merritt. "There, Captain Merritt, we've got the ship positioned and ready for action. Fine work, I'd say, for a crew that's known only whaling for the past three years."

"They've made quick work of it, I'll give ya that, Hamley. N-n-now comes the hard part—usin' them guns in battle. Your men's got their way with spears and such. My men knows guns, so they'll be handlin' the firin' when the t-t-time comes."

"I'm sure there's some of my crew that knows their way with a gun, and—"

"That may be, Hamley, but like I said, my men'll be the ones firin' those d-d-deck guns, end of story!"

With that, Merritt walked away, leaving Hamley with the realization that he was no longer in control of every aspect of the ship. His purpose, like that of the ship, had changed. He turned, and without looking at any of his crew directly, made his way down to his cabin. That's where he was sitting when, at two p.m., the wind sprang up from the northwest and rain began to fall. He felt the ship move and sensed immediately that something was going wrong.

He clambered up the companionway, reached the deck, and yelled, "Fournier, what the devil is going on?"

"The wind, sir," called Fournier, "it's got the best of our broadside. It's pushing us long on those two anchors from shore as well as the stern. The bow's holding firm, though."

"See that it does, Fournier," Hamley growled, "This is no time to be adrift."

The captain returned to his cabin, leaving his second officer to deal with the storm.

Fournier posted a watch on each of the four anchors, and although the ship's bow was now pointed directly at the shore, the anchors held through the evening and into the night.[1]

The next day began with fine weather. The wind was still blowing from the northwest, but a bit lighter. The crew reset the moorings so that the ship was not completely broadside to the shore in order to avoid the same shift that had occurred the day before. The guns were now at an angle but might still be effective if loaded with a proper charge.

Edwin Arthur and Martin Larkins—in their late teens, the youngest men of the crew—were sharing the duty as lookouts, keeping their eyes on the La Playa Trail and watching for any signs of movement by the Californios. A little after four o'clock in the afternoon, as they turned their gaze toward Point Loma, they spotted what looked to be a boat. Rather than call out a warning that might be heard by the enemy, Arthur scrambled down the rigging to alert the captain.

Upon reaching the deck, he saw Alanson Fournier near the mainmast and hurried over to him.

"Mr. Fournier, sir, there appears to be a boat rounding Point Loma and heading our way. Can't say for sure, but it looks to me and Larkins to be the boat that set out for San Pedro a few days back."

"Let's have a look," said Fournier, grabbing his spyglass and heading to the rail. Extending the small brass telescope, he peered through the lens.

"By heaven, Arthur, you and Larkins are seeing clear. I can just make out Bidwell, at the steering oar, no less. Seems he's learned a thing or two about boating on this trip. Let's hope he's got some good news for us."[2]

CHAPTER 18

Brave Action

ALANSON FOURNIER WATCHED AS THE RETURNING BOAT APPROACHED the *Stonington*. Its small crew kept the sail hoisted until they were nearly at the ship, then they brought it down and rowed the rest of the way.

Hamley and Merritt had joined him at the rail, and once the boat was alongside, Fournier could see the haggard looks on the men's faces.

John Bidwell was the first to climb aboard, and Merritt immediately began questioning him.

"What n-n-news, Bidwell?"

Stopping for a moment to catch his breath, he delivered his report.

"We arrived off the coast of San Pedro on the morning of the sixth. The weather was fair on our way there, and we stayed close enough to the shore so that we could make contact with any US forces that we might come across, but there were none in sight.

"The ship *Vandalia* was in port. When we came alongside, we learned that Lieutenant Gillespie was aboard, along with his men. I hadn't seen him since July fourth, when we formalized the California Republic. Seems that he and his forces had to abandon Los Angeles after being driven out by the Californios. We tethered and stayed on the ship overnight."

"Had yourselves a little party, eh, Bidwell?" asked Hamley.

Bidwell ignored Hamley's sarcasm and continued. "That same evening, the *Savannah* sailed into port. Gillespie boarded to meet with Captain Mervine, and they made plans to go ashore and drive the Californios out of Los Angeles. The next morning, we loaded some food and supplies into our boat to bring back here. We left as the boats from the *Savannah* were on their way to shore with three hundred men."

"That must have been a sight to see" said Fournier.

"Indeed it was, sir, and we cheered them on as we rowed," said Bidwell. "Not too long after, a northwest wind began to blow and the sea turned rough. We thought perhaps we could outrun it, but the storm overtook us, knocking the boat about so much that food and supplies fell overboard. We were lucky enough to keep ourselves in the boat. The weather finally calmed down early this morning, and here we are."

"Seems as though you were hit by the same winds that pushed us off our moorings," said Hamley.

"You lost some precious cargo, Bidwell, but you brought back some d-d-damn good n-n-news," said Merritt. "These here Californios'll be thinkin' d-d-different when they hear about their friends' t-t-troubles in Los Angeles. T-t-time for us to start thinkin' about goin' ashore ourselves and givin' 'em the same sort'a t-t-trouble."[1]

Merritt and the others had no way of knowing that the troops led by Mervine and Gillespie were heading toward defeat at the hands of the Californios in the Battle of the Old Woman's Gun, and that they would have to re-board their ships and sail away. All they knew at the moment was that a US force was marching against the enemy—the same enemy that was now occupying San Diego.

"If they can d-d-do it, so can we!" declared Merritt.

His men, who were now standing around him, nodded their bearded, shaggy-haired heads and voiced their agreement. Some of the ship's crew joined them.

"Aye," said one, "and with the men from town what's in the hold, we'll give 'em a fight they won't soon forget."

"Right you are, fella, right you are, but we n-n-need to see what shape those men are in. L-l-let's get 'em up here."

"Captain Merritt," said Fournier, "it would be much quicker if you were to go to the hold to speak with them rather than take the time to bring them all up on deck. It would also be quieter, so we wouldn't be giving the Californios an idea of what we've got in store for them."

"You've got a point there, Fournier. L-l-lead the way."

Fournier brought Merritt to the companionway and down into the hold. As they entered the vast lowest level, Merritt exclaimed, "What in hell is that stench?"

"Their latrine bucket probably needs—"

"N-n-no, not that. I know that smell. The other one. It's up on d-d-deck, t-t-too, but not as strong."

"That'd be the whale oil, sir," Fournier replied.

"But I thought you d-d-dumped all that?"

"Aye, we did, sir, but the smell never leaves a whaleship."

"D-d-don't know how you whalers can stand it."

"I suppose it just becomes a part of us, gets into our blood and our sweat."

"Well, let's see about these men so we can get back up t-t-to some fresh air." Merritt looked around. "Stand up, men, and listen t-t-to what I've got to say."

They brought themselves to their feet, some more easily than others, sensing the urgency in Merritt's voice.

"Right now, as I'm speaking t-t-to you, there's US forces marchin' on Los Angeles to push them Californios outta t-t-town. We're gonna d-d-do the same to them what's in San Diego. Who's ready to j-j-join us?"

Immediately cries of "Me!," "I am," and "*Sí*" mingled and swelled beyond the hold and up through the hatches, causing those on deck to stop and turn their heads in the direction of the sound.

"All right, men, keep your voices low. No warning the enemy, eh?" said Fournier.

"What about the cannons?" one of the men called out.

"We've got them mounted and ready—"

"Not the ones on the ship," said the man. "The ones in the old fort."

"What about them?" asked Merritt.

"There's two guns in that old fort. You know, the presidio. If them Californios gets their hands on 'em, they could do us some serious damage."[2]

Merritt turned to Fournier, then back to the men. "All right, then. Seems t-t-to me that someone's got to get to those guns and spike 'em before them Californios gets a ch-ch-chance to use 'em. Gotta d-d-do it in the d-d-dark to keep from gettin' caught, so it's gotta be someone knows their way real well."

A voice in the middle of the crowd said "I'll do it."

"Who's that?" asked Merritt. "Show yerself plain."

The speaker walked to the front and said, "I'll do it, sir. I'm Albert Smith. I may be from New York, but I've lived here for some time now and know these hills, day or night, and I know guns. You get me to shore with a couple of spikes, I'll get to those guns and fill their vent holes so tight, no flame could ever touch the charge. They'll be useless, and we'll be clear to march and take back our town."

"A fellow New Yorker, eh?" said Fournier, "Whereabouts?"

"Long Island, Suffolk County," answered Smith.

"Same," said Fournier with a smile and a nod.

"All right, enough of that," growled Merritt. "Let's get you up t-t-top and ready, Smith. The rest of you what's gonna j-j-join us, get a good n-n-night's sleep. You'll need it for t-t-tomorrow."

Merritt and Fournier led Smith to the main deck where they explained the situation to Hamley and Bidwell. Fournier saw the blacksmith and said, "Thompson, give this man some suitable metal to spike those guns." Hamley looked at the crewmen. "You four, get a boat ready. Muffle your oars and take Smith to shore at La Playa. Wait for him there and be quick about getting him back when he's done."

Thompson went to his quarters and returned with a canvas pouch that he handed to Smith. "You'll find what you need in there," he said to Smith. "Good luck to ye."

"Much obliged, friend," said Smith, turning and heading for the boat. In the dark of Thursday, October 8, his mission was under way.[3]

The crew had wrapped the oarlocks with canvas strips so the oars wouldn't rattle. They rowed to shore, where Albert Smith hopped out, gave them a wave, and then disappeared into the night.

Smith left the trail, where he could be spotted easily by enemy lookouts on the hills just south of the old fort. He crisscrossed in the scrub brush beyond the trail, taking advantage of any tree that afforded him a slight bit of cover, and being careful to move stealthily in order to avoid kicking up any dust that might reveal his path. Drawing within about one hundred feet of the presidio, he waited and watched to ensure that no one was near the old fort. When he was certain he was alone, he continued, staying as low to the ground as possible while approaching the guns.

Smith reached into his sack and brought out a small hammer and a piece of cloth. Then he took out one of the metal spikes, placed its tip into the vent hole, covered the other end with the cloth, and began to tap the spike with the hammer. The muffled *thup, thup, thup* continued until he had driven the end of the spike flush with the barrel of the gun. Before moving to the next gun, he paused to see if anyone had heard him. Confident he was still undetected, he repeated the spiking process on the second gun. When he was finished, he returned the hammer and cloth to the pouch and made his way carefully back to the boat.[4]

It had been hours since Albert Smith had left the boat, and the crew waiting for him at La Playa were relieved to see him approaching. He gave them a sign to let them know all had gone well, joining them in the boat. They quickly pushed away from shore and rowed quietly back to the ship. The first part of the plan to retake San Diego from the Californios was finished. The next part would begin at daybreak. For now, the small boat crew was happy to be returning to the ship with a successful Smith safely aboard.

As they approached the *Stonington*, they could see Alanson Fournier and some of the crew waiting at the rail to haul the boat up and bring them aboard. Captains Hamley and Merritt soon appeared as well, and when Albert Smith stepped onto the deck, he turned to the expectant Merritt. "Done, sir. Spiked 'em solid."

Merritt clapped him on the back. "Good work, Smith," he said, and the others greeted him with hearty words of approval that they kept muffled in order to avoid arousing the suspicions of the Californios.

"N-n-now get yourself some shut-eye, Smith," instructed Merritt. "You'll n-n-need it for the march to t-t-town."

"Thank you, Captain," replied Smith, "but I'm not sure I'll be able to sleep much given all the excitement."

He turned and made his way to the hold, where he supplied those of his townsmen that were still awake with brief answers to their questions about what he had done, and after receiving more thanks from them, laid down on his blanket for some well-earned rest.

CHAPTER 19

Decisive Moves

IN THE FAINT GLOW OF DAWN ON FRIDAY, OCTOBER 9, MEN WERE SCUR-
rying about the deck of the *Stonington*, carrying out their orders and
exchanging comments that were a mixture of excitement and nervousness.

"High time we get off this stinkin' ship and back on dry land, to do
what we do best—and that's fight," said one of Merritt's men, to which
the others growled their agreement.

The townsmen that would be joining the march were just as eager,
but there was a different edge to their voices. "Our womenfolk best be as
safe and secure as when we left 'em, and same with our houses," said one.

The crewmen were facing a new level of involvement. "We ain't just
whalers no more, fellas. Those of us goin' ashore this time could be in for
a real fight with the enemy."

The situation had taken on an added sense of seriousness after Captain Merritt had decided to take two of the guns ashore. Some of the
crew were busy detaching the lines from the mounts so they could hoist
the guns into the boats.

"Ain't no mistakin' it," said one. "We're truly a part of this war now."

At seven a.m., the combined forces aboard the *Stonington* began loading
the boats. Three crewmen in each boat handled the oars, including the
steering oar, leaving more room for passengers, weapons, and ammunition.

The first few boats landed over a dozen men, soon followed by the
boats carrying the two guns. Several men slid each gun out of its boat
that had been emptied of all other items and then rolled onto its side on

the sandy shore. They then began pulling each gun up to the trail where the rest of the men had gathered. The guns occasionally got stuck in the sand, causing the men to have to lift and carry them part of the way.

Alanson Fournier, who had been in one of the first boats to land, walked among the men and reminded them to stay quiet as they waited for the others to arrive. "The Californios haven't spotted us yet, as far as I can tell, so let's keep it that way. Stay out of sight behind these store-houses until it's time to march." The men nodded in silent acknowledgment as the boats returned to the ship.[1]

By two p.m., those who would be marching to the town, including captains Merritt and Hamley, were all landed and ready to move. Some of the townsmen had remained aboard with several crewmen, to help safeguard the ship.

Merritt called the force of over forty men to attention.

"Listen carefully, men," he began. "Get yourselves into marching formation on that t-t-trail, with four men on each gun in front. We're gonna march our way into that t-t-town, and if any Californios t-t-try to stop us, we'll convince 'em otherwise. All right, then, get movin'."

Merritt and Hamley went to the head of the formation, in front of the guns. Fournier positioned himself in front of the rest of the men behind the guns. Two lines formed behind Fournier, Merritt waved his hand in the air, and the entire force began its march to San Diego.

Within a few yards, the men pulling the guns were forced to stop—not by any opposing army, but by the sandy soil of the path. Each crew, with the help of some of the others behind them, had to lift and carry their gun until they reached a portion of the path that provided more solid ground for them to continue pulling. The columns behind Fournier had to pause as well, until the gun crews were ready and he gave the signal to resume their march.

The entire force had advanced halfway to town when Merritt spotted Californio horsemen approaching in the distance.

"They've seen us, Hamley. T-t-time to ready the guns," Merritt said as he turned to the gun crews. "Enemy's comin'. We'll fire the guns one at a t-t-time so's we can keep movin' forward. Follow my signal. One gun fires then reloads while the other moves ahead and fires. Keep that up and we'll push 'em the hell out of our way."

Serbulo Varela's horsemen drew nearer, moving at a steady trot. Their tall black hats and the long metal-tipped lances that they held upright made them appear larger than they actually were. As they approached, the gun crews loaded their weapons and prepared to fire. The column behind Fournier also readied their rifles. When the Californio horsemen were within one hundred feet, Merritt gave the signal and the first gun fired.

The startled horses twisted and turned, and as the smoke cleared, the Californios could see a second gun advance and fire in front of a column of men with rifles leveled at them. The first gun crew, having reloaded, now advanced and fired its gun. Varela gave a signal, the horses turned as one, and then they galloped away toward the town.

Merritt gave the signal to cease firing the guns and continue forward. By the time they arrived at the town plaza, Varela and his horsemen had ridden away into the northeast hills.[2]

María Antonia Juliana Machado de Silvas had been watching from her home in the plaza as Varela's forces left San Diego for the safety of the hills and Merritt's forces approached the town. Like most of the other nearby buildings, her home was a single-story structure made of white-washed adobe, with a red tile roof. It was situated on the southwest side of the plaza, and from the rear windows, she could see the US forces drawing near.

Her sympathies lay more with the Mexican side of the war because her father, José Manuel Machado, had been one of the original soldiers that the Spanish sent from Mexico in 1781 to settle and protect San Diego, where he eventually became commander of the troops. He remained loyal to his home country, particularly after it gained its independence from Spain in 1821, and it was the Mexican flag flying from the pole in the middle of the plaza that now entered María Machado de Silvas's mind. Determined to keep it from falling into the hands of the enemy, she dashed out the front door of her house and into the plaza. Upon reaching the flagpole, she used the knife she had carried to cut the halyard, pulled the flag down quickly, clutched it to her chest, and ran back inside her house.[3]

Within moments, Merritt and his forces arrived in town and made their way into the plaza, where the flagpole stood empty. In yet another show of bravery, Albert Smith grabbed the US flag that they had brought with them, found a pouch containing a hammer and some nails, shinnied up, and attached the flag to the pole.

As it began to flutter in the breeze, shots rang out. Some of Varela's men, from their perch in the eastern hills, were firing their rifles in indignation at Smith. Seeing that the shots had done no harm to anyone, Smith took his hat from his head, waved it in the air triumphantly, and then made his way back down the flagpole. Ironically, within a few years he would marry the widow María Guadalupe Yldefonsa Machado de Wilder, thus becoming the brother-in-law of the woman with whom he had "traded" flags.[4]

San Diego was no stranger to such shifts of control. Thousands of years ago, various tribes of Indigenous people had jostled for primacy throughout the territory. Sixteenth-century Spanish adventurers explored and laid claim to the land in the name of their country. The people of Mexico took possession after gaining their independence. Presently, it was Americans that held a position of control in San Diego.

PART IV

CHAPTER 20

Again to San Pedro

THE COMBINED FORCES OF CAPTAIN EZEKIEL MERRITT AND HIS MEN, the officers and crew of the *Stonington*, and a group of San Diegans had managed to drive Serbulo Varela and his men out of the town and into the hills surrounding San Diego on Friday, October 9.

The following day, after spending the night aboard their ship, the men of the *Stonington* returned to town and assisted in setting up defensive positions.

"We n-n-need to protect ourselves and these people from the enemy what's up in them hills," Merritt said to Captain Hamley. "They've been t-t-takin' potshots at us already, and I'm figurin' it's bound to get worse."

"Yes, that is true," said the well-dressed gentleman with the neatly parted black hair and finely trimmed mustache standing near Merritt. "Allow me to introduce myself, Captain Hamley. I am Don Miguel de Pedrorena, the *juez de paz*—the justice of the peace—here in San Diego. We did not have time for such pleasantries when I was aboard your ship. I wish to express to you my deepest gratitude for allowing us to come aboard when we were in such a desperate condition."

"We did what was needed," replied Hamley, failing to mention that it was the advice of his second officer that resulted in the *Stonington* becoming a shelter for Pedrorena and the others.

"My wife is also grateful to you for your help," continued Pedrorena. "She and the other women stayed behind here," he added, gesturing to the house behind them. "This is Casa de Estudillo, her childhood home."

"Enough jawin'," Merritt said. "We stand in one spot t-t-too long, we're t-t-targets."

Pedrorena suggested they move their conversation indoors, as he had a matter that he wished to discuss with them. Once they were inside, he began to explain.

"Gentlemen, we are going to need reinforcements and more ammunition if we are to hold San Diego. Serbulo Varela and his men have left town, but they will not give up the area so quickly. They and their families have been living in California for multiple generations. They are the descendants of settlers that came from Mexico as part of Spain's plan to populate the southwestern portions of North America that it had claimed for itself."

"And how d-d-do you know all this?" asked Merritt.

"I may speak your language well, *señor*, but I am not of this country. I was born in Spain, in Madrid. After some schooling there, my family, having the means to do so, sent me to London to continue my education. I then lived in Peru, and eight years ago, I moved here to San Diego. Let us say that, due to my experiences and curiosity, I have gathered a certain amount of knowledge."

"All right, then, go on," said Merritt begrudgingly.

"Three hundred years of Spanish rule ended more than two decades ago," Pedrorena continued, "and the Mexican government that replaced it is disorganized, ineffectual, and plagued with partisan infighting. Yes, *señor*. You see, after three hundred years, the Mexican people had grown weary of being ruled by Spain."

"I wouldn't have lasted three d-d-days," exclaimed Merritt.

"Just over twenty years ago, they rose up and defeated the Spanish, but the country was now much larger," said Pedrorena. "The new Mexican government was unable to control all of its territory, especially the land farthest from Mexico City."

"In other words, here and further north," said Hamley.

"Precisely. And the settlers of these lands, as well as their descendants, developed an independent way of life that is all their own. They call themselves Californios, not Mexicans or Spaniards, and they will fight to keep their land, and to keep their culture alive."

"So you're saying this won't be easy," observed Hamley.

"No, it will not," responded Pedrorena. "Even though there are some Californios, like me, who welcome the opportunity to cooperate with the United States of America, men such as Varela will do everything within their power to drive you out of what they see as their country. That is why I say that we will need more men and more arms."

Merritt and Hamley looked at each other, then at Pedrorena, who continued.

"I am aware that you sent a boat to San Pedro nearly a week ago to seek assistance, and that it returned with only news. If you are willing to send another boat there, I am willing to make the trip and deliver an urgent request for aid and supplies."

Hamley was the first to speak. "There's no telling what the weather may bring, but lately it's been fair, and that's a good sign. I could spare you four men, same as last time."

"If them men in the hills is as set agin' us as you say, then there's n-n-no t-t-time to waste. I expect to see that boat headin' out by t-t-tomorrow morning. I'll have a man ride d-d-down with you to the landing. He'll have messages from me for the officer in charge at San Pedro, and he'll t-t-tend to your horse."

Merritt left to inspect the town's defenses, Hamley made his way back to the ship to make the arrangements for the boat, and Pedrorena went to prepare for the voyage and explain the situation to his wife.[1]

On Sunday morning, October 11, after attending chapel services in the Estudillo house, Miguel de Pedrorena met one of Merritt's men and they made their way down to La Playa where Pedrorena would await a boat from the *Stonington*. Aboard the ship, Alanson Fournier summoned James Holden, Nelson Davis, Gardner Jaques, and John Dias. "The gentleman is on the shore, men. Time to lower your boat and bring him to San Pedro, as the captain ordered last night. Let's hope you return with better results than the last time."

"That would be good, sir, considerin' the effort," said Davis as they lowered the boat.

When the men reached the shore, Pedrorena, looking dignified as always, climbed into the boat and introduced himself. "Tell me, gentlemen, which oar shall I take?" he asked.

Davis and Jaques, both from the small farming town of Preston, Connecticut, glanced at each other with pleasantly surprised looks on their faces.

"Good start," said Jaques to Davis, turning to Pedrorena, and pointing to the available oar, he said, "This one'll do."

Pedrorena sat down, took up the oar, and fell into a rowing pattern with the others as they pulled away from shore and toward Point Loma, where they would hoist the sail and make their way to San Pedro.

CHAPTER 21

Under Siege

VARELA AND HIS MEN HAD TAKEN UP POSITIONS ON THE HILL OVER-
looking the town, the same place from which they had fired at Albert
Smith after his exploit with the flag. Ironically, it was also the same place
into which Smith had crept and spiked the cannons. This was Presidio
Hill, the site of the initial fortification that the Spaniards had built to
protect Mission San Diego de Alcalá, the first of twenty-one such missions that the Franciscan monks established in Alta California from the
late 1700s to the early 1800s. After gaining its independence from Spain
in 1821, Mexico eventually decided in 1833 to secularize the missions in
order to take control of them away from the Catholic Church, convert-
ing them into private lands that the government then sold or granted to
individual citizens. In the case of the San Diego mission, the presidio had
fallen into disrepair and ruin, leaving Varela and his Californios very little
in the way of shelter or concealment.

This did not stop them, however, from waging a campaign of harassment against the town's inhabitants.[1] They used their minimal ammunition sparingly, taking occasional shots at people as they moved about
within the town, especially at the Americans whenever they were raising
or lowering the US flag. They were also attentive to any attempts by the
inhabitants to go beyond the town limits in search of food. Varela's forces
had already driven out into the countryside any livestock, such as cattle
or sheep, that the townspeople could use for food. They had also removed
any food supplies from the dwellings that were situated on the mission

lands. The town was under siege, and those within it would have to act decisively in order to prevent their starvation.[2]

Monday, October 12, began with fine weather. It also began with sporadic gunfire from the hills as the townspeople went outdoors for their daily chores. As the *alcalde* of the town, Henry D. Fitch knew that he had to do something to protect the inhabitants. He sought out Ezekiel Merritt and stated his case.

"Captain Merritt," he began, "this is intolerable. We can't allow the enemy to shoot at us whenever they wish. We've got to coordinate our efforts and push back against them. With your help, as well as that of Captain Hamley and his men, I'm sure we can turn this situation around."

"Couldn't agree with you more, Mr. Fitch," replied Merritt. "My men an' I ain't wantin' t-t-to be sittin' d-d-ducks any more than you and your people are. Hamley and his crew should be here soon. J-j-just a matter of how many muskets we've got, and where to position 'em."

Within the hour, men from the *Stonington*, led by Captain Hamley and Second Officer Fournier, entered the town.

Fitch approached them and explained the situation.

"I'm sure we've got some men that are handy with a gun. Fournier, who comes to mind?" asked Hamley.

"There's Peter McDonnald and Edwin Arthur, sir, and the Comstock brothers."

"Call them up front," said Hamley.

Fournier brought the four men forward, and Fitch told them that after he armed them with muskets, Merritt would place them strategically among the buildings closest to the hills.

"You'll wait for my signal t-t-to fire," said Merritt. "We're gonna let them Californios give away their positions by lettin'"em fire at d-d-decoys. That'll give you a chance to d-d-draw a bead on yer targets. Then we'll give 'em what for."

As the crewmen began to follow Merritt, waiting for their instructions, Peter McDonnald turned to Fournier and said, "I know of one more man who could be helpful in all of this, sir."

"Who might that be?" asked Fournier.

"James Rice, sir."

"All right, McDonnald, I'll take your word for it. Rice!" he called. "Come up and join these men."

James Rice looked puzzled as he made his way up to the front.

McDonnald caught his eye and said, "Come on, you're with me."

As they followed Fitch toward the buildings at the north end of town, Rice said, "Why'd you want—"

"Don't worry, I've got a plan," McDonnald said quietly.[3]

Over a dozen men eventually gathered northeast of the plaza at the two-story building Fitch called home, his living quarters on the second floor and his general store on the first.

"You men that already have muskets, take what you need for charges and shot. Those of you that need guns, let's get you fitted up," said Fitch.

"When yer d-d-done with all that, c'mon over by me so's we can t-t-talk about placement," said Merritt from the back of the store. A few of the townspeople joined the crewmen, who did not have guns aboard the ship, to obtain muskets and ammunition. The rest of them joined Merritt and his men to await their orders.

Once everyone had gathered around him, Merritt explained that they were to spread themselves out among the buildings to the south of the store, taking care to keep out of the direct line of sight from the hills to the east, where the enemy was stationed, but to get into a position where they could view the hills in order to be able to see the flashes of the enemy's guns. After he had given them time to get in place, he would send a few of his men running in the open, from one building to another, to draw fire from the Californios. Once the enemy had exposed their positions, Merritt would give the order to fire, and they were to keep firing as quickly as they could reload, doing their best to take out as many of Varela's men as they could, and possibly break their siege.[4]

Fitch led the men out of his store through a back door, and they began distributing themselves among the buildings of the town.

Peter McDonnald could see the worried look on James Rice's face. "Just stay with me, Rice, and you'll be all right," he said. McDonnald picked a spot behind a house that was midway between Fitch's store and the Estudillo house, at the southern end of the plaza. It afforded them ample cover while also enabling them to peer around the corner at the hills.

"We don't have much time before the fighting starts, so I want you to watch carefully what I do to load this gun," McDonnald told Rice. "Follow my steps and get yours loaded, too. Remember what you did, 'cause I'm gonna want you to reload mine as soon as I fire it. I'll take your loaded gun, shoot, and then trade you for the one you just reloaded. We keep trading like that, we'll be able to keep up a fairly steady stream of fire against those Californios."

Rice nodded, half relieved that he would not have to shoot a gun, and half anxious about reloading quickly. He paid close attention as McDonnald took a paper cartridge from a pouch, tore it open with his teeth, poured a small amount into the pan of the flintlock, and then the rest into the barrel. As McDonnald was moving on to the next step of loading the wadding and shot, Rice took out one of his cartridges and bit into the paper. He pulled so hard that the cartridge burst open, sending black gunpowder into his mouth and all over his face. As he spat out the bitter-tasting powder, he looked worriedly at McDonnald and saw that he was quietly chuckling.

"That's some disguise you've given yourself, Mr. Rice. A bit gentler and steadier oughta do with the next one," he said reassuringly as he finished loading his musket.

Rice nodded, took out another cartridge, and this time performed the loading operation smoothly. With a quick nod of approval from McDonnald, they were ready.[5]

Within moments, the first shot rang out from the hills. The decoys were on the move, and the Californios were responding. All of the men tucked behind buildings took quick looks to pinpoint the enemy gunners and then half-cocked their muskets. They waited patiently for Merritt's signal, and when they heard him bellow "Fire!" they fully cocked their guns, aimed, and squeezed their triggers. The fierce roar of their volley was followed by cries of pain as several of their shots hit their marks.

Peter McDonnald watched intently for another target as some of the Californios returned the fire. He took the gun that James Rice handed to him, aimed calmly, and fired before any of the other men among the buildings had finished reloading. Fully expecting to have to wait before being able to fire a third shot, he turned to his companion who was handing him a reloaded gun.

"You're a quick learner, Rice."

"I don't like the taste of gunpowder, McDonnald."

The skirmish went on for another several minutes. When the enemy's guns grew silent, Merritt yelled, "Hold your fire! Stay put!"

As the smoke cleared, the men in the town looked cautiously to the east, where they could just make out the forms of men carrying other men up and over the crests of the hills. Merritt waited long enough to be sure the enemy had fully withdrawn before calling out, "Fall in!" at which point the men made their way slowly back to Fitch's store, all the while keeping buildings between themselves and the hills.

Fitch and Merritt were glad to see all of the men back safely and unharmed.

The same could not be said of Varela. Two of his men were dead, and others lay wounded. It had been a hard day for him and his Californios, but they remained determined to force the Americans and their allies out of San Diego.

CHAPTER 22

Reinforcements

THE SUNNY, WARM, PLEASANT WEATHER OF TUESDAY MORNING, October 13, belied the tension that clouded the town of San Diego. In the aftermath of the previous day's skirmish, Captain Hamley had ordered all hands ashore to guard the town, leaving only three men to keep watch aboard the *Stonington*. Captain Merritt and his men were on alert, as were the townspeople. Varela and his Californios were cautious in their harassment of the town, firing their muskets less frequently.

Farther up the coast, matters were taking a different turn. The boat that had left San Diego forty hours ago had arrived at San Pedro and approached the USS *Savannah*.

"Identify yourself and your purpose," called a man in uniform standing on the deck of the ship that rose fifteen feet above the water. The gold buttons of his blue single-breasted coat shone brilliantly as they reflected the bright sunshine of the early morning sun.

"I am Don Miguel de Pedrorena, the justice of the peace for San Diego. I respectfully request a meeting with your captain so that I may deliver to him dispatches from Captain Ezekiel Merritt and speak with him about the desperate situation in San Diego. May I have your permission to come aboard, sir?"

"A moment, if you please, sir," the officer called down to Pedrorena. He turned to another officer standing nearby and said, "Duvall, inform the captain that we have a visitor from San Diego who wishes to meet with him."[1]

Midshipman Robert C. Duvall made his way to the captain's quarters astern and knocked on the door of the cabin.

"Yes—what is it?" called a voice from within.

"Midshipman Duvall, sir. There's a gentleman in a boat from San Diego who wishes to speak with you. Shall I allow him aboard, sir?"

"Let me have a look at him first. I'll be right up," answered the captain.

"Aye, sir," said Duvall, and as he turned to go topside, the cabin door opened and out stepped Captain William Mervine, a tall, slender man with wavy brown hair, a high forehead, and a prominent nose, wearing the blue double-breasted coat and white pants uniform of an officer of his rank.

The two men approached the starboard rail, and Mervine gave a careful look at the men in the boat from the *Stonington*.

"Which among you wishes to speak with me?" he asked.

"I do, sir," replied Pedrorena. "I have dispatches for you from Captain Merritt."

After a brief pause, Mervine said, "You may come aboard, sir. Have your men wait in the boat."

Pedrorena looked apologetically at his companions and then climbed up the side of the *Savannah*.

As he stepped onto the deck, Mervine said, "You'll understand my caution regarding your men, sir, when I say that we have just recently been engaged in a bruising encounter with the enemy, and I must safeguard my men and my ship." The action to which Mervine was referring was the Battle of the Old Woman's Gun that had occurred just a few days earlier, in which the Californios had essentially driven the Americans out of Los Angeles.

"As a Californio whose sympathies lie with the United States of America, I am saddened to hear that news, Captain," said Pedrorena. "Please allow me to present to you these dispatches from Captain Merritt. They will, I am sure, confirm for you that San Diego, where I reside with my family, is in a desperate situation. We have driven the enemy into the hills, but they have now laid siege to the town, firing their guns at us from the hills and preventing us from obtaining food. There is a strong possibility that their forces will increase, at which point they could attack us and take control of the town. I am here as the representative for Captain Merritt and the people of San Diego to respectfully request that you provide us with assistance before it is too late."[2]

Mervine had listened intently as Pedrorena was speaking, and remained silent as he opened and read through Merritt's dispatches, nodding his head as he did so.

When he had finished reading, he looked up at Pedrorena. "San Diego is in a bad way indeed, sir, and it is too valuable a port to lose. Tell Captain Merritt that I will send fifty men as reinforcements as soon as they are ready to depart. There is a merchant ship just arrived in port," Mervine said, pointing to a ship moored in the distance that bore a close resemblance to the *Stonington*. "I will charter it for that purpose, as I must keep the *Savannah* stationed here in San Pedro. Godspeed to you on your return to San Diego, and my commendations to Captain Merritt for continuing the fight."

"It is an honor to have met you, Captain Mervine," replied Pedrorena. "I wish you well in your endeavors here in San Pedro, and on behalf of Captain Merritt and the people of San Diego, I thank you most sincerely for your assistance."

Pedrorena climbed down to the boat, and as they began to row away, he pointed to the ship in the distance and said to his companions, "We will see that ship in San Diego soon, and it will bring us the help we need."[3]

The prevailing winds sped the boat on its return to San Diego, and it arrived at La Playa early Wednesday morning, October 14. Before climbing out onto shore, Miguel de Pedrorena spoke to the men of the *Stonington*.

"I thank you, gentlemen, for your assistance on this journey, and for allowing me to be a part of this crew."

"You done right by us, sir," said Gardner Jaques, one of the two men from Preston, Connecticut, "pitchin' in the way you did. You're welcome to join us if you've a mind to go whaling."

"I am flattered by your offer," replied Pedrorena humbly, "but there is much that keeps me here in San Diego, especially now, conditions being what they are. Until we meet again."

He bowed to them, they nodded in response, and he made his way into town to deliver the good news from San Pedro.[4]

Pedrorena immediately sought out Ezekiel Merritt, who was pleased to hear that help was on the way. Hamley and Fitch were heartened as well when they heard the news, and as word spread throughout the town, the spirits of the inhabitants lifted at the thought of the siege soon coming to an end.

Their sense of relief would be short-lived, however, as the following morning, another warm and sunny San Diego day, a lone rider appeared on Presidio Hill.

"Enemy's comin'! Get yer guns ready!" cried one of Merritt's men.

Captain Merritt took a careful look and said, "Hold, men. I'm seein' somethin' white in his hand. He may be wantin' t-t-to talk."

As the rider approached, it became clear to all those watching that in one hand he held the reins, and in the other, a white cloth, which he was slowly waving.

"Go t-t-tell Fitch he n-n-needs to get over here," said Merritt to one of his men.

Meanwhile, the rider had reached the base of the hill, drawing closer to town.

Several men took up defensive positions alongside buildings as a precaution, while most of the inhabitants remained indoors, watching warily.

Fitch had by now joined the group that was gathered by the buildings on the edge of town. As the *alcalde*, he stepped to the front and waited.

The rider stopped his horse near the group, dismounted, and walked slowly toward Fitch. When he was within a few feet, he began to speak, and Fitch immediately waved his hands in the air, signaling him to stop. Despite being married to a woman, Josefa Carrillo, whose family was among the most prominent in San Diego, and serving as a leading official of the town, Henry D. Fitch had never learned to speak Spanish fluently, and therefore could not understand what the rider was saying. He turned, looked at Miguel de Pedrorena, and said bluntly, "If you will, please."[5]

Pedrorena stepped forward and addressed the rider, who began to speak deliberately. As the rider spoke, Pedrorena's posture grew tense, his shoulders shifting backward, his chin tucking inward. His face showed increasing concern, and he was motionless as the rider finished speaking, mounted his horse, and rode slowly toward the hill.

Pedrorena stood silently for a moment, then turned to speak to the group.

"I am afraid I have disturbing news for you and for the town. The Californios on the hill have received reinforcements, more than doubling their numbers. They say that we must gather our arms and deliver them to their camp. If we have not done so by tomorrow morning, they will come down and butcher all of us, with no distinction."

"I ain't givin' up my gun t-t-to no one—n-n-neither's any o' my men!" exclaimed Merritt.

"I say that we must cooperate with their demands; otherwise, we will jeopardize the lives of our families," stated Pedrorena firmly.

"I don't like the notion of being unarmed against an enemy that's ready to slaughter us," said Fitch.

"I agree," said Hamley.

"How would they know?" said someone in a calm, confident voice.

The others turned to see that it was Fournier who had asked the question.

"What do you mean, my good man?" replied Pedrorena.

"With all due respect, sir, how would they know if we've turned over all of our guns? We could keep enough of them to give us some protection, and we could make the pile we give them bigger by adding any guns people might have that are in need of some repair," explained Fournier.

"Your suggestion is a clever one, sir," said Pedrorena. "I admire your reasoning. However, I would want to be certain that the number of guns we collect to relinquish is sufficient to avoid arousing any suspicions."

"Ain't n-n-none o' my men givin' up their guns, I'm t-t-tellin' ya," insisted Merritt.

"I say it's worth a try, even if you and your men keep your guns," replied Fitch. He looked around at the group and saw they were all nodding in agreement. "All right then," he said, "let's get started."

As they began to go their separate ways, Fitch called out, "Mr. Fournier."

"Yes, sir, Mr. Fitch?"

"Well done."

"Thank you, sir."[6]

CHAPTER 23

Timely Arrival

As the sun rose Friday morning on another beautifully clear day, it shone its light on a most welcome sight for the Americans. A ship flying the US flag was rounding Point Loma.

"Sail, ho!" called a crewman on watch aboard the *Stonington*.

"Where away?" replied Captain Hamley, who had returned to the ship the previous afternoon, following the meeting in which Alanson Fournier had made such a favorable impression.

"Heading for the harbor, sir."

Hamley took out his spyglass and, looking carefully, could see that in addition to the Stars and Stripes, the ship was flying a blue flag with a blue "M" on a white diamond, indicating that it was a part of the fleet belonging to the Charles W. Morgan whaling firm in New Bedford, Massachusetts, the whaling capital of the world. Hamley anticipated speaking to its captain once the ship drew near enough.

Meanwhile, people in the town had spotted its sails and had spread the news to their officials. For Miguel de Pedrorena, it was a moment of great relief, for he was certain that this was the ship from San Pedro bringing reinforcements and supplies.[1]

The ship drew nearer to the *Stonington*, enabling Hamley to see that there were many men on deck wearing uniforms of blue and white.

"Those are the uniforms we saw at San Pedro, Captain," said James Holden excitedly as he looked toward the approaching ship.

"Yes, it seems the navy has kept its word and sent the reinforcements it promised," replied Hamley.

When the two ships were within speaking distance, Hamley called out, "George Hamley here, captain of the ship *Stonington* out of New London. And you?"

A man in common whaler's clothes came to the larboard side of the ship that was passing the stern of the *Stonington*.

"Bezer Simmons, sir, captain of the *Magnolia* out of New Bedford," he answered.

"You and your passengers are a welcome sight, Captain Simmons," shouted Hamley.

"Fifty men from the USS *Savannah*, Captain Hamley, with three officers in charge. That ought to improve your situation!" replied Simmons.

"Certain it will, Captain Simmons, certain it will!" responded Hamley. "Seems the navy is fond of whaleships."

"They know good help when they see it!" called out Simmons with a laugh as his ship passed beyond the *Stonington*, on its way to a mooring spot. They would soon begin disembarking the sailors and volunteers that would then march to the town, much to the relief of its inhabitants, who had not as yet surrendered their arms.

The Californios in the hills had seen the *Magnolia* making its way into the harbor, too.

The sight of so many men in uniform on board led them to reconsider their threatened attack on the town.[2]

Lieutenant George Minor of the *Savannah* called for Captain Simmons to prepare the *Magnolia*'s boats for lowering, then called his forces to attention.

"Listen carefully, men. We will take the boats toward shore and then up the small creek that runs through the grassy flats. The ground there will be too boggy for the enemy to stage a charge at us. When we have landed, we will make our way to town, to a place where we can establish our barracks and store our ammunition and supplies. Be on your guard as we approach the town. Our visitor at San Pedro informed us that the enemy has made a habit of firing randomly from the hills. Take cover when necessary. All right, then, board your boats. Midshipmen Duvall and Morgan, lead the way."[3]

It was well into the night by the time the entire force had landed and finished transporting their equipment to the barracks they had established in a storehouse on the west side of town, close to running water and beyond the firing range of the enemy.

On Saturday morning, October 17, Lieutenant Minor assessed his situation and decided it would be best to strengthen the barracks. He directed his men to go into town and collect adobe bricks to use in constructing bastions at the corners, on the east side of the barracks, and to build a protective wall on the west side. Minor also reminded them to be wary of enemy gunfire from the hills.[4]

Alanson Fournier was already in town with some of the crew from the *Stonington* as the men from the *Savannah* approached. He could see a column of a dozen or so men wearing blue uniforms. At its head was a fairly tall man of sturdy build whose uniform was also blue, but beneath his jacket he wore a white vest.

Fournier strode forward to introduce himself. "Good morning, sir. I am Alanson Fournier, second officer of the ship *Stonington*. Whom do I have the pleasure of addressing?"

"I am Midshipman Robert Duvall of the USS *Savannah*, sir. My men and I are in search of adobe bricks that we will use to fortify our position," he said, pointing in the direction of the barracks. "Are you familiar enough with this town that you could tell me where I could find such bricks?"

Fournier turned his head toward his crewmen, grinned, then turned back to face Duvall. "I'd say we've been here long enough to know our way around. Evacuating and then retaking a town brings a certain amount of familiarity," he replied, causing some of his crewmen to nod their heads and chuckle.

"Ah," said Duvall, "you must be those whalemen we've been hearing about, that helped to save this town."

"The very same, sir, and knowing this town's situation as we do, I'd suggest that we all move ourselves behind some buildings to continue our conversation before those fellows in the hills get a chance to take aim at us."

"Wise advice, sir," said Duvall, waving his men forward as he followed Fournier to a safe spot.

"The man that you'll want to speak with about the bricks is Henry Fitch, the *alcalde*. He's likely at his store over that way," said Fournier, pointing to Fitch's place. "Is there anything else we can help you with?"

"Actually, yes, there is," replied Duvall. "The captain of the ship that brought us here has been whaling in these waters for several years now, and he mentioned something about an old fort at the mouth of the harbor, where there may be some guns lying about. If they are indeed there, it would be far easier to ferry them on the water than to drag them on the trail."

"We've got some boats already ashore at La Playa," said Fournier, pointing toward the harbor entrance. "We could make our way down there while you're getting your bricks, then you could meet us when you're ready."

"I'll have this detail fetch the bricks to the barracks, and then I'll bring another group to you and your boats. Much obliged, Mr. Fournier," said Duvall, extending his right hand.

"Pleased to be of assistance, Mr. Duvall," said Fournier as he shook the midshipman's hand.

Duvall and his men went off toward Henry Fitch's store as Fournier and his crew took to the La Playa Trail. The old fort they were heading toward was Fort Guijarros, Spanish for "cobblestones," located at what became known as Ballast Point. It was a peninsula about a quarter of a mile long, just over two miles south of La Playa, jutting out from Point Loma at the very mouth of the harbor. It had acquired its current name through the practice of merchant ships using the cobblestones as ballast in the holds of their ships in order to balance their loads. The Spanish, realizing that it was an ideal spot for a fortification to guard San Diego, constructed it in 1797 using the plentiful gray rocks, or cobbles, that the action of the Pacific waters had tumbled into smooth, rounded stones. Atop the walls of their fort, they had placed ten bronze cannons.[5]

Those guns had seen action only twice, both times involving American ships smuggling goods. Through the ravages of time and the changes of governments, the fort had deteriorated and was now abandoned, but within its remains lay weapons that, with a bit of rehabilitation, would prove to be quite useful to the US forces that now occupied San Diego.

CHAPTER 24

A Convenient Encounter

ON THE SAME DAY THAT MEN FROM THE *STONINGTON* WERE ASSISTING Duvall and his men with the guns at Fort Guijarros, Captain Bezer Simmons was helping himself.

"How do you do, sir," said Simmons to the town official who had just come aboard the *Magnolia*. "You say that you have some business to attend to with me?"

"That is correct, Captain," replied Pedro Carrillo. "As the customs collector for the town of San Diego, it is my duty to assess the fee that you will need to pay with regard to your cargo."

"I see," said Simmons with a slight smirk. "Well, Señor Carrillo, before settling that account, I wonder if you could answer a few questions for me regarding that island over there," he said, pointing to the large peninsula that formed a protective barrier between the Pacific Ocean and the mainland.

"You are interested in Isla Coronado?" asked Carrillo, squinting his eyes with obvious curiosity.

"Yes, sir, I am," said Simmons. "You see, I've been whaling this coast for some time, and I've often thought that if I could find a spot with just the right conditions, I'd have my own whaling station where ships could replenish their water and other provisions before continuing their hunts. What can you tell me about that island?"

"The island has its own freshwater spring," replied Carrillo, "and there is a bight on the eastern side that provides a convenient and safe harbor. What we often refer to as an island is actually a peninsula that extends southward from here for approximately ten miles and then connects to the mainland. Ships that stop here would have many resources available to them for replenishing their supplies before continuing with their voyages."

"This all sounds very promising, Señor Carrillo. Tell me, is there anyone that already has a claim on that land?"

"Yes, there is."

"Could you please put me in communication with this person so that I might express my interest in the property?"

"I certainly can, Captain," said Carrillo, lifting his head.

"How soon do you think you could arrange that?"

"Immediately," said Carrillo.

"If that's so, then I do not wish to detain you any longer. Let's settle my ship's account so that you may be on your way," said Simmons. "I have not come to deliver any goods. I am under charter of the United States Navy to deliver reinforcements for your town's protection."

"Yes, Captain, I understand, and your fee will reflect that."

"In that case, our business here is done, and you will now please inform the owner of the island that I wish to speak with him about a possible purchase."

"You have already done so, Captain."

"I'm not quite sure what you mean."

"You see, sir," said Carrillo with a slight chuckle, "*I* am the owner of the island."

"You?!"

"Yes, sir, it is true. Governor Pío Pico, for whom my father-in-law, Don Juan Bandini, worked as his secretary, gave it to me as a wedding present when I married Don Juan's daughter, Josefa. I was, of course, very grateful to him, but my thoughts about my future are now such that I am planning to make a new life in San Francisco, and the sale of this property would surely help in that endeavor."

The two men continued their discussion and negotiated a price of one thousand dollars in silver, providing Don Pedro Carrillo with the means to make his move, and leaving Captain Bezer Simmons in possession of his longed-for whaling station.[1]

CHAPTER 25

Full and Varied Service

FOURNIER AND DUVALL HAD JOINED FORCES AT FORT GUIJARROS ON Saturday, October 17, unearthing, cleaning, and removing spikes from two of the cannons, then transporting them to the barracks. It wasn't only the supply of weapons that needed attention, however; they also had to find food. The old adage that an army travels on its stomach certainly applied to the Americans in San Diego. When the Californios had fled the town, they had driven most of the nearby livestock into the hills and beyond. They had also taken with them any available provisions of food. The Americans and the remaining townspeople may have retaken control of the town, but there was little left to sustain them, and their situation was growing desperate.

"A word, sir?" asked Alanson Fournier, after knocking on Captain Hamley's door and being summoned into his cabin. It was Sunday, October 18.

"What's on your mind, Fournier?" said Hamley.

"Well, sir, having been in town recently and working with Midshipman Duvall and his men, it's become clear to me that those folks are in a bad way. They'll soon be out of food."

"And you've got some idea for helping them, do you?" responded Hamley, a slight hint of disdain in his voice.

"Yes, sir, I do. It would help us, too. If I may?" said Fournier, calmly and politely.

"Go on," grunted Hamley.

"The enemy may have been clever in driving cattle into the hills when they left, but they didn't get them all. I've seen plenty of strays, including bullocks, that we could get to without having to fight those Californios. Using the guns that we got from Mr. Fitch, we could take down some of those young bulls and provide meat for ourselves as well as the folks in town. Instead of hunting whales at sea, we'd be hunting cattle on land," said Fournier with a glint in his eye.

"Very clever, Mr. Fournier, very clever," said Hamley. He thought for a moment and then said, "I suppose you could take a few men with you on this hunting expedition of yours. It would keep them busy, at least, seeing as I'm not expecting to take us to sea anytime soon."

"Thank you, sir. If it's agreeable to you, I'll likely take the same men that were in the fight with the enemy, as they've already handled the guns."

"That will be fine, Fournier."

"Yes, sir. There is just one more thing, Captain."

"What is it?"

"With your permission, sir, I'd also like to send some of our provisions to town to ease their hunger. As I said, they really are in a bad way."

"Confound it, Fournier, I've got a ship to tend to! My first responsibility is to see that my own men have the food they need."

"I understand, sir. Whatever you think you could spare, I'm sure the townsfolk will welcome."

Hamley turned away from Fournier and stood shaking his head. He seemed to be struggling with his thoughts. "All right," he said after a moment. "Go check with the steward to see what he thinks we could give them—but keep in mind my concerns about the men of this ship."

"I will, sir. Thank you."

Fournier went to find the steward, and Hamley stood quietly, gazing out the stern windows at the deceivingly placid waters of San Diego harbor.[1]

It was now Monday, October 19. Alanson Fournier and his small crew, made up of young Edwin Arthur, the Comstock brothers, Peter McDonnald, and James Rice, boarded one of the boats and headed for shore.

Fournier supplied them with the muskets and ammunition that had been secured safely in Captain Hamley's cabin following the skirmish with the enemy. They also brought with them a few sacks of flour and beans that the steward had provided after listening to Fournier's explanation of the situation in town.

When they landed, Fournier explained how they would proceed.

"Comstocks, you carry the food sacks; we'll carry the weapons. We'll all make our way along the trail until we get to a fork that leads up into the hills at the head of Point Loma. At that spot, the Comstocks will continue into town and deliver the food to Mr. Fitch at his store—tell him compliments of Captain Hamley. The rest of us will turn left. After you've delivered the food, come back down the trail and bear right at that fork and catch up to us. We'll be searching for those bullocks I mentioned as we were rowing in. They like the vegetation up there, so we're bound to come across some of them. Let's get moving!"

"Aye, sir," they said as they hefted their loads and began making their way up the trail.

At the fork, Mark and Samuel Comstock waved and continued along the main trail as the others turned onto the narrower, less traveled path and began walking uphill, sweating in the warm, sunny weather. When they reached the top, they stopped to admire the spectacular views that spread around them. Toward the east, the serene waters of San Diego harbor lapped gently against the shore, beyond which lay the buildings of the town and the hills that rose behind them. To the south, the harbor waters curved around the flat, lengthy peninsula that extended from the mainland, shielding the harbor from the vast Pacific Ocean that filled their gaze as they looked west toward their former hunting place. As they looked north, they saw the rugged coastline of towering cliffs that ran all the way up to San Francisco and beyond. It had been less than a month since they had left San Francisco, and they each reflected in their own way on the changes that had happened to them and their ship since coming to San Diego.

It was Peter McDonnald that broke the reverential silence.

"Excuse me, gentlemen, but as grand as this view is, it just got a sight better. Lookee there," he said, pointing to a small group of bullocks that had come from behind a slight rise to the south and were now grazing near the edge of the cliffs to the west.

"Easy, now, men," said Fournier in a hushed tone. "We don't want to scare them off before we've had a chance to take a shot at them."

Quietly and quickly, they unshouldered their muskets and began loading them. As they did so, Peter McDonnald nudged James Rice with his elbow.

"Mr. Fournier, if it's all the same to you," McDonnald said, "I'd like to suggest we give Rice here the opportunity to take the first shot."

James Rice jerked his head wide-eyed toward McDonnald.

Fournier looked approvingly at McDonnald and said, "I believe that's a fine idea. Rice, pick your target and take your shot."

"But, sir—" Rice said.

"The moment is yours, Rice. Take your shot."

Summoning his courage, James Rice lifted his musket, aimed at one of the bullocks, and pulled the trigger. The blast of the gunpowder filled the air as the ball flew from the barrel. The bullocks looked up as the ball landed in front of their hooves, and they ran several yards to the north.

James Rice's shoulders slumped dejectedly, but as he dropped his musket to the ground, he felt another one replacing it in his hands. He looked behind him and saw Peter McDonnald.

"It's loaded and ready," said McDonnald. "Time for your next shot."

Rice nodded with a look of resolve. The bullocks had settled down to continue their grazing. The men from the *Stonington* moved stealthily closer, each of them preparing to shoot if Rice missed again. With the sun shining brightly over his left shoulder, James Rice hoisted the musket that Peter McDonnald had handed to him, took a deep breath, and squeezed the trigger. He watched as the ball shot through the air and straightened as a bullock crumpled to the ground.

"I did it!" he cried as another gun fired and a second bullock fell.

"You caught on mighty quick after that first shot," said McDonnald, clapping Rice on the back.

As the rest of the animals ran northward, Fournier said, "Let's tend to our catch, men," and they made their way over to the fallen beasts.

"That's a clean kill, Rice," said Fournier upon reaching the motionless bullock that Rice had shot. "Unlike mine," he continued, as they moved toward the second bullock. Fournier had mortally wounded the creature he'd shot, but it was still breathing. "Finish him off, Arthur—your gun's still loaded."

Edwin Arthur, the young harpooner, aimed his musket in the middle of the animal's forehead and fired, rendering it lifeless.

Just as he did so, the Comstock brothers strode up the hill and joined the group. They approached Fournier, and Mark, the older brother, said, "Mr. Fitch sends his thanks to Captain Hamley for the food. He hopes there'll be more where that came from, 'cause his people are mighty hungry."

"Yes," replied Fournier, "they are certainly in need of help."

"Should we get our guns ready for more hunting?" asked Samuel Comstock.

"No," said Fournier, "we'd best deal with what we've got. It'll take some doing on our part to haul them to the barracks."

The six men took turns carrying the slaughtered bullocks for two and a half miles until they reached the barracks of Lieutenant George Minor and the men of the *Savannah*.

Minor, Duvall, and some others came out to greet the hunters as they approached.

"Which of you is Fournier?" asked Minor.

"That would be me, sir," said the second officer of the *Stonington*. He wiped his sweaty, grimy right hand on the front of his shirt and extended it toward Minor, who hesitated before snapping his own right hand to his forehead in a crisp salute.

Fournier shrugged and returned Minor's salute.

"Midshipman Duvall tells me you've been quite helpful in our efforts to secure this town," said Minor.

"Yes, sir," said Fournier, "and we figured you might like to add some meat to your meals, so we've brought you these two bullocks."

"That's very generous of you, Mr. Fournier. My thanks to you and your men."

"The way I see it, sir," responded Fournier, "we're all in this fight together, and it's to our benefit if you and your men keep your strength up. We'll be heading back to our ship now. Enjoy the meat!"

"We will, Mr. Fournier. Again, thank you," said Minor, saluting once more.

Fournier returned the salute, and then he and his men headed down the trail to their boat at La Playa.

For the next week or so, men from the *Stonington* made regular visits to shore that were, for the most part, aimed at fortifying the town of San Diego to safeguard its inhabitants. Among the items they brought to town were more guns that they had reclaimed from Fort Guijarros, more bullocks that they had hunted and killed, and more food provisions from the ship, particularly fish and meat that had been preserved in salt. They also brought shooks of wooden staves and a large quantity of metal hoops that they assembled into one-hundred-twenty-gallon barrels that they and others filled with dirt and put into place as defensive breastworks. In some cases, their trips to shore were for the purpose of supplying men as reinforcements in response to the continuing harassment from the Californios in the hills, who seemed to have grown in numbers.[2]

On board the *Stonington*, Captain Hamley saw to some basic maintenance.

"All hands," he called out on Friday, October 23. When the crew had gathered around him, he gave his orders. "We may not have done much sailing lately, men, but I want this ship to be ready when the time comes. Form yourselves into three groups, one for each mast. Go up and loose those sails, give 'em a chance to dry out. With the weather as fine as it is, it shouldn't be long before you're ready to furl them again, so keep your positions once you're up there." Looking straight at Alexander Anthony and recalling the incident that had led to his flogging, Hamley continued. "I expect you to do your work cleanly and efficiently. Mind you don't let the sails catch wind and pull us loose from our mooring. Now get to it."

The men dispersed, and Anthony found himself in a group with McDonnald, Rice, and William Fisher, the Black man from Philadelphia who had watched in silent anger while Hamley flogged Anthony. As they began their climb up the mainmast, McDonnald looked toward Anthony with a jaunty smile and then said to all of them, "C'mon, fellas, let's go do some *clean* work." They responded with hearty chuckles, including Anthony, and continued their climb.[3]

When they had reached their stations, they began to unfurl the sails. McDonnald and Rice were working on the starboard side of the mainsail. As the sail moved lower, the bottom corner, held loosely by the slackened clew line, caught a slight breeze and flapped upward, causing the line to fly toward Rice. McDonnald heard a loud snapping sound and, seeing Rice lose his balance, reached over quickly, grabbed him firmly under the arm, and held him in place until he was steady. Rice looked at McDonnald, then down at the deck far below, and the water, even farther, then back at McDonnald.

"I—" began Rice, his face pale with fear.

"Just breathe," said McDonnald calmly.

His heart racing, Rice took a few deep breaths. As the blood returned to his face and he regained his color, his breathing became smoother.

"You're okay, Rice. Saved me from having to go down and clean up a terrible mess on the deck, which I appreciate," said McDonnald with a glint in his eye.

"My pleasure," replied Rice with a faint smile; then, in a lower tone, "Thanks."

McDonnald gave a slight nod. "Let's get back to work."

At four o'clock that afternoon, just as they were finishing with the sails and were about to make their way down to the deck, the men in the foremast spotted a boat entering the harbor.

"Mr. Fournier," called one to the second officer, visible below. "There's a boat comin' in."

Fournier strode to the larboard rail and watched carefully. Using his spyglass, he could see that the boat's crew were wearing US Navy uniforms.

"Jaques," he called to one of his crewmen standing nearby, "let the captain know there's a navy boat approaching. No need for concern, but he ought to know, just the same."

"Aye, sir," replied Gardner Jaques as he turned and headed for the captain's cabin.

Fournier waited until the boat drew near enough for conversation. "This is the ship *Stonington*, and I am its second officer. With whom do I have the pleasure of speaking?"

"We are from the USS *Savannah* at San Pedro, sir," replied one of the sailors, "come to check on our men that came here last week aboard the *Magnolia*."

"Ah, Minor, Duvall, and the rest," said Fournier knowingly.

"You're acquainted with them, then?" asked the sailor somewhat incredulously.

"Well enough to admit it, aye," said Fournier wryly.

"Where might we find 'em?"

"Pull in at La Playa," said Fournier, pointing to the shore, "then walk the trail inland for two miles or so. You'll come upon their barracks soon enough."

"Much obliged, sir," called the sailor.

Fournier waved as the boat headed toward La Playa.

He was somewhat surprised the very next day when he saw the same boat and its crew on the way out of the harbor.

"What ho, there, men," called Fournier jokingly as the boat was passing by the *Stonington*. "Couldn't find your shipmates?"

"Oh, we found them, all right," replied one of the sailors.

"Just not the sort you want to spend much time with, then?" asked Fournier with a smile.

"Not when they've so little in the way of refreshments!" shouted the sailor. "We're heading back to our ship with a full order for provisions. See if we can get those men back to a civilized state!"

"And you're the proper gentlemen for the job, I'm sure," replied Fournier.

"Aye, we're the refined type," answered the sailor as he and his mates laughed.

"Smooth sailing to you!" called Fournier as the boat passed beyond the ship.

"As a baby's arse!" cried the sailor, and the jolly exchange drifted to a close.

Despite the lightheartedness, Fournier knew that the condition of the besieged people at San Diego was no laughing matter. Fortunately for them, they were about to receive aid from an unexpected source.[4]

CHAPTER 26

Herding with a Vengeance

DURING THE FINAL WEEK OF OCTOBER, 1846, THE SIEGE OF THE CALIfornios on the town of San Diego was proving to be quite effective. With most of the livestock driven away and stores depleted at the ranchos, the civilians and US military sheltering in town had little to eat. The men who had just visited their shipmates from the USS *Savannah* had seen the desperate situation firsthand and hurried back to their ship to sound the alert. While the men of the *Stonington* had done a good deal of hunting in order to provide some meat for those in town, as well as themselves, there was now very little left for them to hunt.

In the midst of this crisis, there was a group of people that had previously experienced deprivation at the hands of the Californios and who were ready to strike back somehow. They were the Kumeyaay, the Indigenous tribe that had been living in the area for over ten thousand years.

When the Spanish had ventured from Central America into California in the later 1700s, they had established a series of settlements, or missions, through which they intended to indoctrinate the Indigenous inhabitants to Christianity, lead them to adopt Spanish agricultural and livestock practices, and eventually develop them into loyal citizens of New Spain. That process of acculturation would, according to Spanish law, take ten years, after which time the purpose of the mission would be completed and the government would assign plots of mission lands to the local Indigenous people that had been working the land during those years.

All did not go as smoothly as planned, however. Many of the Indigenous people refused to change their ways, resulting in harsh treatment by the Spanish Franciscan monks that were in charge of the missions. Those who cooperated with the new system often took longer to adapt than had been expected. Friction developed between the monks and the Spanish military personnel that were stationed in forts on mission land and resented the control that the religious authorities had over the missions.

The Mexican Revolution of 1821 ended Spanish rule, and the new Mexican government gradually eliminated religious control of the missions, handing them over to civilian magistrates in a process known as secularization. Those magistrates then sold or auctioned the lands, in many cases for little or no money, to their closest friends and allies. The Indigenous people who had cultivated the land—and were due to receive portions of that land under the previous law—were now left with the prospect of working as veritable slaves to the new landholders, or retreating to what was left of their former villages.[1]

The Kumeyaay people viewed the Californios who were aligned with Mexico as their enemies, invaders who had brought disease and oppression to their tribe. They had a clear preference for which side should be victorious in the present conflict, and there were those among them that were willing to contribute to the success of the US forces. A portion of the tribe was located in the territory surrounding the barracks of the men from the *Savannah*. The Californios had been mostly successful in their surveillance of the town and preventing Lieutenant Minor from sending scouts to search for food. Eventually, though, one man had made his way far enough and back to report that there was a large herd of sheep some thirty-five miles or so to the south.

"That's well and good," said Minor to his scout on hearing the news, "but we've got to find a way to get those animals here without alerting the enemy. We haven't been able to reconnoiter the area, thanks to those damned snipers, to know it well enough to keep that herd hidden while we move them."

"That's true, sir," said Midshipman Duvall, who was standing nearby, "but if I might suggest?"

"Go on, Duvall," said Minor.

"I imagine these local Indians around here know the land better than anyone, and from what I've heard, they'd welcome the chance to help us against those Californios."

Minor paused for a moment, and then said, "You raise some interesting points, Duvall. Take a couple of men with you over to the Indian camp and see if you can raise some volunteers to herd those sheep."

Duvall saluted and then set out with two others for the Kumeyaay village.

They returned within a few hours, accompanied by two men of the tribe, one of them the village chief. Duvall had explained to them the situation regarding the sheep, and when they realized that their participation would help in the fight against the Californios, the two Kumeyaay men readily agreed to make the journey. Their migratory lifestyle had resulted in an intimate knowledge of the territory, and they were confident that they could find the sheep and then herd them northward through the many ravines that cut deep into the landscape and would keep them safely out of sight. They would then drive the animals onto Coronado Island, the very same peninsula that had been the subject of negotiation between Bezer Simmons and Pedro Carrillo. High tide would isolate the peninsula from the mainland and provide the sheep with protection and land where they could graze. The chief and his companion would signal Lieutenant Minor from the island when all the sheep were there and ready to be ferried to the mainland.

Lieutenant Minor agreed to the plan and bade farewell to the two men, telling them that his own men would be on watch for their signal.[2]

The Kumeyaay used their knowledge of the terrain to keep themselves out of the sightlines of the Californios as they made their way south during the night toward the sheep. By daybreak, they had located the herd of nearly six hundred sheep and positioned themselves, the chief in front and the other in back, to begin maneuvering the easily guided animals along the route that would keep them hidden. The terrain was dry and rocky, which made for slow going in the heat of the day. There were some occasional shaded spots, but the men chose not to linger in order to complete their journey as quickly as possible.

After a couple of days they were within a few miles of the base of the peninsula. The chief continued to lead the herd, while his companion trailed well behind. Too far behind and too much in the open, unfortunately, as some Californios spotted him, then captured and killed him. The chief was far enough ahead of the large herd, maintaining his stealthy advance so that he was out of sight of the enemy. By the end of the day on Wednesday, October 28, he had managed to guide all of the sheep onto the island, build himself a small fire, and send his signal to Lieutenant Minor.

Captain Hamley was ashore that day, conducting some business with Henry Fitch.

Minor found Hamley at Fitch's store. "Good evening, Captain Hamley," he began. "Quite advantageous to see you here."

"How so?"

"You may recall, Captain, that I informed you some days ago of a mission that two local Indians were undertaking on our behalf."

"Yes, I do remember that."

"Well, sir, they have succeeded, and there is now a large number of sheep on the island ready to be transported to the mainland. Please have your boats ready to begin ferrying the animals at daybreak tomorrow."

Hamley stared straight at Minor for a moment, turned his head and looked at Fitch with the same blank stare, then turned back to Minor. "Sheep in the boats," he said plainly, then started to chuckle, and as he did, Fitch joined him. Soon, both men were laughing out loud.

Minor looked at the two of them with a straight face, waiting, and when they had quieted, said sternly, "Yes, Hamley, sheep in the boats. I'll have some of Captain Merritt's force join my men at the shore to assist with the unloading. Daybreak tomorrow."

With that, Minor turned and left the store.

When he was some distance away, Hamley looked at Fitch. The two of them shook their heads and, laughing quietly, said to each other simultaneously, "Sheep in the boats," and then Hamley left to return to his ship and prepare his men for their next duty.[3]

CHAPTER 27

Sheep in the Boats

ON THE MORNING OF THURSDAY, OCTOBER 29, 1846, CAPTAIN GEORGE Hamley had complied with Lieutenant George Minor's orders, and the boats of the ship *Stonington* were at the northeast coast of Coronado Island, preparing to transport to the mainland six hundred sheep that would provide much-needed sustenance for the besieged people of San Diego. Hamley had put Second Officer Alanson Fournier in charge of the operation, and it was Fournier who was giving directions to his crew in the early morning hours.

"I chose you for this job because you are the sturdiest and hardiest of rowers. We have to limit ourselves to two rowers per boat instead of five, plus the steering oar, to make room for the cargo, and we'll be making multiple trips throughout the day, as you can see by the size of the herd," he said, turning from the fourteen men gathered on the sandy beach and sweeping his right arm through the air, parallel with the expansive grassy meadow in which the sheep were grazing. "I figure we can fit about a dozen of the creatures at a time in each boat, and that means we'll need to make about fifty trips. We've got five boats, so that'll be at least ten trips per boat. Let's see how many trips we can get done today. I know I can count on your cooperation. As for the sheep . . ." He trailed off, shrugging his shoulders and raising his hands in the air.

The men chuckled. A few of them responded.

"We'll take care of 'em."

"Remember, they're sheep!"

"How much trouble could they be?"

"I'm glad you're ready for them," said Fournier. "Let's see if they're ready for us."

Fournier turned and walked up from the beach to the edge of the meadow so he could see both the near and the far ends of the herd. Captain Hamley had told him there would be two Indians watching over the sheep, but Fournier could see only one, and he was at the far end. Fournier waved his hand in the air and made a beckoning motion to let the Indian know it was time to begin moving the sheep toward the boats.

The Kumeyaay chief clapped his hands and made a clucking sound with his tongue.

The sheep began moving forward, and the rowers worked in pairs, guiding the sheep toward their boats that were being held steady by their boatheaders.

"I've got these three!" said John Dias, a tall man from Cape Verde, to his partner, Jason Freeman, a Black man from Montville, Connecticut, who, at exactly six feet, was an inch taller than Dias.

"You sure about that?" said Freeman as he guided another three sheep toward their boat.

Dias saw that one of his sheep was getting away from him. He reached out to grab it, slipped, and fell face-first on the damp grass.

"You're a lucky man, Dias," said Freeman as he reached out his long arm and cradled the stray sheep.

" 'Cause you stopped my sheep?" said Dias, still lying on the ground.

"No," said Freeman with a laugh, " 'cause you landed just right. Coulda been a whole different mess than what you've got on you now."

Dias twisted his head and spotted a pile of dark pellets just beyond where he had fallen. He rose quickly to his feet, stepping away from the sheep droppings.

"I see what you mean," he said, brushing dirt off his hands and clothes. "Let's hope my luck holds out beyond this first batch!" he said with a grin, and they resumed leading their sheep.

When they got to their craft, their boatheader, Aaron Peters, steadied it as Freeman led the first sheep aboard. He coaxed the animal toward the gunwale, and after a slight hesitation, it hopped gracefully over the rail and into the boat. Once the first sheep was aboard, the others naturally followed. Peters, whose copper-colored skin and tightly curled black hair suggested a combination of Native and African American heritage, spoke to the sheep in a low, resonant voice that kept the creatures calm and relatively still while Freeman and Dias went to retrieve six more.[1]

The other crewmen were delivering sheep to their boats with varying degrees of success. In one case, a sheep leapt into a boat and then out the other side, into the water, causing James Holden to humorously give chase around and around the boat until it finally got on board and stayed there. At another boat, the sheep took a while to settle, and the vessel rocked back and forth so much that one of the sheep actually became seasick and vomited into the boat.

Nelson Davis boarded his boat to get into rowing position, pushing sheep out of the way to ready his oar, and had to clear his seat of sheep dung. When he sat down and braced his feet, he found that his shoes were mired in more of the muck. In an unwitting echo of Captain Hamley, Davis shook his head and muttered, "Sheep in the boats."

Within a half-hour, each vessel was making its way across the bay, where men from Minor's and Merritt's forces awaited them. Some of those forces were facing in the opposite direction of the oncoming boats. With muskets at the ready, they were keeping a close watch on the hills to the east in case of possible sniper fire from the Californios.

The boats eased onto the shore, one after another, and as the sheep leapt onto the sand, some of the waiting men grouped them and guided them onto the coastline path to lead them toward the barracks and the town, where newly constructed corrals would hold some of the animals before they were slaughtered to provide food for the townsfolk and the American forces.

When Fournier arrived onshore, he spoke to the men that greeted his boat.

"The Indian chief who brought the sheep onto the island seems fairly worn out. I learned from him that the enemy caught and killed his companion, so he had to guide the herd by himself. He's going to stay on the island until we're finished boating them, which by the look of it might not be until tomorrow. He sure could use some food and water. Whatever you can manage to find would be much appreciated. I'll get it from you on my next trip to bring to him."

The men looked at Fournier hesitantly.

Sensing their resistance, he added, "Taking a look around at what he's brought everyone, I'd say he's earned a bit of thanks in return."

The men grumbled in agreement, and the work continued.[2]

The boats returned to the island, and by the time they arrived again at the mainland with their loads, there were men waiting to help unload and guide the next batch of sheep toward town. The process continued until it grew dark, and gathering clouds made it difficult to see.

"We've done a good day's work, men," said Fournier. "Let's head back to the ship while we've still got a bit of light. We'll finish the job tomorrow, although by the look of it, the weather's going to be more of a challenge."

While the men cleaned their boats in preparation for boarding, Fournier walked toward the remaining herd and the Kumeyaay chief who was standing nearby them. He thanked the chief, who in turn thanked Fournier again for the food and water that he had brought him from town earlier. Fournier explained that the boats would be back in the morning. The two men waved briefly to one another, and then Fournier made his way to his boat.

The crews shoved off and began rowing back to the ship. As the crewmen aboard the ship hoisted the boats, they began to smell a foul odor that grew stronger as the boats came closer to the rails.

"What in the hell is that smell?" exclaimed William Elliot, a young man from Boston, Massachusetts. The men in the boat nearest to Elliot scowled at him and said in near unison, as if they had rehearsed it: "Sheep in the boats."

Friday, October 30, began with weather that was even worse than what Fournier had predicted the previous evening. Gale-force winds were blowing as early as two a.m. and rain was pouring. The strong winds and ebb tide caused the ship to drag its anchor, and the crew had to heave short and run a kedge to windward. They used that smaller anchor to pull the ship back toward its mooring spot while they retrieved and then reset the main anchor.

The storm conditions gradually diminished, and later in the morning the crew lowered the boats and their men so they could complete the job they had begun the day before.

William Elliot was once again tending to a boat. As he was helping to lower it, he thought he would wish the men well. Instead of the customary "Greasy luck," he began to say, "Sheep in—" when immediately the three men in the boat raised their hands and shouted "Ahh!," stopping Elliot in mid-sentence.

The five boats made their way to the island, where the chief greeted them and again assisted them by keeping the herd together and close to the boats. The men resumed loading and ferrying the sheep. At one point, Peter McDonnald and James Rice were gathering a load when they noticed one of the animals lying on its side. As they approached it, Rice went to lift it onto its feet when McDonnald stopped him.

"Why?" asked a puzzled Rice. "We've got to finish."

"Not until she's finished."

"Finished with what, a nap?" said Rice sarcastically.

"Not hardly," said McDonnald, shaking his head. "She's lambing."

"She's what?"

"Just wait. You're about to see something special. It may be out of season," said McDonnald, "but she's giving birth."

"Why now?" moaned Rice in an exasperated tone.

"Not exactly something that's in our control, is it?"

"How long will this take?"

"As long as she needs."

They stood and watched silently as the ewe went through a series of contractions and a lamb began to emerge from the birthing canal. Two hooves appeared, then a head, and then the movement halted. Rice looked worriedly at McDonnald, who patted him on the shoulder and said, "Don't worry, she's still working." The ewe eventually rose and stood, allowing gravity to assist in the delivery. More of the lamb's body slid out, and the ewe laid back down. A few more contractions occurred, and the lamb was almost completely visible. The ewe stood again, causing the last portion of the lamb to slip out onto the ground.

Now the ewe began the process of cleaning and stimulating the lamb in order to ensure its viability and safety. It licked the amniotic fluid off of the lamb's mouth and nose to promote its breathing, then began a combination of licking and prodding to encourage the lamb to stand. The newborn shivered at first, seemingly in resistance, then slowly and unsteadily pushed itself up onto its hind legs, its forelegs still tucked under its body. It stood there wobbling for a while as its mother licked some more of the fluid, prodding it at the same time. Eventually, the lamb unfolded its forelegs, rocked back and forth, and then rose fully on all four tiny hooves. Within a few seconds, it began to take its first tentative steps, making its way to its mother's teats and the nourishment they would provide.

McDonnald looked over at Rice, saw him staring in amazement, and said in a reverential tone, "Beautiful, isn't it, how life just keeps on, no matter what."

"Sure is," replied Rice in a hushed voice. Then he added, "And it's already on its feet and walking."

"They've got to be ready for danger right away."

"Compared to them, I guess we've got it pretty easy when we start out."

"You're catchin' on, Rice, you're catchin' on," said McDonnald approvingly. "Now let's see about finishing *our* work."[3]

They left the lamb while it was nursing from its mother and gathered some other sheep to bring to their boat. As they approached the shore with their load, they saw Joseph Frank, the Portuguese boatheader who had explained to Rice how to row while they were on a whale hunt, standing by their boat with his arms crossed over his chest. All the other boats were across the bay unloading.

"So," he said, "you finally decide to come back."

"Yes, Joseph, I'm sorry, we—" began Rice.

"No need for sorry. I see from here why you stay so long. Is a good thing you see this happen, this miracle. Nothing more important. More important for us, because we take life so much. We need have respect for what we take."

"True enough," said McDonnald, as Rice nodded in agreement.

"Yes, yes," said Joseph. "Now, we load the boat."

When their boat was full, the three men pushed off and headed to the mainland to unload their cargo. The other four boats were already returning to the island for their next loads. As they passed his boat, McDonnald called out to each of them, "There's one sheep just gave birth. Leave her and her lamb to us. We'll take care of 'em." The crews acknowledged his request and continued toward the island.

By late afternoon, the men of the *Stonington* had ferried all but about a dozen of the sheep to the mainland.

Midshipman Duvall was supervising the work onshore when Alanson Fournier approached with his final load.

"You've done us a great service today, Fournier," called out Duvall as Fournier's boat landed on the beach.

"Thank you, sir," replied Fournier. "With your permission, this will be our final load. There are about a dozen sheep left on the island that we'd like to take back to the ship for our own use."

"You've more than earned them, sir," said Duvall. "Take them, by all means."

"Much obliged, Mr. Duvall."

"Much obliged in turn, Mr. Fournier."

The men onshore gathered the unloaded sheep as Fournier's crew shoved off toward the island, where they met the rest of the boats.[4]

"You've done fine work these past two days, men," said Fournier, addressing the crews as they stood at their boats. "The last part of it will be taking these remaining sheep back to the ship. When we've got them unloaded, I'll see to it that you have some rest while the men who stayed on board will have the pleasure of cleaning out the boats. Fair enough?"

They responded with a rousing chorus of "Aye, sir!"

"All right, then," continued Fournier, "each boat take two or three sheep and prepare to head back."

While the men collected the sheep, Fournier approached the Kumey-aay chief who, as before, had remained with the herd. Fournier expressed his thanks to the chief and then made his way to his boat as the chief walked away, toward the southern end of the peninsula.

Fournier checked to see that each boat was ready, then pointed in the direction of the ship. With a gentle scraping sound, each boat left the sandy beach and began its return. As they approached the ship, one of the boats veered off toward La Playa. Those in the other four boats could see it in the distance as they drew closer to the ship. When it reached the shore, they saw a full-grown sheep and a lamb leave the boat and bound onto the path and up the hillside of Point Loma. Then the boat left the shore and headed their way, still carrying a couple of sheep for the ship's use.

When all five boats reached the ship, the men on board began the process of hoisting them, and saw that they contained not only men, but sheep as well.

"So, you've brought us some presents, have you!" shouted one of the haulers. "More than you know!" came a voice from one of the boats. Some of the haulers looked at each other with quizzical expressions as they continued hoisting.

When Fournier came aboard, he went straight to the captain's cabin and then returned shortly to the deck. As the last of the sheep came clattering onto the ship, he called out, "All hands!" and delivered his orders. "Milnor, these sheep need a corral. You and your detail see to that. Those of you who've been ferrying the sheep these two days, get yourselves forward to your quarters. The rest of you, see to it that these boats are cleaned and stowed properly," he said, gesturing to larboard and starboard.

There was a pause among the men as his words registered with each group. The first to move were those who had done the ferrying, and they walked toward the fo'c'sle. Next were Milnor and his crew, heading to gather supplies. Those left stood silently in place, as if stunned.

"Well?" queried Fournier in a deeply resonant tone as he swept his gaze across the group.

With downcast looks, the men began shuffling their way toward the boats, gathering the supplies they would need to remove two days' worth of sheep excrement.

The men in the fo'c'sle had cleaned themselves as well as they could and were settling in for some well-deserved rest. As they lay back in their bunks, drifting off to sleep, they could hear unhappy voices on deck muttering "Sheep in the boats!"

PART V

Chapter 28

Stockton Arrives

Monday, October 31, 1846, was a warm, sunny day in San Diego. The men of the *Stonington* were engaged in regular ship's duty when those on the larboard side spotted a vessel off Point Loma.

"Ship comin' in, Mr. Fournier," shouted Samuel Comstock, "and it's a big one!"

Alanson Fournier pulled out his spyglass and looked toward the Point.

"You're quite right, Comstock," he said with a touch of seriousness in his voice. "That's one of our navy warships. Go to the captain's cabin and let him know what's coming."

"Aye, sir," said Comstock, and away he went.

Within minutes, Captain Hamley joined Fournier at the larboard rail. He, too, used his spyglass to view the ship.

"Looks to be nearly twice our size, Fournier," said Hamley. "With that deep a draft, it's going to have a hard time getting over the bar at the mouth of the harbor."

As Hamley was speaking, Fournier swept his spyglass from the Point toward La Playa.

"Look there," he said, pointing toward the landing area. "There's a boat heading out toward the ship," said Fournier, "and I believe that's Lieutenant Minor in the stern."[1]

Fournier was correct. It was indeed Lieutenant Minor heading toward the imposing ship whose crew was now in the process of mooring off the Point.

As the boat drew nearer, Minor caught a glimpse of the ship's stern and saw that this was not the USS *Savannah* as he'd thought it might have been. This was the USS *Congress*, flagship of the Pacific Squadron, of which the *Savannah* was a part. The *Congress* was nearly one hundred eighty feet long with a beam of almost forty-eight feet. It carried forty-eight guns that fired thirty-two-pound balls, as well as four Paixhans guns that fired explosive shells.

Minor realized that the captain of the ship, to whom he was intending to deliver a report on conditions in San Diego, was none other than Robert F. Stockton, commodore of the entire Squadron. Stockton was a storied figure with an impressive lineage. His grandfather, Richard Stockton, was a member of the Second Continental Congress and a signer of the Declaration of Independence, and his father, also named Richard, had served as a US senator and representative from New Jersey.

Stockton himself had entered the US Navy as a midshipman in 1811 at the age of sixteen. Following his service in the War of 1812, he patrolled the Windward Coast of West Africa to prevent US ships from participating in the by-then-outlawed transatlantic slave trade. In 1821, he and an agent for the American Colonization Society negotiated in West Africa with tribal leaders for the purchase of land that would become the African nation of Liberia, where the Society planned to settle free Blacks from the United States. In the early 1840s, he promoted the development of a heavily armed navy steamship that would be propelled by a screw rather than paddlewheels. Upon its completion, now-captain Stockton became commander of the ship, named the USS *Princeton* after the New Jersey home of the Stockton family. During an 1844 demonstration cruise for dignitaries on the Potomac River, one of the two very large guns was fired a third and fatal time, causing the overheated gun to explode and kill six people, including the US secretaries of state and navy. Nearly twenty others were injured, but President John Tyler, who was belowdecks at the time, escaped unharmed.[2]

When Robert F. Stockton had sailed into Monterey harbor on July 23, 1846, aboard the USS *Congress*, John D. Sloat was in charge of the US Pacific Squadron, and the flagship of the fleet was the USS *Savannah*. It was on that same late-July day that Sloat, in acknowledgment of his poor health, had named Stockton as his successor. Stockton became the commodore of the Squadron, and the *Congress* became its flagship. Sloat made his departure for home on July 29 aboard the USS *Levant*.

Stockton was now at San Diego to assess the situation there before making preparations to retake Los Angeles. On board the *Congress* with him was marine captain Archibald H. Gillespie, whose imposition of martial law on Los Angeles during his occupation of that city had led to a revolt by the Californios that resulted in Gillespie and his forces withdrawing from Los Angeles and leaving it under the control of the Californios.

It was to these two men that Lieutenant Minor would be making his report.[3]

"Who approaches, and for what purpose?" was the call from the deck of the *Congress* as the boat drew near.

Minor looked up the side of the ship that rose nearly twenty feet from the waterline and answered the uniformed man standing at the rail. "Lieutenant George Minor of the USS *Savannah* to deliver a report to Commodore Stockton."

The man turned away for a moment and seemed to be conferring with others near him, before turning back and saying, "Come aboard."

Minor climbed the rope ladder and, when he had stepped on the deck, was led to the stern and down to the commodore's cabin.

"Lieutenant Minor to see you, sir," said his escort after knocking on the cabin door.

"Show him in," responded a deep, resonant voice from within.

The escort opened the door and motioned for Minor to enter.

Minor walked in and immediately saluted the two men standing before him. At a glance, he noticed that both of them wore blue jackets over white trousers, but the man on the right had gold buttons trimmed in dark blue, whereas the gold buttons on the jacket of the man on the left were trimmed with bright gold brocade. Minor shifted his stance slightly in order to face more toward the left.

"Lieutenant Minor, sir, with a report for the commodore," he announced, a slight quaver in his voice. The two men before him ended their salutes, at which point Minor ended his own.

"I am Commodore Stockton, and this is Captain Gillespie," said the man on the left. "What have you to report, Minor?"

Gillespie was of average height, with brown hair parted in the middle, longish sideburns, and a mustache and goatee on a relatively plain face. Stockton, a slender man, was a bit taller, with thick, wavy dark hair, a straight nose, strong chin, and piercing gaze.

Minor began his report. "We're in a troubled state, sir. Although we've occupied the town along with Captain Merritt and his men, as well as the townspeople, the enemy controls the high ground beyond the town. They have driven away the nearby livestock and made off with the food that was at the ranchos," explained Minor.

"Yes," interjected Stockton, "the same tactics they used at Los Angeles before we first took control of that town, and I left Captain Gillespie in charge there," he said, with what seemed to be a slight hint of exasperation.

"Yes, sir," continued Minor. "If I may, sir?"

"Go on," replied Stockton.

"In addition to the deprivations regarding food, sir, the enemy has also besieged us with persistent sniper fire, causing our movements to be restricted. Despite the additional assistance from the whaleship *Stonington*, we are still in need of reinforcements if we are to properly control San Diego."

"I see," said Stockton. "And if I were to agree to your request for an additional force, how do you propose we supply them to you? There is a bar at the mouth of the harbor, is there not?"

"Yes, sir, there is, but I believe that your ship, large as it is, will be able to clear it in order to make a convenient mooring in the harbor," responded Minor confidently.

"All right, then, Minor. I shall give this entire matter some thought and act accordingly. If there is nothing further, you are dismissed," stated

Stockton, at which point Minor saluted smartly, left the cabin under the guidance of his escort, and went to his boat.

As they rowed their boat to La Playa, Minor said to his crew, "He's a tough one, that Stockton, but I believe I impressed upon him the severity of our situation. We'll know soon enough."

CHAPTER 29

Stockton Leaves

THE BOAT CARRYING LIEUTENANT MINOR LANDED SAFELY AT LA Playa. As the men were stowing their oars, Minor looked in the direction of the *Congress* and saw promising signs. Sails on its masts were unfurled and filled with air, and its bow began to point toward the harbor.

"Look, men," cried Minor. "Help is on the way!"

The crew watched the movement of the *Congress* and began shaking their fists in the air triumphantly. The ship drew visibly closer to Ballast Point, and then stopped.

"No!" gasped Minor.

The crew stopped their work and stood silently, staring at the *Congress* as it stood eerily motionless and slightly tilted to starboard.

"They've hit the bar, haven't they," said one of the men. Minor nodded his head in dejected agreement.

They watched as the ship remained in the same place for minutes on end, then began to sway slowly, eventually breaking free and returning to its earlier mooring position.

For a variety of reasons, Lieutenant Minor felt a great sense of relief. "In spite of that obstacle," said Minor, as they began heading back to their barracks, "let's hope that they'll still see clear to providing us with some help."

The next day affirmed that hope, as boats from the *Congress* began heading into the harbor. Three of them went straight to La Playa, and one of them went toward the *Stonington*. The boat approached the ship, and a uniformed sailor called up.

"Ahoy! This is the ship *Stonington*?" he asked.

"It is indeed, sir," replied Alanson Fournier, who was standing at the starboard rail. "How can I help you?"

"Well, sir, this is more about how we can help you, and how you can help yourselves," replied the sailor.

"You've certainly got my attention," said Fournier with a smile.

"We've got some provisions for you, courtesy of Commodore Stockton and the USS *Congress*, and there's more for you and the town if you're willing to furnish the boats to get them," said the sailor. "Our ship is too big to bring them in directly."

"I'll have to speak with the captain about the boats," continued Fournier, "but we'll be happy to lighten your load for now."

"That'll be fine," said the sailor. "Drop us a line for hoisting when you're ready."[1]

While the crew of the *Stonington* lifted the welcomed provisions aboard, the boats at La Playa were unloading more than food.

"Welcome to San Diego, sir," said Lieutenant Minor, saluting Captain Gillespie as he stepped out of the boat and onto the shore.

"Thank you, Lieutenant Minor," replied Gillespie as he finished the salute. "My men and I," he said, gesturing to the forty marines who were now disembarking and forming columns, "will see about making this town a bit more hospitable."

When Gillespie's men were ready to march, they followed Minor and his force to the barracks, carrying food and ammunition that, together with the reinforcements, would soon lift the spirits of the besieged occupants of San Diego.[2]

On Monday morning, November 2, boats from the *Stonington* began heading out to the *Congress*. Alanson Fournier had conferred with Captain Hamley the previous day, and Hamley had agreed to using the boats to transfer provisions from the *Congress* to the town, as well as to the *Stonington*. The weather that Monday was very fine, with clear skies and calm seas.

At about eleven a.m., while they were ferrying goods, the men of the *Stonington* spotted a two-masted ship making its way around the stern of the *Congress* and heading into the harbor. It was the *Malek Adhel*, an eighty-foot-long, ten-gun brig named for a sultan of Turkey. The ship had been a part of the Mexican navy until about two months ago, when the USS *Warren* had captured it at the Mexican west-coast town of Mazatlán, across the Gulf of California from the southern tip of the Baja peninsula, and designated it as part of the Pacific Squadron.

As soon as the *Malek Adhel* had secured its mooring in San Diego Bay, a boat rowed out from the ship toward the *Congress* to deliver dispatches that it was carrying from Lieutenant-Colonel John C. Frémont to Commodore Stockton. The messages informed Stockton that because of the unavailability of horses at Santa Barbara, Frémont would have to journey farther north to Monterey in order to obtain enough horses to march to Los Angeles to retake that city.

Upon receiving that news from Frémont, Stockton decided to return to Los Angeles to confer with Captain Mervine of the *Savannah*. The departure of the *Congress* on Tuesday, November 3, only three days after its arrival at San Diego, was a surprise to many, including Captain Hamley.

"Confound it!" shouted Hamley when Alanson Fournier came to the captain's cabin to inform him that the ship was leaving. "I was expecting to go aboard that ship to talk business with the commodore. I need to know how the navy plans to compensate us. Without the oil that we had to pitch overboard, there'll be no profit for Mr. Williams or Mr. Barns to use as a basis for paying anyone's lay on this voyage, making those shares worthless."

"I venture to say, Captain," responded Fournier, "that given the value of this port, we're likely to see the commodore return to San Diego before the war is over."

"I certainly hope so," replied an annoyed Hamley.[3]

CHAPTER 30

A Southern Excursion

ALTHOUGH THE *STONINGTON* REMAINED AT ITS MOORING THROUGHOUT the day of Wednesday, November 4, it experienced a good deal of activity. A group of the volunteers that were onshore came aboard as lookouts for the *Congress*, and members of the *Stonington*'s crew that had been ashore within the military camp came back on board for ship's duty. Some of the crew went aloft to loose the sails for drying, while others went ashore to look for freshwater to bring back to the ship.

The next day, however, brought a true change of scenery. That afternoon, a boat from shore arrived with a message for Captain Hamley.

"What's your news," called Alanson Fournier from the starboard rail.

"Orders from Lieutenant Minor, sir," replied a uniformed sailor. "Tell Captain Hamley he's to ready his ship for sea and prepare to take on board forty men."

"Another evacuation?"

"No, sir," answered the sailor, "they'll be going after horses and cattle."

"Ah, a hunting expedition. All right, then, I'll relay the orders to the captain."

The sailor waved to Fournier, and the boat's crew rowed back to shore.[1]

Fournier went below to deliver the news to Captain Hamley, a bounce in his step at the thought of actually heading out to sea after nearly a month of being moored in the bay. As he approached Hamley's cabin, however, he remembered that the rudder head was still sprung and in need of repair.

After delivering the initial orders to Hamley, Fournier raised the rudder head issue.

"No time to deal with that now, Fournier," said Hamley brusquely. "We'll just have to make do as we can. Set the crew to work."

"Aye, sir," replied Fournier, with a hint of doubt in his voice.

He made his way back to the deck and called "All hands!" When the crew had gathered, he said, "We've got orders to head to sea, men," at which most of the crew cheered. "Get yourselves aloft and prepare to set sail."

The men clambered to their stations in the rigging and went about their work. At about ten o'clock that evening, they saw boats leaving the shore and heading toward the ship. Once they arrived, between thirty-five and forty men boarded the *Stonington*, along with Lieutenant Minor, Captain Gillespie, and their weapons and artillery.

"Mr. Fournier," said Minor as he approached the *Stonington*'s second officer, "I need you to set a course for Ensenada. Upon our arrival there, we will disembark and begin herding horses and cattle northward to San Diego. We nearly had them two days ago when we marched southward twenty miles, but an informant in the enemy's camp alerted them to our approach and they dispersed beyond our reach. We'll be coming at them in the dark from the south this time."

"Aye, sir," replied Fournier, "that's a trip of about eighty miles," he said, with thoughts of the rudder head running through his mind.

"Yes, and we'll be ready for them this time."

"I'm sure you will, sir," said Fournier, hoping for smooth seas.[2]

At eleven p.m., the sound of clanking chains could be heard as the crew weighed anchor and the *Stonington* began moving out to sea. Peter McDonnald expressed the thoughts of many of the men when he turned to James Rice as they trimmed sail at starboard, saying, "It's good to be under way again, breathing life back into this ship."

"Yes," replied Rice, "but I sure wish our destination was different. I stowed away on this ship thinking that I'd be getting home quicker. When I heard the captain say we were going to sea, I thought to myself,

'Finally!' Turns out we're just doing more work for the navy. Damned war changed everything."

"War has a way of doing that," said McDonnald, "making it better for some, worse for others. Won't know how this one balances out 'til it's over."

"Well, I hope it's over soon—or at least our part of it," said Rice, "so we can balance our way back home."

While they and the other men stood at the ready, Captain Hamley watched intently as he maneuvered the ship beyond Ballast Point, out of the harbor, and past the bar that had grounded the *Congress*. The winds were light, and by one p.m. the next day, the *Stonington* was only two miles south of Point Loma.

Fournier welcomed the gentle winds, concerned as he was about how the rudder would perform. All had gone well so far, but now the winds were beginning to pick up and the sky was growing dark as clouds began approaching from the northwest. Within the next two hours, rain and squalls were upon them. Fournier monitored the ship's movement closely, and as he looked astern, he was glad that he had put Mark Comstock at the helm. Comstock knew the steering mechanism well enough to sense how much pressure it could take and when it was time to let the sails adjust the ship's direction.[3]

The stronger winds had increased the *Stonington*'s speed, and at ten p.m. that night they sighted Islas de Todos Santos, the islands that lay just five miles off the coast of Ensenada.

At eleven o'clock on the morning of November 7, with the winds having moderated, the crew anchored the ship in All Saints Bay, furled the sails, and began ferrying Minor, Gillespie, and their men to shore. The waves that had earlier been crashing in rapid succession along the broad arc of the sandy beach were now reduced to gentle rollers that allowed the boats to make easy landings onto the shore. Those conditions did not last, however, as the wind shifted to the northeast, causing the ship to sway uneasily, which made it difficult to deliver the final items of the landing—the artillery.

Captain Hamley hesitated a moment, wondering if it might be best to wait until the winds again grew weaker. His hesitation led Lieutenant

Minor and Captain Gillespie to begin shouting from the shore to "Get those guns landed!" The offshore wind carried their exhortations clearly to Hamley, who relented, waved to them, and gave the order to deliver the guns. It was well that he did so, because by the time the guns were ashore and the boats had returned, the wind, rather than abate, had gradually strengthened and the sea had become rough. Those conditions continued through the next day, leading Hamley to keep the ship moored in the bay until the evening of Monday, November 9, when the ship finally got under way for San Diego.

For the next three days, breezes were light, sometimes calm, and persistently from the northwest, making it difficult for the *Stonington* to achieve any headway. On Friday the 13th, a thick fog had settled in, causing Hamley to anchor the ship that evening until the early morning hours of Saturday, when the fog finally lifted. The weather held for most of the day, but in the evening the fog returned, this time accompanied by light breezes from the southeast. Captain Hamley decided to take advantage of the favorable winds and continue northward, finally coming to anchor at San Diego on Sunday morning, November 15.[4]

CHAPTER 31

Californios Attack

It had been more than a week since the *Stonington*'s crew had ferried Minor, Gillespie, their men, and their equipment ashore at Ensenada, and they were eager to hear if there had been any word from them.

Fournier requested and received permission from Hamley to take a boat to shore later that Sunday. He brought with him some provisions for the barracks in exchange for any news that they might have to share. What he was about to learn would be quite surprising.

The boat landed at La Playa, and Fournier and his crew began their march to the barracks. As they drew nearer to town, they began hearing what seemed to be animal noises. The closer they got, the more defined those noises became, until it was obvious that what they were hearing was the whinnying of horses and the lowing of cattle.

"They're back already!" exclaimed Fournier to his men. "They were traveling on foot through rugged country and dealing with herds of animals while we were sailing on the open sea, and they still beat us back here!"

Upon reaching the barracks, Fournier spotted Lieutenant Duvall and called out to him.

"Mr. Duvall! Or should I call you Odysseus?"

"How's that, Mr. Fournier?"

"I hear plentiful animal noises. Did you and your men encounter Circe on the way back?" Fournier asked.

"No, sir, no Greek mythological magic here," Duvall said as Fournier and his men drew closer. "I see we beat that old tub of yours, despite increasing our size more than sixfold."

Fournier looked at Duvall, puzzled. "You recruited more men along the way?"

"No, sir," said Duvall with a laugh. "Livestock—ninety horses and two hundred cattle, to be exact."

"And no magic, you say?"

"No magic, although some of our men showed some special talents with controlling the creatures, moving them as they did through the ravines while avoiding the enemy."

"Well, my men and I may as well hand over these provisions we brought you, although you seem to be well supplied at this point."

"Somewhat," said Duvall. "The majority of these animals are for Commodore Stockton's purposes. He plans to march from here northward to retake Los Angeles, in combination with Major Frémont marching southward from Monterey. In order to do that, he needs horses for transport and beeves for food. That's why he sent us to Ensenada to get those animals."

"I see," said Fournier. "But that doesn't explain his sudden departure from here."

"I would have to agree. Still, it's not for me to say why Commodore Stockton makes his decisions."[1]

Neither man knew about the dispatches that Stockton had received from Frémont that had caused Stockton to take the *Congress* back to San Pedro to confer with Mervine. They knew enough, however, to realize that a major offensive was in the works. Two days later, on Tuesday, November 17, Stockton and the *Congress* returned to San Diego, only to find themselves in the midst of a double predicament—a grounding and an attack. The grounding occurred when Stockton insisted on bringing his ship into the harbor rather than mooring in the area outside of it where he had done so on his earlier visit. This time, after surveying and marking the bar and the channel, he successfully brought his ship across the bar, but then got it stuck in the channel, where it listed to one side.

The crew had to work quickly to adjust the spars so that they would keep the ship from tipping over.

In the midst of that predicament, the second one arose.[2]

The Californios, who had been continuing their sporadic sniper fire on the town, launched a full-force attack. Nearly one hundred men on horseback appeared at the top of the hill, led by José Antonio Carrillo, the man who was second in command of the force that defeated Mervine and Gillespie at Dominguez Rancho over a month ago in the Battle of the Old Woman's Gun. Then, Carrillo was among those that had prevented the Americans from retaking Los Angeles. Now, he was intent on retaking San Diego from the Americans who were consistently increasing their supplies, most notably their recent acquisitions of livestock. The return of the *Congress* lent even greater urgency to Carrillo's attack, as while part of the ship's crew were working to prevent it from capsizing, others had already landed ashore and were advancing to join in the fight.[3]

Carrillo led the charge down the hillside, his mounted horsemen brandishing their deadly lances. As they approached, Lieutenant Minor, Captain Gillespie, and a force of forty men opened fire from the base of the hill. In addition to those musket shots, men at the barracks fired the guns that had been brought from Fort Guijarros. One of the nine-pound balls struck a Californio, tore off his foot, and then passed through his horse's body. The rider fell to the ground but the horse continued to run into the Americans' ranks, with its intestines hanging out of its belly. The American forces held, however, and prevented the Californios from entering the town.

Carrillo, realizing that the Americans had the advantage with their weaponry and the approaching reinforcements, called off the attack and led his men back up the hill and into the countryside beyond. In the process of doing so, they rounded up about forty cattle and took them along. Four of Carrillo's men died that day, while the Americans had no casualties.

The Californios continued their sniper fire throughout the following days, keeping the inhabitants of San Diego on edge and in a continual state of preparedness in the event of another attack.[4]

CHAPTER 32

Taking Care of Business

SPURRED BY THE RETURN OF THE *CONGRESS*, THE ENSUING SKIRMISH, and the information that he had gleaned from Duvall, Fournier made a visit to Captain Hamley's cabin. Upon knocking and being granted entrance, Fournier shared his thoughts.

"Sir," he began, "I believe there is sufficient reason for us to see immediately to the repair of the rudder head."

"And what might that be," replied Hamley gruffly.

Fournier conveyed Stockton's plan for marching northward, and he reviewed the amount of sail adjustment that had to be made in compensation for the faulty rudder head during the trip to and from Ensenada. "It is highly likely," he continued, "that Stockton will order us to sea again in some capacity. Without a fully functional rudder, we may find ourselves in a vulnerable position that could result in preventing our return to New London."

Hamley straightened and stood silent at that last statement. The thought of being responsible for the loss of the ship, and the effect that it would have on his reputation and livelihood, was more than he was willing to risk. In a forcibly calm and deliberate voice, he said, "Well, then, Fournier, given Stockton's apparent intentions, I believe we should address the repair of that rudder head. See to it at once."

"Aye, sir," replied Fournier, and he left the cabin, relieved that the issue that had caused him no end of worry about the safety of the crew and the integrity of the ship would soon be resolved.

He immediately sought out Henry Thompson, the blacksmith.

"Thompson, we're finally going to repair that sprung rudder head," stated Fournier triumphantly.

"A sensible move, if I do say so myself, sir. Too bad we had to toss the tryworks overboard, or I could do the work right here."

"Agreed on both counts. I need you to go to the helm and remove that bent metal strap so we can take it to town tomorrow to get it fixed, or replace it. We'll be leaving first thing in the morning."

"I'll be ready with it," said Thompson.

Fournier and Thompson took one of the boats to La Playa Wednesday morning. With them was Mark Comstock, whom Fournier had brought along due to his familiarity with the rudder-head machinery. They went straight to the town's blacksmith and showed him the damaged metal and explained its purpose.

"I could reshape it for you," said the smith, taking a careful look at the part, "but there's no guarantee that it won't spring on you again, seeing as how it's already weakened. My suggestion is to get a whole new piece."

As Fournier considered the smith's suggestion, Thompson looked around at the shop to get a sense of the man's competence. He could see all the proper smithing tools as well as pieces that had been shaped with skill.

"This is all your work?" asked Thompson.

"It is. Been working on my own for over fifteen years now."

"Do much ship's work?"

"Regular part of the trade, this being a port and all," answered the smith matter-of-factly.

Thompson looked the smith in the eye, sized him up, then turned to Fournier and nodded.

"All right," said Fournier. "How soon can you get started on a new piece?"

"Business has been a bit slow lately," said the smith wryly. "I could get to work on it right now, if you like."

"That suits us just fine," said Fournier. "How long will it take?"

"No more than a couple of hours."

"Mind if we wait?" asked Fournier.

"Suit yourselves," said the smith as he selected a piece of metal to begin shaping.

The men watched as the smith worked deftly, heating, bending, hammering, and drilling until he had fashioned a replacement for the sprung rudder head that they had brought him.

"Comstock," said Fournier, "you know this piece and what it needs to do better than any of us. How does it look to you?"

Comstock hefted the angled metal with both hands and inspected it carefully, bearing in mind how well it would have to fit in order to withstand the pressures put upon it. Having eyed the entire piece, he handed it to Fournier. "I'd say he's done a fine job, sir."

Thompson agreed. "The man knows his craft," he said, and the smith acknowledged the compliment with a nod.

Fournier turned to the smith and said, "How much do we owe you?"

"No charge."

"Did I hear you right?" said Fournier in surprise. "No charge?"

"That's right, no charge," said the smith. "I know your ship full well. Without it there to take us in, I might not be standing here talking with you. Fashioning this piece of metal is the least I can do to thank you for saving us."

Fournier extended his right arm, the two men shook hands, and then Thompson and Comstock each did the same. The three men said good-bye to the blacksmith and headed down the trail to La Playa and their boat.

When they got back to the ship, Fournier went to the captain's cabin and reported what had happened with the blacksmith.

"It's a good thing he didn't charge us," said Hamley in a caustic tone. "I don't know how we would have paid him."

"Aye, sir," said Fournier with quiet disappointment, then left to find the ship's carpenter.

"Milnor," said Fournier when he had found him, "I want you to go to the helm. Comstock is waiting for you there with the new piece for the rudder head. He'll give you whatever assistance you may need. Take your time with it. We'll make the final adjustments tomorrow."

Milnor tapped his forehead with his right hand in a modified salute, gathered some tools, and made his way astern.

Fournier went onto the deck and looked up at the late-afternoon sky, took in a deep breath, and exhaled. For a moment, he could relax.[1]

CHAPTER 33

Casks for Tasks

ON THURSDAY MORNING, NOVEMBER 19, WHILE THOMAS MILNOR AND Mark Comstock were finishing the adjustments on the rudder head, a boat from the *Congress* approached the *Stonington*. Alanson Fournier went to the starboard rail and greeted them.

"What business brings you to us on this fine San Diego morning?" he called down to the sailors.

"Orders from Commodore Stockton."

"And what might those be?" asked Fournier.

"Water," said one sailor.

"We've not much," said Fournier.

"Ah, but you will," said the sailor. "The commodore wants you to collect freshwater from shore, stockpile it in your hold, and have it ready for his ship's use when he needs it."

"So, we're to be his supply ship, now, are we?" asked Fournier some-what impatiently.

"That'd be the size of it."

"I'll go see what the captain has to say about this," said Fournier.

"Do that if you must," said the sailor, "but take it from me, Stockton isn't a man to trifle with. This isn't a request from him—it's an order."

"I'll pass that along to the captain for his consideration," said Fournier as he waved to the sailor, then turned and made his way to Captain Hamley's cabin.[1]

"He what?!" shouted Hamley after Fournier had delivered Stockton's order. "That's rich, it is," he continued. "First they make us empty our hold of all our oil, and now they want us to fill it for them with their water. I've a mind to set sail and leave this place, now that we've taken care of that rudder head."

"I don't know that you'd want to run afoul of Stockton, sir," said Fournier when Hamley had paused in his rant. "He'd likely have his entire fleet after us if we tried to make a run for it. We're in the government's service now. They could hang us as deserters."

"Let 'em try," snarled Hamley. He grew silent and paced the floor of his cabin. It took him a while to calm down, but as he did, he realized the futility of going against Stockton's order. Hard as it was for him to accept, he was not the ultimate authority for his ship at this point. If he was to make it through this period, he would have to follow someone else's orders for a time.

Hamley relaxed his hunched shoulders as he looked out his cabin windows. "Have the cooper begin preparing casks for water, Fournier," he said.

"Aye, sir," responded a relieved Fournier.

He left the cabin to find Selden Maynard, a young man from Sag Harbor, New York, who had developed the skill of coopering at an early age.

"Whatever shooks we've got in the forehold, Maynard, you'll need to get them assembled for water," Fournier told him. "If there are any empty casks lying about, prepare them as well. We're about to become a reservoir of sorts for Commodore Stockton."

"All right, then, Mr. Fournier," said Maynard as he gathered his tools and began making his way forward, "casks it is."

Maynard spent the rest of the day hauling shooks, hoops, heads, and bungs to his work area in the fore 'tween deck. There he unbound each shook and, starting with the bung-hole stave, stood each pre-formed wooden slat inside a metal hoop at its top end. When all the staves were fitted inside that hoop, he tapped along the top end with his hammer to even them out, then slipped another hoop over the top and drove it down tight with his hoop driver until he heard a ringing sound from the hoop that let him know he had gotten it to just the right spot. After flipping the cask over and adding two more hoops at the other end, he set a wooden head into each open end. Then he lightly tapped a wooden bung into the bung hole to plug the cask until it was time to remove the bung and fill the cask with water.

The sounds of clanging metal and thunking wood resonated within the *Stonington* and made their way out to the main deck, producing a sense of vibrant energy throughout the ship. Evening approached, and Maynard was finishing his last cask of the day when Fournier came in to check on his progress.

"Well, now, Maynard," exclaimed the second officer, surveying the nearly twenty casks that filled more than half the space, "you've done a fair piece of work today."

"Aye, sir," replied Maynard, wiping the last touch of sweat from his brow. "I reckon this is enough to get the watering started."

"Enough to earn yourself a bit of grub," said Fournier with a nod. "Go on up. Cook's got it ready. You'll need your strength for another round of this tomorrow."

"Appreciate it, sir. Tell the truth, feels good to be doin' the work again."

With that, Maynard went to the main cabin to get his meal with Milnor, Thompson, and the other middle-class men, while Fournier, having already been served in the first round with the captain and the other officers, continued making his rounds about the ship.[2]

The next day, Maynard continued his coopering while crewmen hauled the completed casks up onto the deck through the main hatch. They lowered them to the sides of the awaiting boats that towed them to shore, where crew members then rolled them as close as possible to freshwater streams and springs. Using wooden buckets from the boats, the men filled the casks, set the bungs, and rolled the casks back to the boats. They then tied the casks together, creating a raft, and towed them back to the ship, where they were lifted to the deck and then lowered into the hold. This process continued for the next two days, with the crew bringing casks to shore, filling them with water, towing them back to the ship, and then storing them in the hold.

On Sunday morning, with the thick fog of the previous day lifted and the skies fair, a boat from the *Congress* approached the *Stonington*.

"Boat's comin', Mr. Fournier," cried one of the crew on deck.

Fournier went to the larboard rail and saw that in the boat was the same sailor that had delivered Stockton's order for water.

"Good morning to you, sir," called the sailor.

"Morning it is," replied Fournier, "but seeing you again makes me wonder if it is indeed a good one. I hesitate to ask, but what purpose brings you here?"

"We're here to lighten your load," said the sailor.

"How so?" asked Fournier.

"Commodore Stockton wants you to deliver a batch of water to his ship."

"Good enough. Is that all, then?"

"No, sir," answered the sailor. "The commodore wants you to send casks to town."

"Bring the water back to shore?" asked a puzzled Fournier.

"Just casks, sir," said the sailor. "Big ones."

"Empty casks? What the devil for?"

"Now that we've chased the enemy off the hill, the commodore wants to build a new fort there, to replace the old one. Plans to fill the casks with sand and put 'em side by side to make the outer fort walls," explained the sailor. "Then he'll pile dirt and gravel on their fronts, and dig a ditch all along the backside of 'em."

Fournier stood in silence and thought about the state of affairs that now existed, where sand was considered a more precious commodity than whale oil for the *Stonington*'s casks.

"I don't suppose this is going to sit too well with the captain—or the cooper, for that matter—but I'll relay the message," said Fournier.

"Mind, same as before. It's more than just a message—it's an order."

"Yes, and as I said before," replied Fournier, "morning it is."

The two men waved to each other as the boat pulled away and headed back to the *Congress*.

Fournier put some of his crew in charge of delivering a raft of water to Stockton, then he made his way to Captain Hamley to convey the latest order from the commodore.

"Sand," said Hamley incredulously when Fournier delivered his news. "He wants to put sand in our whale-oil casks." He stared at Fournier and then shook his head. "I'd like to tell him to go pound that sand somewhere else, but I don't suppose that would go over too well with the mighty commodore, would it?" said an annoyed Hamley. Fournier shook his head in agreement. "Well, then, Fournier," said the captain resignedly, "time for you to go to the cooper and give him his orders. I'm sure he'll find them amusing."

Fournier left the cabin and headed to the fore 'tween deck. Selden Maynard was there, busily assembling casks, and he continued his work as Fournier approached and began to speak.[3]

"You're certainly an industrious sort, Maynard," said Fournier as the tap-tap-tap of Maynard's hammer on the hoop driver rang out.

"That I am, sir," said Maynard, continuing to tap hoops into place.

"And you're able to carry on a conversation without stopping your work," said Fournier admiringly.

"Wouldn't get much done if I let my talking get in the way, now, would I, sir?" Maynard said, turning the cask end for end and tapping on another hoop.

"No, I don't suppose you'd have nearly enough casks ready for the commodore, especially now that he wants even more so he can fill 'em with sand."

The tapping stopped. Maynard looked up to the planks above his head, then returned his gaze to his hands and resumed his tapping. "Sand, you say," Maynard said, clearing his throat. "Oil. Water. Sand?" He continued tapping.

"That's right," said Fournier, "sand. The commodore wants to build a fort on the hill, and he plans to surround it with casks full of sand."

Maynard finished with the hoops but his tapping continued as he began putting one of the heads in place. He was silent for a moment, then said, "I can see that. Clever. This oak'll withstand musket shot. Guns are another matter, though." He turned the cask over and began tapping the other head in place.

"He's going to pile dirt up against them."

"That could turn into a handy ramp for scaling the wall," said Maynard as he finished the cask and began assembling another one.

"He's going to have a ditch all along the other side," responded Fournier, gazing with admiration at the work that was continuing in front of him.

"This commodore fellow thinks of everything," said Maynard, chuckling. "Sounds like he's got some engineering blood in his veins."

"I believe he does, Maynard. I believe he does."

"Well, then, Mr. Fournier," Maynard said as he tapped on another hoop, "I guess I'll be working on casks for a few more days."

"Seems so. I'll leave you to it, Maynard."

"Aye, sir."

Fournier shook his head in wonder as he walked away to the continued tap-tap-tapping of a hammer on a hoop driver.[4]

CHAPTER 34

Triple Duty

On Monday morning, November 23, three boats left the *Ston-ington* and headed for shore, each towing a raft of empty casks, each raft meant for a different purpose.

The first raft consisted of a half-dozen medium-sized casks, the same as those that had gone ashore in the previous few days. Crewmen would fill them with freshwater and then tow them back to the ship where they would be added to the supply being held for Commodore Stockton.

The other two rafts also consisted of six casks each, but these casks were larger, each one capable of holding three hundred gallons. The crews of those boats rowed past La Playa and further northward until they had reached the edge of where the coastal area became too sandy for them to be able to roll the casks onto the trail that led into town. There they were met by men from Lieutenant Minor's and Captain Merritt's forces that had ridden from town.

The crewmen landed the boats and began untying the casks.

"Roll 'em onto the sleds and we'll take 'em to the hill," called out one of the men onshore, pointing to the simple, wooden carriers that were attached to their horses.

After they had unloaded all of the casks, the crewmen prepared to row back to the ship. One of them called out to the men onshore, "We'll be back in a day or two with another load once our cooper's got 'em ready." The men waved to each other, and the boats headed off to the ship.[1]

As they rode their horses along the trail, the Americans of those combined forces were in the beginning stage of what would prove to be an arduous process. They and their fellow sailors and soldiers would spend the next three weeks hauling casks, lumber, and adobe bricks to the construction site. There they would arrange the casks in a rectangle measuring thirty by twenty yards square and fill them with sand. Within the rectangle they would build a ball-proof house of adobe covered on its exterior with wooden planks. On top of the house they would mount a swivel gun. They would then dig a ditch around the blockhouse and behind the casks, fighting their way through rocks and dirt with rudimentary tools. They would pile the excavated material against the front of the casks to strengthen the wall, and then they would construct a gate and drawbridge at the front.

When it was finished, the officers would commend the men for having worked so long and hard under conditions made difficult by food rationing and, for many, no proper shoes for their feet. All too predictably, it would eventually be known as Fort Stockton.[2]

The crew of the *Stonington* continued its water-gathering activities during the last week of November and made another delivery of empty casks for use in the construction of the fort.

At two o'clock in the afternoon of November 27, the Friday of that week, while part of the crew was ashore getting water, a boat from the *Congress* approached. Alanson Fournier was already at larboard when it drew near enough for him to see that it was the same sailor aboard who had been delivering messages from Commodore Stockton.

"Remarkable how the water covers the traces of a well-worn path, isn't it, sir?" called Fournier to the sailor.

"No path necessary, sir. I believe we could make the trip blindfolded by now."

"What is it this time, my friend?"

"Commodore wants you to prepare to go to sea."

"Where to this time?"

"Can't say for certain, sir, but I believe you'll be heading southward."

"Another southern excursion, eh?" quipped Fournier. "Well, I'll inform the captain after I've finished checking the repairs that my crew made to the bulwarks the past couple of days."

"You'll want to make that a quick inspection, sir."

"Oh, and why is that?"

"Because the men you'll be transporting will arrive at your ship later today."

"The commodore certainly has high expectations regarding timetables."

"That he does, sir. Well, I'll be off now."

"Yes, back to your ship. Enough with your visits," Fournier said with a slight smile.

"Ah, you know you'll miss me, sir," called the sailor with a laugh as his boat returned to the *Congress*.[3]

At eight o'clock that evening, forty men from shore came aboard the *Stonington*, led by Captain Samuel J. Hensley, a wiry man with a receding hairline, high cheekbones, and a long, sharp nose. Hensley, originally from Kentucky, had been a settler in California near Sutter Buttes when John C. Frémont entered the area with his expeditionary force in the spring of 1846. Hensley soon joined the Osos and became a participant in the revolt that led to the Bear Flag Republic. He had ridden with Ezekiel Merritt and the other Osos when they came to San Diego at the end of September.

"Who's the captain of this ship?" asked Hensley in a nasal, reedy voice.

"I am," responded Hamley as he stepped forward. "Captain George Hamley. And you, sir?"

"I am Captain Samuel Hensley, proud member of the California Battalion, as are many of the men with me. Our mission is to head south, get as many horses and cattle as we can find, and bring 'em back here to San Diego for Commodore Stockton's use."

"So, another trip to Ensenada, eh?"

"Yes, sir, but only after you bring half of us to San Ramón, about a hundred miles farther down the coast."

"I see," said Hamley hesitantly. "Well, you and your men make your-selves comfortable here on the deck. We'll get under way first thing in the morning."

"The sooner the better," replied Hensley curtly as he turned to orga-nize his men.[4]

Night passed quietly except for the loud snoring of the men sleeping on deck. Saturday morning, November 28, dawned with fair weather. Hensley and his men awakened to the sounds of crewmen climbing into the rigging and preparing the *Stonington* for departure. Sailors from the *Savannah* that were among Hensley's men were all too familiar with the activity occurring that morning, but the men of the California Battalion were duly impressed with the smooth efficiency of the crewmen as they handled the sails and the sheets, or ropes, that controlled them.

Another group of men was watching the action. They were the crew of the merchant ship *Sterling* that had come into the harbor about a week ago after having delivered John C. Frémont and his men to Monterey. The ship was moored not too far starboard of the *Stonington*.[5]

Alanson Fournier called out the orders while George Hamley observed from the stern. "Heave short! Prepare to haul anchor!" he shouted.

The current was running very strong, and before the ship drew near enough to begin hauling, the anchor broke ground. The ship, now caught by the incoming current, began drifting, its stern swinging toward the bow of the *Sterling*.

Hamley yelled "What the devil is going on?" as Fournier shouted to the crew to reset the anchor. As the men at the anchor worked furiously, all others watched helplessly as the stern of the *Stonington* collided with the *Sterling*, tearing away the jibboom and flying jibboom that extended from its bow and doing considerable damage to other portions of that section.

Men aboard the *Sterling* were yelling all sorts of obscenities at the *Stonington*'s crew. One voice rose above all the others.

"What in blazing hell have you done to my ship?!"

"I take it you are the captain?" shouted Hamley.

"I am, sir," came the reply. "And you?"

"The same as well, sir."

"Not so well, by the look of it, sir."

"My deepest apologies, Captain," said Hamley. "Our anchor broke loose as we were heaving short, and the current got the best of us."

"And we, the worst," came the tart reply.

Hamley raised his eyebrows and shrugged his shoulders apologetically. "I'll lower a boat to help you retrieve the booms, and I'll send our carpenter over to assist with the repairs to your bulwarks."

"Aye, the boat would be helpful. The booms are in a tangled mess with all the loosened rigging," said the *Sterling*'s captain. "As for the carpenter, I'll keep to my own, thank you very much."

"As you wish, sir," replied Hamley. "Again, my apology for the mishap."

The *Sterling*'s captain went about inspecting the damage to his ship, and Hamley called to his crew to lower a boat to assist with the retrieval of the booms.

It wasn't until later that Saturday evening that the *Stonington* made its way safely out of San Diego harbor and toward its southerly destination . . . and another mishap.[6]

The ship *Stonington*. (Spencer Emanuel)

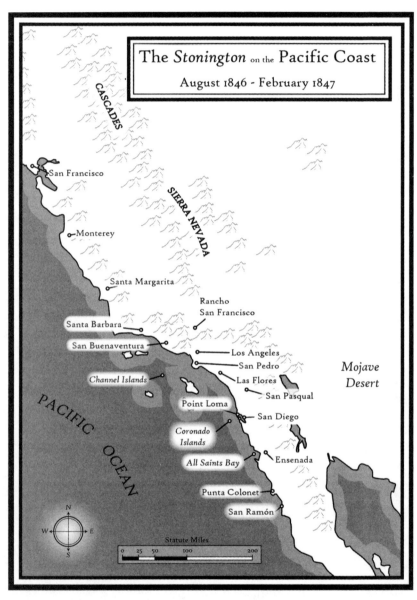

Map of the Pacific coast showing places of significance to the *Stonington* during its service in the Mexican-American War. (Spencer Emanuel)

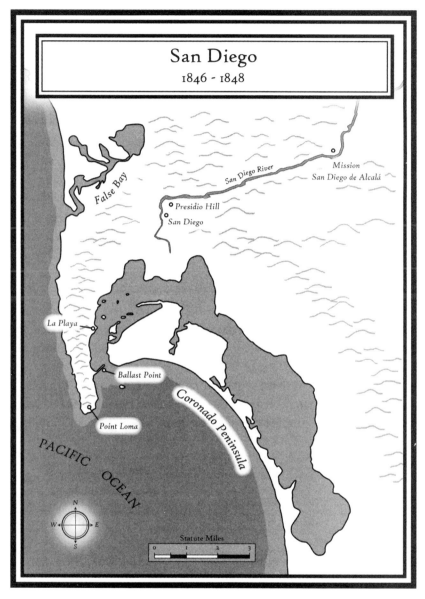

Map showing the port of San Diego and surrounding area during the *Stonington*'s time there. (Spencer Emanuel)

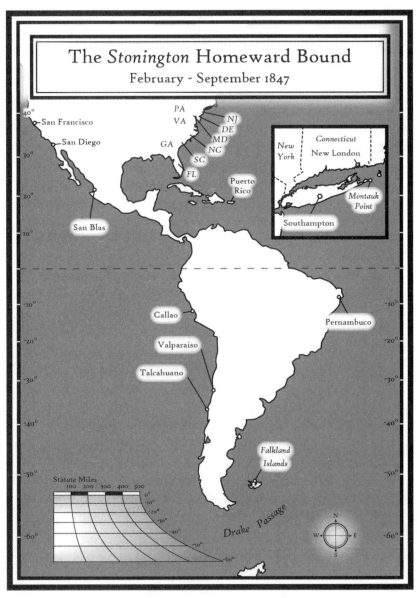

The *Stonington* Homeward Bound
February - September 1847

40° San Francisco

San Diego

30°

20°

10° San Blas

PA
VA
GA
SC
FL

NJ
DE
MD
NC

Puerto
Rico

New
York

Connecticut
New London

Southampton

Montauk
Point

-10° Callao

Pernambuco

-20° Valparaiso

-30° Talcahuano

-40°

Falkland
Islands

-50°

Statute Miles
100 200 300 400 500

Drake Passage

N
W E
S

-60°

Map showing places of significance during the *Stonington*'s voyage home from San Diego, California to New London, Connecticut. (Spencer Emanuel)

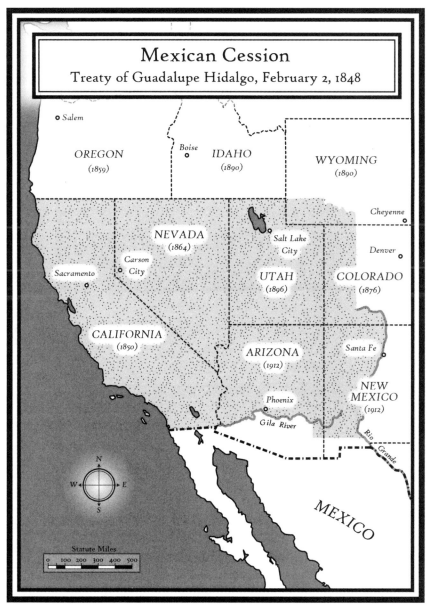

Mexican Cession
Treaty of Guadalupe Hidalgo, February 2, 1848

Salem

OREGON
(1859)

Boise

IDAHO
(1890)

WYOMING
(1890)

Cheyenne

NEVADA
(1864)

Salt Lake
City

Denver

Carson
City

Sacramento

UTAH
(1896)

COLORADO
(1876)

CALIFORNIA
(1850)

ARIZONA
(1912)

Santa Fe

NEW
MEXICO
(1912)

Phoenix

Gila River

Rio Grande

N
W E
S

MEXICO

Statute Miles
0   100 200 300 400 500

Map showing the territory Mexico ceded to the United States according to the
Treaty of Guadalupe Hidalgo that ended the Mexican-American War of 1846–1848.
(Spencer Emanuel)

Pages from the *Stonington*'s logbook written by Alanson Fournier showing him to be the keeper of the log, including information for February 28, March 1–2, 1846 (left); and describing the ship's arrival at San Diego, including information for September 28–30, 1846 (right). (Log 335, courtesy Mystic Seaport Museum)

Pages from the *Stonington*'s logbook written by Alanson Fournier describing circumstances in San Diego, meetings with Captain Ezekiel Merritt and customs collector Don Pedro Carrillo, and the beginning of the *Stonington*'s service for the United States government, including information for September 30, October 1–2, 1846 (left); and showing Fournier's final entries before another officer assumed the duty of keeping the log, including information for June 6–11, 1847 (right). (Log 335, courtesy Mystic Seaport Museum)

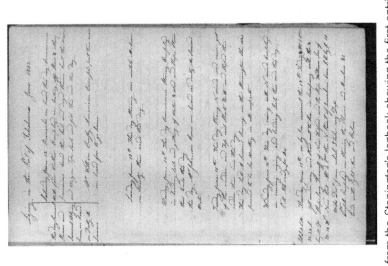

Pages from the *Stonington's* logbook showing the first entries written by the unidentified officer who assumed the duty of keeping the log, including information for June 12–17, 1847 (left); and the first identification of Alanson Fournier as master of the *Stonington*, including information for August 4–11, 1847 (right). (Log 335, courtesy Mystic Seaport Museum)

CHAPTER 35

A Rough Landing

SUNDAY, NOVEMBER 29, BEGAN WITH FAIR SKIES AND A GENTLE BREEZE. By midday, however, the ship was becalmed, and Hamley, mindful of the need to deliver his passengers as soon as possible, ordered a boat lowered to tow the ship until the winds increased. As the crew rowed the boat, with a line extending from its stern to the bow of the ship, they neared the Islas Coronado, a small group of islands about fifteen miles south of Point Loma. The closer they came to the islands, the more they could hear a barking sound. When they were near enough to see clearly the shoreline of North Coronado, they spotted a large number of sea lions, some staying still, others apparently jockeying for a better position among the crowd, and nearly every one of them making the barking sound that filled the air.

The winds returned the next day, but they blew from the southeast, accompanied by rain, and they made it difficult for the *Stonington* to maintain its course. At eleven o'clock that morning, however, the winds shifted suddenly to the northwest and blew stronger, making for much easier sailing through the remainder of Monday and into the next day.[1]

Tuesday, December 1, dawned with even stronger northwest winds. Ocean waves were rolling toward the shore, some of them cresting and crashing well before they reached the sandy beach. The result was a fierce jumble of white and blue surf that would make landing a boat difficult.

"Fournier," called Captain Hamley to his second officer, "get this ship moored safely beyond those breakers. Once you've got us anchored firmly, prepare boats to go ashore."

"Aye, sir," responded Fournier.

Looking at the surf conditions, Fournier decided that it would be best to send just two boats at first in order to minimize the chances of a collision. After the ship was secured, two boats were lowered, each with a crew of three and carrying about ten soldiers, along with their weapons and ammunition, as well as saddles and other equipment that they would need for herding animals northward to San Diego.

As the boats approached the breaking waves, one of them capsized, the pounding surf cracking open its hull and spilling its contents into the roiling water. The men gurgled and sputtered as they struggled to gather as much of their strewn equipment as possible while making their way to shore. Six guns were among the items that the powerful rip current pulled out to sea. Men from the other boat that had already landed waded out to help their beleaguered comrades. Once everyone was safely onshore, the crewmen of the *Stonington* salvaged what they could of the equipment that had fallen from the broken boat and rowed back to the ship.

The *Stonington* remained moored off the coast for the rest of Tuesday and all through Wednesday, waiting for a signal from shore. Captain Hensley and a few of the men that had landed would be returning to the ship in order to join the rest of the force for another landing to the north. The winds had continued to be strong, and Fournier, thinking back to the chaotic departure from San Diego, was concerned about the anchor holding firm.

On Thursday morning, with the winds still blowing, Fournier finally saw the signal and, with a sense of relief, ordered a boat to shore to retrieve the men. The process went smoothly, and as Hensley came aboard, Fournier approached him and said, "Welcome back, sir. I hope you enjoyed your stay."

Hensley just grunted, unamused by the attempted humor.

Hamley, who had come on deck to greet Hensley, walked over and asked, "Now to Ensenada, sir?"

"That is the plan," replied Hensley matter-of-factly.

"Set the course, Fournier," said Hamley, and returned to his cabin.[2]

The *Stonington* set sail northward for Ensenada on Friday morning, December 4. The winds were light but the seas were heavy, and both were coming from the north/northwest, making it necessary for the ship to tack and move in a zigzag pattern rather than a straight line. Still, it managed to advance almost thirty miles toward its destination. The next three days did not bring as much progress. The winds were calm, then light, and then baffling, shifting their direction so frequently that it was difficult to catch a breeze. Heavy rain poured through the first two of those days, and the sea was filled with large swells on all three. By Monday night, the ship was still about sixty miles south of All Saints Bay.

Tuesday morning, December 8, began with clear skies and light winds, but by two o'clock that afternoon the winds had died away and the ship was too close to shore for Hamley's liking. Once again, he ordered a boat lowered to tow the ship, this time not only to speed the delivery of Captain Hensley's men, but also to bring the ship into safer waters. By six p.m., there were strong winds from the northeast that continued into Wednesday. After beating through a series of tacks on Thursday, the *Stonington* finally anchored in All Saints Bay on Friday afternoon, December 11.[3]

It had taken three days to go southward from San Diego to San Ramón, then nearly three times as many days to go northward to Ensenada, prevailing winds being the major cause of the difference. Fournier thought it best to take advantage of this stop, so he made his way to the captain's quarters.

"A word, sir?" said Fournier after Hamley had allowed him into his cabin.

"What is it, Fournier?"

"With your permission, sir, I'd like to send along some casks for water when we take Captain Hensley and his men to shore. Our supply is low after being out so many days with extra men on board."

"Yes, that's a good idea," said Hamley. "We've also got orders to take on a load of hides. With the number of horses that Stockton's anticipating from this trip, he wants enough leather for saddles and other gear, more than what's available at the hide houses in San Diego."

"Aye, sir. I'll send all four boats ashore, seeing as the surf in this place is far more manageable."

"That'll be fine. One other duty, Fournier. Get some men to pump the bilge. Let's see how well the hull has held up on this trip."

"Yes, sir. Will that be all?"

"All for now, Fournier," replied Hamley.[4]

Alanson Fournier made Selden Maynard his first stop among the activities that he had to coordinate. "Maynard," he said, when he'd reached the cooper's quarters, "we're going to need some casks to take ashore for water, enough for a raft. Time to get tapping on that hoop driver again."

"Right, sir," said Maynard, and Fournier continued on his rounds.

Next he sought out four men to pump the bilge. The men he had in mind—Nelson Davis, Gardner Jaques, Aaron Peters, and William Harry—were strong and in their twenties, and at about five-foot-eight or -nine, at a good height to push down and pull up on the handles of the pump. He found them on deck and called them over to the fife rail at the mainmast.

"Men," he said, "I've chosen you for a scientific task."

"And what might that be, sir?" asked Jaques in a wary tone.

"I want you to determine just how much water is in the bilge," replied Fournier with a straight face.

"And is there a special piece of equipment that you'd like us to use for this, sir?" asked Harry with a half grin.

"There is, indeed."

"And might that be this here bilge pump?" asked Peters, pointing to the dual-tube structure rising up nearly two feet from the deck just behind the mast.

"Yes, men, this is the illustrious device," answered Fournier with a full smile. "In consideration of the scientific nature of this endeavor, I ask that you keep a count of the number of strokes it takes to pump this ship dry. Are you up to it?"

"I believe we're talented enough to pump and count at the same time, sir," said Davis. "Might even catch us adding some singing to the mix."

"I knew I asked the right people. Carry on, then," he said as he went off to coordinate boat crews.

The four men formed two pairs, one at each pump handle. After priming each tube by pouring water into them from a nearby bucket, they began to pump, each man taking a turn at the handles while counting out thirty strokes in alternating beats that soon formed the rhythmic basis of the song that the two men standing by began to sing. Fournier could hear its strains as he went to make arrangements for the boats:

The *ocean* we all *do* adore
So *come* on, lads, let's *pump* some more
Don't *worry* if you're *stiff* and sore
I'm *sure* we've pumped this *bit* before.

Pump me boys, *pump* 'er dry
Down to hell and *up* to the sky
Bend your back and *break* your bones
We're *just* a thousand *miles* from home.

Fournier found the boatheaders at the foredeck. He told them to select a couple of men each to row the boats to shore in the morning, and said they would be landing Hensley and his men, along with their equipment and a raft of casks for gathering water. As he did this, the singing at the pump continued:

Yes, *how* I wish that *I* could die
The *swine* who built this *tub* to find
I'd *drag* him back from *where* he fries
To *pump* until the *beggar's* dry.

Pump me boys, *pump* 'er dry
Down to hell and *up* to the sky
Bend your back and *break* your bones
We're *just* a thousand *miles* from home.

Fournier then found Hensley and explained the arrangements.

"Captain Hensley, tomorrow morning the larboard boats will take you and your men to shore. The starboard boats will carry your artillery and other equipment to you. The breakers are much gentler here than they were at San Ramón, so the landings should go much smoother."

"I certainly hope so, Mr. Fournier," replied Hensley sternly. "We've already lost time—I don't care to lose anything else."

Fournier nodded coolly, noticing that the singing had stopped.

He made his way to the pump, where the four men were now standing, sweat glistening on their bare forearms.

"So, you've concluded your investigation," said Fournier to the group.

"Aye, sir, we have indeed," replied Nelson Davis.

"And how many strokes' worth of water did you determine was in the ship?"

"Well, sir," said Aaron Peters, "our finding was three hundred."

"Is that so?" Fournier exclaimed, surprised. "A full month since the last pumping and only three hundred strokes?"

"That'd be it, sir," said Gardner Jaques.

"Well, then, let's see," said Fournier. "Roughly thirty days to a month—three hundred strokes? We could dispense with the three hundred load and do just ten each day, couldn't we?"

"Ah, but sir," answered William Harry with a grin, "that'd give us just barely enough time to sing one verse. Not quite worth the effort, now, is it?"

"No, I don't suppose it is, Harry," replied Fournier. "What say the rest of you?"

The other three men smiled and shook their heads.

"All right, men," said Fournier cheerily, "that's all for now. Well done, and I'll look forward to your next performance."

The four men bowed exaggeratedly, as if having completed a grand concert, and walked away toward the bow.

Fournier made his way to the captain's cabin where he would deliver the good news about the integrity of the hull.[5]

CHAPTER 36

An Eventful Return

As Hensley and his men began boarding their boats on the morning of Saturday, December 12, Fournier supervised the loading of the starboard boats and the tethering of the cask raft. The light southeast winds interacted with the waves in such a way as to keep the surf relatively calm and affirm Fournier's prediction to Hensley of a smooth landing. The two boats carrying men delivered their passengers successfully. The boatheaders remained onshore with their boats while the other crew members went to the hide houses to gather the leather for Commodore Stockton. The crews in the other two boats landed Hensley's artillery and equipment and then brought the casks ashore. Here, too, the boatheaders stayed while their companions sought freshwater sources and then filled the casks.

All four boats returned to the ship with their respective cargoes and stowed them on board, and the rest of the crew prepared the ship for leaving the next morning to head back to San Diego.[1]

The hull of the *Stonington* was holding up very well throughout all of its newly acquired duties, as had been determined by Alanson Fournier and the bilge-pump quartet. The same could not be said, however, about its anchor.

"Something just don't feel right," said Jason Freeman, a Black man from Montville, Connecticut, who at forty-seven was the oldest member of the crew. Freeman and the other three men at the windlass were

163

pumping the seesaw-style hand crank that drew in the anchor chain. "It's too easy," he added, and the others nodded in agreement.

As they continued pumping, the anchor broke through the water's surface.

"Lookee there, Freeman," hollered William Fisher. "The flukes are gone!"

The entire curved portion with the blades that dug into the sea bottom and held the ship in place had snapped off. What remained looked like a large capital "T."

"Won't be holdin' much with that, now, will we, boys," said John Brown, an Englishman from Liverpool.

"We're good for sailin' to San Diego," said Sidney Cheever, the fourth man of the group, "but stayin' put once we get there is gonna take some doin'."

"Mr. Fournier," called Freeman to the second officer, "you need to take a look at what's left of this anchor."

Fournier made his way over and looked with dismay at the damage. "We're going to have to think of something right quick, as we'll be back in San Diego soon," he said.

"Somethin' least as heavy as an anchor," said Cheever in response.

They paused, then Freeman spoke. "May be a war goin' on, but we ain't seen no enemy ships in all our time on the water. Figure we could spare one o' them guns we got on deck?"

The five men looked at each other with raised eyebrows.

"Seems as though there's good reason to keep old buggers like us on board," said Brown, who was thirty-seven.

"Aye to that!" said Fisher, age forty.

"What say you, Mr. Fournier?" asked Cheever, age thirty-five.

"Freeman," said Fournier in response, "I may be less than half your age, but I know a wise man when I hear one. You pick the gun, I'll see to the rest."[2]

At sundown on Monday, December 14, the Coronado Islands, home to hundreds of sea lions, were visible to the northwest. The weather had been clear all day, with light breezes from the southeast, but around eleven p.m. that night it became squally with heavy rains.

Near dawn on Tuesday, the *Stonington* began its entrance into San Diego harbor. Commodore Stockton, who was observing from his cabin, and the men on the deck of the USS *Congress* paused for a moment, watching in disbelief as crewmen in the whaleship's bow tossed an artillery gun overboard. Could this be a desperate attempt at getting even for all the whale oil they had lost, they wondered? Looking closer, they saw that there was a chain attached to the gun, and as the chain tightened, the ship stopped drifting.

When a cheer went up among the just-arrived crew, Stockton made a quick assessment of the situation and promptly ordered an anchor to be sent to the *Stonington*. "Tell them we offer any other assistance they might stand in need of," he added.

Within the hour, a boat left the *Congress* to deliver the anchor, and as it drew near, Fournier heard a familiar voice.

"Hello again, sir," cried the sailor.

"Visiting us so soon?" called Fournier. "Seems you've missed us since we've been gone."

"I believe it's more a case of what *you're* missing, sir. We've brought you a welcome-home gift of sorts, compliments of the commodore," he said, gesturing to the anchor.

"Thoughtful of him. I suppose it's been fairly quiet around here without us."

"Quite the contrary, sir," said the sailor, as a crewman aboard the *Stonington* lowered a line down the starboard side to haul up the anchor. "General Kearny and his army came into town a couple of days ago after fighting a difficult battle last week, just to the east of here. From what I've heard, they were lucky to get out of it alive."

The line grew taut, and as the anchor rose up to the deck, crewmen worked to keep it from striking the side of the ship.

"Much obliged for the news," Fournier called down to the sailor, "and be sure to relay our thanks to the commodore," he said, pointing to the anchor that was now on the deck.

"Aye, sir," called the sailor. "I'm sure the gun thanks him, too," he said, gesturing toward the water beyond the bow of the *Stonington* as his boat began heading back to the *Congress*.[3]

PART VI

CHAPTER 37

The Bloodiest Battle

On December 6 and 7, 1846, during the time that the *Stonington* had been making its way north from San Ramón toward All Saints Bay through heavy weather, a fierce battle had taken place just thirty-five miles northeast of San Diego, in the San Pasqual Valley. The battle would prove to be the bloodiest one fought in California during the war.

A force of about one hundred fifty Californio lancers led by General Andrés Pico was positioned near the Kumeyaay pueblo of San Pasqual, from which the valley derived its name, to defend their homeland. Pico, the younger brother of California governor Pío Pico, was a short, sturdy man with dark hair, side whiskers that joined with a mustache, and dark, piercing eyes. He was a native of San Diego with extensive knowledge of the territory, well aware of the US military presence in his hometown and the likelihood of an attack from that direction.

What he did not know, however, was that troops commanded by General Stephen W. Kearny had been riding westward to San Diego from Santa Fé since September 25, on a mission to take control of California. On October 6, Kearny and his forces crossed paths with noted mountain man and scout Christopher "Kit" Carson, about one hundred forty miles south of Santa Fé. Carson, who had come to California with John C. Frémont as a member of the expedition that led to the Bear Flag Revolt, was on his way to Washington, DC, with messages from Commodore Stockton. Hearing from Carson that, according to his latest information, California was already under US control, Kearny decided to send two hundred members of his Army of the West back to Santa

Fé, leaving him with only one hundred men, most of them mounted on recently acquired mules, to continue the westward march. Kearny also convinced Carson to join him as his scout and lead him to San Diego.[1]

Under Carson's guidance, Kearny and his troops arrived at Warner's Ranch in San Diego County on December 2. The owner of the ranch was Jonathan Trumbull Warner, a settler originally from Lyme, Connecticut, who had come to California in 1831. His grandfather, Colonel Samuel Selden, had been the commander of the 4th Connecticut Regiment in the American Revolutionary War. Jonathan Warner, a naturalized citizen of Mexico who became known as Juan Largo due to his height of six-foot-three, had allied himself with the Californios that supported the Americans. His ranch, and the trading post that he established there, had become a frequent stop and gathering place for travelers and local inhabitants.

Another local landowner, Edward Stokes, who was at the ranch and on his way to the town of San Diego when Kearny arrived, agreed to take a message from the general to Commodore Stockton, in which Kearny requested that Stockton send a party to join and assist his travel-weary troops as they continued their westward march. Upon receipt of that message, Stockton consented, sending a group of fifty men led by Captain Gillespie and including Midshipman Edward F. "Ned" Beale, an officer on Stockton's ship USS *Congress*.[2]

Kearny and Gillespie met and joined forces on December 5 at Santa Ysabel, just over forty miles northeast of San Diego. Gillespie informed Kearny about the presence of Andrés Pico and his forces about eighteen miles to the west. A bungled attempt that night at scouting the Californios' position eliminated the element of surprise, and the next morning, December 6, the Americans rode out in battle formation. Rain-soaked gunpowder reduced the effectiveness of muzzle-loaded firearms for both sides, and the fighting quickly developed into harsh hand-to-hand combat. The Californios, expert horsemen and formidable opponents with their lariats and lances, held the advantage. The fighting lasted for approximately fifteen minutes, and when it was over, nineteen Americans lay dead, and eighteen, including General Kearny, were seriously wounded, reducing the US forces by nearly one-third. General Pico reported no Californio deaths and only eleven wounded.[3]

The Americans' situation was precarious, and they needed to get themselves to a safe position in order to protect themselves from any further attacks by the Californios. They eventually made their way to the top of a hill where, lacking food, they proceeded to butcher those mules with enough meat left on their bones to provide at least some nourishment. Fittingly, they called their encampment Mule Hill. They now needed to get word of their predicament to Stockton so that he could send reinforcements.

Four men left that evening on the twenty-six-mile hike to San Diego, making their way surreptitiously around Pico's encampment. Among the four was the same Kumeyaay chief that had so effectively herded the sheep onto Coronado Island just over a month ago, and who was now continuing his efforts to assist the Americans. Upon reaching San Diego, they delivered their message to Stockton and immediately set out with his reply. The Californios spotted them this time, captured them, and brought them to their encampment.

The next morning, December 8, Andrés Pico arranged a prisoner exchange, sending over one of the Americans, Thomas Burgess (a member of the Osos), for the lone Californio, Pablo Véjar, that Kearny's men had captured. The news that Burgess brought from San Diego was disappointing: Stockton declined to send troops, indicating there were not enough horses for them, nor for the wounded men and the artillery that would need to be brought along.

Undeterred, Kearny drew up another letter to Stockton. Ned Beale, Kit Carson, and Panto, a Kumeyaay guide, volunteered for the mission. Kearny hesitated to send Carson, not wanting to be left without his scouting skills, but Carson thought it best that he accompany the twenty-four-year-old, relatively inexperienced Beale. Kearny eventually acquiesced, and the three men set out on their mission that night. They crawled down the hill and made their way stealthily past the Californios, eventually discarding anything, including boots and canteens, that might make unwanted noise.

The trio separated onto individual routes through thirty miles of desert land filled with cacti that tore at their feet. They arrived at San Diego separately—first Panto and then Beale, on the evening of December 9, then Carson, a day later. Beale was in the worst condition of all three, bleeding, sunbaked, parched, and delirious from the grueling trek. He managed, however, to deliver Kearny's urgent request for help.

Stockton, recognizing the severity of the situation, responded by immediately sending nearly two hundred men, led by his aide-de-camp, Lieutenant Andrew F. V. Gray, to assist the survivors of the Battle of San Pasqual.[4]

While Lieutenant Gray and his troops were marching toward San Pasqual, General Pico had received reinforcements of his own, courtesy of Leonardo Cota and his horsemen. Pico, emboldened by his success against Kearny and by the near doubling of his force, was planning to assault the battered and weakened Americans when they left Mule Hill and continued on to San Diego. Lieutenant Gray and his men had circumvented the Californio encampment on December 9 and had concealed themselves on a nearby hill during the daylight hours of the following day. In the predawn hours of December 11, they entered General Kearny's camp on Mule Hill with much-welcomed supplies.

The combined US force of over two hundred fifty men began their march to San Diego at daybreak. Stunned by what was now a much larger and better equipped number of men than he had expected, General Pico reassessed his previous plan and rode away with his lancers.

On Saturday, December 12, while the *Stonington* was in All Saints Bay landing the remainder of the soldiers that it had transported along the coast, General Kearny and his men were experiencing a thankful sense of relief as they spotted the vast Pacific Ocean on their way into San Diego. It had been a long journey since leaving Santa Fé on September 25. They had traveled over eight hundred miles across mountains and through deserts, and they would soon enjoy the basic comforts of shelter and food.[5]

CHAPTER 38

Time for Liberty

DURING THE DAYS IMMEDIATELY AFTER THEIR RETURN TO SAN DIEGO on Monday, December 14, the men of the *Stonington*, having taken care of the anchor situation, went about giving the ship a fresh coat of paint, including the spars. They also spent some time catching fish to replenish their food supply.

"The men have been working hard, sir," said Alanson Fournier to George Hamley as they stood in the captain's cabin. "Been at one thing or another steady since we got here, almost two months ago."

"Mmm," grunted Hamley.

"Been through some tough, unusual situations, too," added Fournier, to which Hamley once again simply grunted.

"I'm thinking, sir—"

"Something you do all too well, Fournier," interrupted Hamley coarsely.

"I'm thinking," continued Fournier, "that now might be a proper time to grant them a day of liberty."

"Is that so?"

"Yes, sir. And with your permission, tomorrow would be a fitting day, it being Sunday and all."

"Is there any part of this idea of yours that you *haven't* thought about yet?" asked Hamley with a hint of annoyance.

"There may be, sir, but I'll be sure to do so if need be."

"Full ship's liberty?" asked Hamley, "sunup to sundown?"

"That'd be fine, sir."

"I'm asking, Fournier, not granting," growled Hamley.

"Yes to both, then, sir," said Fournier pleasantly.

"I'll think on it. Will that be all?"

"That's all, sir."

"You may go, then."

Fournier left the cabin unsure of whether the captain would grant his request.[1]

On Sunday morning, December 20, as the sun began to rise on a fine fair-weather day in San Diego, the men aboard the *Stonington* heard their captain call "All hands!" Once they were gathered on deck, George Hamley began to speak.

"Men," he said, "I know this has been a long two months, and you've been working hard, sometimes in ways beyond your normal duties."

As he spoke, some of the men noticed that Second Officer Fournier, standing near the captain, was smiling and nodding his head.

"With that in mind," Hamley continued, "I have concluded that this being Sunday, it is appropriate that I, as your captain, grant you a day of liberty."

The men looked at each other as if unsure of what they had just heard, then many of them looked at Alanson Fournier, who was looking down at the deck but still nodding and smiling. Putting two and two together, they cheered loudly while focusing their gazes not on Captain Hamley but on Second Officer Fournier.

"You may take the boats ashore, but I expect each and every last one of you to be back aboard this ship by sundown. Is that clear?" Hamley shouted.

"Aye, sir," came the chorus of replies.

"All right, then," said Hamley, "off you go."

As the men dispersed to gather a few necessities before heading ashore, they nodded their thanks, mostly in the direction of Alanson Fournier.[2]

It was quite an assortment of nearly forty individuals that set out for San Diego from the *Stonington* that Sunday. The crew had been ashore in various groupings and for a variety of purposes, but this was the first time they would be in town without a chore to complete or an officer supervising their activity. They were free for the day, with the expectation that they would be back on board and ready for duty the next day.

Ranging in age from eighteen to forty-seven, the majority of them had been born in the United States, mostly Connecticut, Rhode Island, and Massachusetts, with a few from New York and Pennsylvania. Others hailed from Nova Scotia, England, the Azores, Cape Verde, and the Sandwich Islands. About a half-dozen were Black, and a couple were Indigenous people. As was the case with most whaleships, the number of men in the crew fluctuated throughout the voyage. Whenever the ship came into a port, one or more might desert, only to be replaced with recruits from that same—or another—port. Ships such as the *Stonington* would often depart New England with a shorthanded crew, expecting to add more as they stopped at the Azores and Cape Verde. Some of the men had signed on because it was an available job. Others were seeking adventure and a chance to see the world. In the case of many Blacks, it was an opportunity to be judged not by the color of their skin, but, just as with all the others, by their ability to work cooperatively to keep the ship running smoothly and safely.[3]

The boats were full of expectant chatter as the men rowed their boats to La Playa.

"Soon as I get to town," said Nelson Davis, "I'm heading straight for the nearest grog shop."

"I'll be right along with you," said Gardner Jaques. "High time we did our own scientific investigation of liquids."

"Aye to that!" chimed in fellow bilge pumpers Aaron Peters and William Harry.

"I'm gonna find myself a sweet little *señorita* I can cozy up with all day long," said Mark Comstock in another boat.

"Second prettiest to the one I'll find before you," challenged his younger brother Samuel.

"Who'll be your lookouts?" asked John Brown.

The brothers squinted at him questioningly.

"Pretty young girls in this town bound to have mothers and fathers keeping a close watch on their daughters," he said. "Might want to find a different sort of woman for what it seems you're after."

In a nearby boat, as Peter McDonnald rowed steadily, he could see a pensive look on the face of James Rice, who was seated just in front of him to the right.

"What's on your mind, Rice?" he asked.

"Hearing all that talk in the other boat has me thinking of my girl back home. I don't want to get caught up in doing anything I'll be ashamed of later."

"I see," said McDonnald. "Well, if you don't mind hanging around with an old codger like me, I'm sure we can find something to do that'll keep you out of trouble."

"I'd be much obliged, McDonnald," said Rice, relieved.

CHAPTER 39

Into Town

As each boat landed at La Playa, its crew tied it up securely and then began walking to town. The steady stream of various-sized groups of men caught the attention of Captain Ezekiel Merritt, who watched from his barracks as they drew near.

"L-l-let's go see what this is all about," he said to his fellow Osos.

A few of them joined him and went out to meet the crewmen as they entered the town.

"Well, n-n-now," said Merritt to the first few groups, "what brings you fellas t' t-t-town?"

"We've got some important business to take care of," said Alexander Anthony, the steward that had suffered the flogging.

"Oh, and what might that be?" asked Merritt.

"Captain's given us liberty for the day!" said the young Martin Larkins excitedly.

"And we're gonna enjoy every minute of it," Anthony said emphatically.

"To the last drop," added Thomas Milnor, the carpenter.

"That explains the spring in your steps," said Merritt, causing his men to chuckle, and he turned to them. "What say you, boys? Should we show these whalers what the t-t-town has to offer?"

"Why not, Captain?" said one of them. "They might even find it in their hearts to buy us a drink or two on account of our hospitality."

"As the good Lord says," responded Milnor with a smile, "do unto others as you'd have them do unto you."

There was a bit more chuckling among the men before Merritt said, "All right, then, l-l-let's be on our way."

The large group of men made its way into town, with Zeke Merritt and his Osos leading the way. As they drew closer to the first grog shop, Peter McDonnald nudged James Rice with his elbow and said, "Follow me." The two men went down a side road that was lined on each side with whitewashed adobe houses with red-tile roofs. The din of the large group of Osos and whalers faded, and the two men relaxed their pace.

"Where are we going?" asked Rice as they continued southward along the dusty road. The morning sun was arcing out of the east, shining its full light between the houses without favoring either side with more shadows than the other.

"I'm following my nose," said McDonnald. "It's got a good memory."

"Why would your nose . . . ," Rice began, then paused. There was something familiar about where they were, but he could not quite determine what it was. Walking a little farther, there was a gap between the buildings on his left, and he saw the hillside rising toward the east.

"We've been here before, haven't we?" he said to McDonnald, whose frame was perfectly erect as he walked, his head tilted slightly upward in order to accentuate his sense of smell. Rice noticed that a portion of the corner of the building on the left of the gap had a large chip in one of the adobe bricks. "Wait," he gasped, looking at McDonnald and then at the brick, "is this the . . . ," and as he looked again at McDonnald, he could see him nodding and grinning.

" . . . where you were loading and I was shooting," said McDonnald, completing Rice's question by turning it into a statement. "In the middle of that skirmish, I began to smell the most delicious aromas, but I had to tuck them into the back of my mind. Otherwise, we wouldn't have lived long enough to be standing here talking about it." Rice looked around as McDonnald continued. "When the captain announced our liberty, which I'm more than certain is thanks to Mr. Fournier, I decided right then and there that I was going to find the source of those delicious smells."

"Excuse me, *señores*," said a soft female voice. They turned, startled, and saw a Californian woman of between thirty and forty years of age. "Is there something I can help you with?"

"*Buenos días, señora*," replied McDonnald, using some of the little Spanish he knew in hopes of making a good impression on the woman. "My friend and I are from the whaleship *Stonington* that's anchored in the harbor," he said, gesturing toward the water. "More than two months ago, we were involved in a fight with the Californios when they came down the hill, and I still remember the delicious food smells that were coming from this building while we were using it as a shield." The woman nodded knowingly as he continued. "Our captain let us come to town today, and the first thing I thought of was those smells. I was hoping we might be lucky enough to find more of that same food cooking today, and that we might be able to buy a meal or two. By the smell of it," at which point he paused, closed his eyes, and inhaled deeply through his nose, "I'd say that luck is with us so far."

"I believe your luck will go even further, *señor*," said the woman.

"That's kind of you to say, *señora*. Why would that be so?" asked McDonnald.

"Because it is my cooking that you are smelling," she said, smiling, "and I will be pleased to offer it to you and your friend."

"This is indeed a happy day, Rice," said McDonnald as he clapped his companion on the shoulder.

"Yes," the woman added, "there is rice as well."

"Oh, no, excuse me, *señora*," said McDonnald, "Rice is the name of my friend."

"Ah, Señor Arroz," she said laughingly, using the Spanish word for rice. "Well, the two of you wait here, please, while I go fix you some bowls. I would invite you in, but as I am by myself at the moment, it would not be proper custom for me to do so."

"Oh, we understand, *señora*," said Rice. "Please don't be concerned about that."

"Yes," added McDonnald, "I don't care where I sit—I'd even stand if it means I get to sample your cooking."

The woman curtsied slightly, then went into her house. She returned within a few minutes, bringing out two stools for the men, then went back inside again.

When she returned, she was carrying two medium-sized bowls, each containing a hot and hearty serving of *chile colorado*, a stew with browned beef, dried red chili peppers, onions, and spices. The bowls also contained some rice, and tortillas for the men to use to scoop the food.

"*Señora*, I think I may be in heaven," exclaimed McDonnald as he held the bowl to his nose to absorb the rich aroma. Rice did the same, simply saying "Mmm."

"I will leave you to enjoy," said the woman, and went back into her house.[1]

The two men savored their meal, allowing each mouthful to linger on their tongues before swallowing, extending their time with the flavors as long as possible. They grinned and nodded at each other as they ate, acknowledging their good fortune at being able to sit in the warmth of the sun and enjoy food so fresh and delectable.

As they were scraping the lingering bits from their bowls with the last pieces of their tortillas, the woman emerged from her house with a mug of coffee for each of them.

"*Muchas gracias*," said McDonnald as he exchanged his bowl for the mug that she offered. "This was the most delicious meal I have had in a very long time. We are both very grateful. How much would you like us to pay you?"

The woman looked at them and said, "You do not need to pay me any more than you have already."

The two men looked at each other, puzzled.

"I don't quite understand," McDonnald said.

"The help that you and the other men of your ship have provided for us since you came to our harbor is worth far more than the food and drink I have provided for you today," said the woman with deep sincerity. "There may be some of my people," she said, pointing toward the eastern hills, "that do not welcome the presence of you and your people in our lands, but there are those of us who believe there is great promise in what we may accomplish together."

The men stood, and as they raised their mugs, Peter McDonnald said, "May there be friendship among us long after this meal has ended."

Finishing their coffee, they placed their mugs on their stools, bowed, and said together this time, "*Muchas gracias, señora.*"

The woman curtsied and said, "*De nada, señores.*" She watched as they walked away from her house, happy to have contributed in her own way to the prospect of peaceful relations with the Americans.

CHAPTER 40

Exploring the Point

"I HAVE AN IDEA, RICE," SAID McDONNALD.

"What might that be?"

"You recall that hilltop where we shot those bullocks?"

"I'm not in much of a mood for hunting right now."

"Neither am I," responded McDonnald quickly. "That involves some work, and I don't want to be working today. I was thinking of what we could see when we were up there—remember?"

"A bit. Most of my attention was on making that shot after you told Mr. Fournier that I should go first."

"Yes, you did yourself proud that day," observed McDonnald. "We had quite a view when we were up there, though, which we didn't really take much time to appreciate. I'm thinking it'd be good to go back there and take in the natural beauty of it all."

"I suppose so," said Rice, "but that's quite a ways from here. It'd take a lot of walking to get there, and I thought you said you didn't want to be working today."

"That's where the other part of my idea comes in. I'm thinking that Lieutenant Minor and Midshipman Duvall might remember us from bringing them those bullocks and be willing to let us borrow a couple of horses for a few hours."

"It's worth a try," agreed Rice. "No harm in asking."[1]

McDonnald's assessment of the situation proved to be correct. When he and Rice reached the barracks, Minor and Duvall were there. They recognized the two men, and readily supplied them with two horses.

"They're not racehorses," said Minor, "but they'll get you where you want to go. Just have them back by sundown."

"Aye, sir," replied McDonnald, and he and Rice began their trip. They followed the La Playa Trail and took the turnoff that led to the spot where they had done their hunting. As the horses walked up the path, the men could feel the change in the air. The breeze that blew in from the Pacific Ocean was cool and carried with it the scent of salt water. When they reached the top of the hill, they paused. McDonnald took in a deep breath through his nose and then exhaled a relaxed sigh. Rice took in his surroundings and nodded, acknowledging what he had missed on his first trip to this place.

"Let's ride the entire length of this point, Rice," suggested McDonnald, "as far north and south as we can go."

"Sounds like a good plan to me."

They tapped the sides of their horses with their heels and guided them with their reins northward along a path of pale yellow, sun-bleached sand that meandered through a variety of coastal sage scrub plants that were no more than three feet tall. The plants had leaves that were mostly dark green, others gray-green, and some had small yellow or pink flowers. To their right, the men could see the top end of the harbor and the sandy flats that formed the delta of the San Diego River. As they rode farther north, they could see that the land ahead of them began sloping downward toward a sandy beach area that formed one bank of what appeared to be a river that wound circuitously inland.

"Look!" exclaimed Rice. "That river looks like it comes to a full stop."

"Aye, that's what they call False Bay. Bring a ship in there, you'll soon find yourself wishing you hadn't."

They rode their horses down the slope until they reached the water's edge. The tide was flowing inward, creating a smooth trail through the center of the water's surface while the edges rippled with the force of the incoming ocean.

"Well," said McDonnald after watching the water flow, "this is our northern stop. Ready to head south?"

Rice nodded, and the two began their ascent to high ground. They soon reached the top, where, seated on their horses, they had a commanding view of the Pacific Ocean. The water varied in hue, from greenish close to the shore to light blue a bit farther out, and then eventually dark blue far beyond. At the edge of the dark blue area, however, there was a thick band of brown that extended from just past the entrance to False Bay all the way down to the end of the Point.

"It looks as though dead leaves have piled up in the water," said Rice, as they paused their horses, "but there don't seem to be enough trees in these parts to cause all that."

"Those are leaves, all right. But they're still attached to their trees."

"Has the sun gotten to you already, McDonnald?"

"No, I'm not any more out of my mind than I normally am," he replied, chuckling. "What you're seeing are the kelp beds. It's a whole forest of plants that have their roots on the ocean bottom. We passed them when we first sailed into San Diego and made our way into the harbor through a break in the beds, down off the Point."

"I wonder how it would be to see them underwater," said Rice.

"Cold," said McDonnald, "too cold to stay in very long. Maybe just long enough, though, to see a mermaid. They like living in these forests. Easy to keep themselves hidden."

"Do they . . . ," Rice began, then stopped when he saw McDonnald's shoulders bouncing. "All right, you got me."

McDonnald let out a short laugh, looked over at his companion, and said, "Let's keep moving."[2]

They moved at an easy pace, and a bit further along, McDonnald stopped his horse and stared toward the harbor.

Rice halted as well, and after a moment, asked, "What is it?"

"You hear that?" said McDonnald, his head tilted upward.

Rice paused intently. "I don't hear anything."

"That's just it," said McDonnald in a soft voice. "It's quiet."

Waves breaking, breezes blowing, and their own breathing were the only sounds they heard. They could see their ship, among others, anchored in the harbor, yet it was silent, as was the island where they had wrangled the sheep. There was no sporadic gunfire from the hillside beyond the town now that the Californios had ridden north to consolidate their forces in the event of a US advance on Los Angeles. The two knew otherwise, but for now, all seemed peaceful.

Rice broke the stillness. "Look," he said, pointing toward the western edge of the ridge, "there's a path that leads downward. If it's not too steep, maybe we could get closer to the edge of this land."

"Worth a try," said McDonnald. "Lead on."

Rice guided his horse slowly onto the path, and McDonnald followed. The descent was gradual enough, and the ground sturdy enough, that the horses had little trouble negotiating their way through the scrub brush. Rice made a point of steering clear of the agave plants, whose broad, thick, green leaves were fringed with sharp teeth that would tear harshly at the horses' legs. The path eventually leveled out onto a flat plain that extended along the Point.

The men brought their horses toward the water but stopped well before the edge. As they looked north- and southward, they could see that they were atop a dramatic line of sandstone cliffs that rose one hundred feet above the ocean. The constant breaking of the waves directly below was mesmerizing as the two men sat on their horses and contemplated the grandeur of the scenery.

After a while, McDonnald dismounted and handed the reins to Rice, saying, "Hold my horse for me, will you? I want to get a closer look."

He made his way to the edge, stood there for a moment, and then lowered himself to the ground so that he was lying flat on his belly, his head peering over the cliff and down to the water. *That's a long way down,* he thought, watching the waves crash and swirl against the earthen wall that was dark brown at its base but yellow and orange as it rose to where he lay.

Within a few minutes, he got to his feet, brushed himself off, and returned to his horse.

"See much?" asked Rice.

"Enough to know I wouldn't want to fall from that height," answered McDonnald. "Let's ride to the southern end of this plain. We've got time to make it down there and then backtrack a bit to a path that we can take up to the top of the Point," he said, looking up at the land that was another three hundred feet above them.

They nudged their horses and meandered on the flat terrain whose scrub brush gave way at times to bare ground that was a mixture of surprisingly solid sand and rock. When they made it to the end of the plain, this time it was Rice who alighted from his horse and laid down at the edge. He did so briefly, and as he re-mounted his horse, he saw McDonnald looking at him expectantly.

"I see what you mean," said Rice.

McDonnald raised his eyebrows and nodded, then the two of them turned their horses around and rode for about a mile until they reached a place where the slope of the hillside was gradual enough for their horses to make the climb without much difficulty. As they began their ascent, they noticed the nearly imperceptible traces of a deer trail and guided their horses along it until they reached the top, where they stopped and faced southward.

"There it is," said McDonnald, looking toward the very end of Point Loma, "the tip of the spine. And we thought those sand cliffs were tall. Ready?"

Rice nodded, and they started their horses walking on the ridge that ran down the center of the Point. The land sloped down on either side toward the sea, but to their left, they could see that it ended abruptly rather than leveling off to the plain they had just explored, on their right. The breeze was stiffer at this height, and they had to be more conscious of keeping their horses centered to avoid a slide down either side.

As they came within a hundred feet or so from the end of the land, the horses began to snort. "They can tell we're getting close," said McDonnald. "Best not to spook 'em. Let's stop here. We can take turns holding them while one of us walks out to the edge."

"You look all you want," replied Rice. "I can see just fine from here."

"Suit yourself," said McDonnald as he handed his horse's reins to Rice and began walking. When he came within three feet of the edge of the cliff, he stopped and stood still. With the wind whistling past his ears, he looked down the coastline of California until it disappeared into the distance, where it began to form the Baja peninsula. Turning his head to the left, he saw the waters of the harbor as they curved around the upper portion of the Coronado peninsula. Beyond that, the low-lying land rose into hills and then a line of mountains. To his right, he saw the vast expanse of the Pacific Ocean and the sun that was arcing gradually lower in the bright blue sky. He peered over the edge in front of where he stood and saw that it was a sheer drop of nearly four hundred feet to the ocean below. After spending several minutes taking in the impressive sights around him, he began walking back toward Rice and the horses.

"I think I understand now," said McDonnald.

"Understand what?"

"Why so many people have fought each other over this land."

"They're still fighting."

"Yes, they are," said McDonnald, "and we're in it with them. Be interesting to see how it all ends," he mused.

"Soon, I hope," said Rice emphatically. "I've got someone back home waiting for me. Don't you?"

"I did at one time, but that's over now."

"Oh," said Rice. "I'm sorry."

"Don't be," said McDonnald, "it's better this way." His gaze drifted for a moment, then he said, "Sun drops quickly once it starts getting low, so we'd better start making our way back to the barracks."

Rice nodded, and he and McDonnald nudged their horses northward along the spine of Point Loma, absorbing the views as they went along and storing them for future use when they would help make the cramped quarters of the *Stonington* seem more tolerable.

The sun had dipped far enough that its light was dimming as the two men reached the barracks and dismounted. Midshipman Duvall greeted them, and when McDonnald said that he and Rice would be willing to rub the horses down, Duvall replied, "I appreciate it, but we've got groomers to take care of that. Besides, you've got a bit of a walk ahead of you to get down to La Playa and your boats."

"Well, sir," said McDonnald, "we certainly do appreciate your letting us ride these horses. It was as fine a day as I've had in some time."

"Yes, sir, it was," said Rice in agreement, as they shook hands with Duvall.

"I'm glad you enjoyed your liberty. From what I've heard, your shipmates have had quite a day themselves."

"Oh, I'm sure they did, sir, I'm sure they did," said McDonnald with a grin.

"Give my regards to Mr. Fournier," said Duvall, and the two men waved as they began their walk to the boats.

CHAPTER 41

Back from Liberty

PETER McDONNALD AND JAMES RICE REACHED LA PLAYA IN THE afterglow of the sun that had already set. They were the first of the *Stonington*'s crew to arrive at the boats, so they found a comfortable place to sit and wait for the others.

Within fifteen minutes, they began to hear the sound of approaching voices. As the sound came closer, they could hear a boisterous commingling of talk and laughter, and they were soon able to recognize individual voices. The Comstock brothers were boasting competitively with each other about the talents of the women with whom they had spent their time and energy. The four bilge pumpers were comparing and ranking the grog shops they had patronized. While the rest of the crew arrived and began filling the boats, one voice in particular was louder and more resonant than all the others. It was Thomas Milnor, the ship's carpenter, explaining the proper method for consuming large quantities of alcohol in order to maintain a certain level of control while still achieving inebriation.

"It's all a matter of pacin', you see, and for that you've got to know the proof percent," said Milnor, slurring through those last two words. His shipmates, accustomed by now to his authoritative-sounding explanations on any number of subjects, helped him into the nearest boat. As they did, the ditty bag hanging from his waist made a slight thud against the gunwale. "Typical carpenter," said one of them. "They just can't seem to let go of their tools." Milnor paused his explanation just long enough to let out one of his trademark *hee-hee* giggles.

The boats left the shore, some not as steadily as the others, and none of them in a particularly straight path toward the *Stonington*.

Alanson Fournier, who as second officer had remained aboard the ship with Captain Hamley, chuckled to himself as he saw the boats weaving their way toward the ship.

"Looks as though they've managed to blow off some steam," he said quietly.

When the boats reached the side, some of the men climbed out and up onto the deck. Others, after considering their conditions, decided to stay in the boats until their crewmates hauled them up to their davits. Thomas Milnor, who was still explaining the benefits of his definitive approach to drinking, held his ditty bag protectively as he climbed out of his boat.

"Don't grab your sack too tightly," called Fournier to the carpenter, who let out another giggle on the way to his quarters.

Fournier greeted the rest of the men with similar good humor and watched amusedly as they headed belowdecks.

"You two seem to be faring better than the others," he said as McDonnald and Rice climbed over the rail. "Grog shops run dry before you got to them?"

"No, sir," said McDonnald, "we took a different route."

"Got us a good home-cooked meal and then rode to the Point," said Rice.

Fournier cocked his head quizzically.

"Borrowed a couple of horses from the barracks," explained McDonnald. "Mr. Duvall sends his regards."

"Well done," replied Fournier as he nodded his head in approval.

When all of the crewmen had gone below, Fournier went to the captain's cabin. "A moment, sir?" he asked, after tapping on the cabin door.

"Come in, Fournier," said Hamley. "What is it?"

"Crew's all in and accounted for."

"Good to know. Be sure to put them straight to work in the morning. Don't want them getting any ideas about extending their liberty."

"Aye, sir," said Fournier. "Will there be anything else?"

"No. You may go."

"Good night, sir," said Fournier as he left and went to his own quarters.

The next two days were fair, weatherwise, and Fournier, in line with the captain's orders, had the men take advantage of them, bending sails and painting the ship.

On Wednesday, December 23, the weather turned somewhat, and so did one of the crew.

Strong winds began to blow from the northeast, and loud noises began to flow from the carpenter's quarters. Evidently, Thomas Milnor had decided to open the bottle that he had stashed in his ditty bag while on liberty. One sip led to another, and before long he was downright drunk.

By the afternoon, pieces of wood were hurtling out of his quarters and into the passageway, accompanied by loud denunciations of their quality. Milnor made his way onto the deck, where he proceeded to intrude on every work crew, pushing them aside and criticizing their work as "Shabby! Downright shabby!"

Fournier saw what was happening, went to the captain's quarters, and returned quickly with a set of irons. He went to the work detail that Milnor was currently accosting and, enlisting their help, clapped the irons on his hands and feet.

"Let me go! Let me go!" shouted Milnor as Fournier and the others carried him down to his quarters. After they had laid him down on his bunk, Fournier spotted the bottle and grabbed it, causing another outburst from Milnor.

"Milnor," said Fournier sternly, "you're lucky you're in your bunk and not over the side. Let it wear off or sleep it off, makes no matter. Either way, you don't leave until you're sober."

With that, Fournier and the other men left the carpenter and went back on deck.

The following morning, Fournier went to Milnor's quarters. "I see you're awake," he said to the carpenter, who was lying on his side in his bunk. "Are you sober yet?"

"Far as I can tell, sir," replied Milnor, "though I'll know better once I'm up and about."

"Before I take those irons off, hear me well," said Fournier. "You need to keep yourself under control. No more behavior such as yesterday, or you'll bring worse upon yourself than a set of irons. Captain used the word 'severe' when speaking of what he'd do to you if it happens again, and that's without his knowing about the incident back in April at Tubuai, when I checked you for insubordination. You catch his meaning?"

"You never told him?" asked Milnor, somewhat astonished.

"No, Milnor. I gave you my word that I wouldn't, and you promised to do better. Remember?"

"I do, sir," said Milnor apologetically.

"All right, then. I've given you as much warning as I can. The rest is up to you."

With that, Fournier unlocked and removed the irons, then went back to his cabin, leaving Milnor to contemplate what he had just said to him.[1]

PART VII

CHAPTER 42

Preparing for the March

COMMODORE STOCKTON'S MAIN OBJECTIVE WAS TO CONQUER CALIFOR-
nia and make it a possession of the United States. In order to do that, he
knew that he would have to regain control of Los Angeles. He was determined to use every means available to do so, and for the past two months,
that is exactly what he had done. One of the key elements toward his
success, he knew, would be a sufficient number of horses to be used
as mounts for the dragoons, as well as for hauling supply wagons and
artillery. He would also need cattle for food and for the hides that would
provide leather to make saddles and harnesses for those horses. Stockton
had relied heavily upon the *Stonington* to transport men southward to
gather those animals and drive them to San Diego. He had also relied
upon that ship to ferry sheep and other supplies to the town. Stockton's
reliance on the *Stonington* would continue as he finalized his plans to
march on Los Angeles.[1]

The *Stonington's* crew spent Friday, December 25, ferrying provisions
from the USS *Congress* to town.

"This sure is a lot of supplies," said Martin Larkins, rowing on his
third trip to town, "and it's not just food. Some of these boxes got ammunition in 'em."

"Seems like they're getting ready for something special," said George
Hopkins.

"Some kinda big battle, be my guess," said Jason Freeman.

"You think there'll be fighting in the town again?" asked Larkins.

"With all them horses they've gotten, I'd say they's thinking 'bout takin' the fight elsewhere," answered Freeman.

"Considering the wagons they got lined up to haul everything, I'd say you're thinking right, Freeman," said Hopkins.

The following day brought more signs that something major was in the works.

"Mr. Fournier, sir," called John Jennings that afternoon, "there's a boat comin' from the *Congress*, and there looks to be a big ship comin' 'round the Point."

Fournier took out his spyglass and, looking toward Point Loma, he could see a three-masted ship that was a bit smaller than the *Congress* but still considerably larger than the *Stonington*. As the boat drew closer, he spotted a familiar face.

"It's been over a week since your last visit," Fournier called down to the returning sailor. "I was beginning to wonder if perhaps you had forgotten us."

"Nothing of the sort, sir," the sailor called up to Fournier. "The commodore's quite aware of your presence. He's got a new mission for you."

"And what might that be?"

"He's sent a pilot," said the sailor, pointing to the passenger in his boat. "He wants you to take him out to the *Cyane* to bring the ship safely into harbor."

"He thinks his own boats are too delicate for that type of work?"

"No, sir," replied the sailor, "it's a matter of size and speed. Ours may be bigger, but yours are faster."

"Interesting," said Fournier, grinning.

"That it is, sir," responded the sailor with a chuckle. "Permission for the pilot to come aboard?"

"Send him up. I'll get a boat started for him and let the captain know of the commodore's latest request"—he paused as he saw the sailor raise his index finger—"er, order."

The sailor smiled and nodded. "Always a pleasure, sir," he said, and as the pilot climbed over the rail, the boat headed back to the *Congress*.[2]

The USS *Cyane* was a sloop-of-war, just over one hundred thirty-two feet long, with a beam of a bit more than twenty-six feet, and it carried two hundred men and twenty-two guns, less than half as many in each category as the *Congress* carried. As a result, its draft was sixteen and a half feet, six feet less than the *Congress*, which meant that the pilot would have a slightly easier time maneuvering the ship into the harbor than he would have if he were aboard the *Congress*.

The commander of the *Cyane* was Samuel F. Du Pont, the man whom Commodore Stockton had selected as commander of the *Congress*, the one to sail him and his flagship around Cape Horn from Norfolk, Virginia, to Monterey, California, in 1845. Upon reaching California, Stockton had granted Du Pont command of the *Cyane*.[3]

Saturday, December 26, was the second time that Du Pont had sailed the *Cyane* to San Diego, and both instances involved the delivery of troops. In July of 1846, the ship had carried and disembarked John C. Frémont and his California Battalion to take control of the town after Du Pont's men had made a preliminary scouting survey. Now the *Cyane* would be contributing its men to the force that Commodore Stockton and General Kearny were gathering for the march to Los Angeles.

Two days after the *Cyane* had anchored successfully in San Diego harbor, Thomas Folger, a harpooner aboard the *Stonington*, noticed a familiar sight. "Mr. Fournier," he called, "boat from the *Congress* coming this way."

Fournier made his way to the rail and waited. "So soon?" he called to the sailor.

"Urgent matters call for quick action."

"What now?"

"I bring two orders from the commodore. One is fairly common, the other, a bit unusual," said the sailor. "Which would you prefer to hear first?"

"Let's get the easy one out of the way."

"All right. You're to send two boats to ferry stores from the *Cyane* to the town."

"Simple enough," responded Fournier. "Now to the unusual."

"The commodore wants your captain to be among the troops marching to Los Angeles," announced the sailor. "He's to report to the town this evening."

Fournier stared at the sailor for a moment, then said, "Unusual indeed. What reason does he give for wanting Captain Hamley to join him?"

"No reason necessary, sir. He's the commodore," said the sailor matter-of-factly.

"I see. Well, then, I'd best be about passing along these orders," he said, with an emphasis on the last word.

"Well said, sir," responded the sailor. "I'll be off, then."

"Will you be marching?" asked Fournier as the boat rowed away.

"No, sir, I'll be remaining aboard. You'll not be rid of me that easily."[4]

Fournier gave the orders for two boats to go to the *Cyane*, then went to deliver the news to Captain Hamley.

"He what? Why?" asked Hamley, with a mixture of incredulity and annoyance. After letting Fournier's words register, however, his sense of self-importance began to overcome his initial resistance. "I suppose I'd best be getting myself ready to leave, then. Fournier, this means that you'll be in charge during my absence. Any questions before I go?"

"None that I can think of at the moment," replied Fournier, eagerly anticipating the chance to show his readiness to take on the responsibilities of being a captain.

"Don't get too comfortable in your new position," Hamley said. "I'll be back as soon as this fight is over."

"Aye, sir, and good luck to you," responded Fournier.

On Tuesday morning, December 29, over six hundred men assembled in town in parade formation. Most of them were sailors and marines from the three warships—*Congress*, *Portsmouth*, and *Cyane*—currently in the harbor. Some were sailors and marines sent from the *Savannah* over two months ago, while others were soldiers in General Kearny's army. Still more were from the Osos and Frémont's California Battalion. One, Captain Hamley, was from the *Stonington*.

Also among the force were Californians in allegiance with the Americans, one of whom was Captain Miguel de Pedrorena, the refined gentleman who had gone to San Pedro in October in one of the *Stonington*'s boats to seek help from the *Savannah*, and was now serving as an aide-de-camp to Commodore Stockton. Others were members of a company of soldiers that Santiago Argüello, a former *alcalde* of San Diego, had organized. In addition to the men, there were six artillery pieces, supply wagons, packhorses and -mules, beef cattle, and spare oxen. On Kearny's command, the march to Los Angeles began.[5]

CHAPTER 43

Meanwhile, in San Diego

ON JANUARY 1, 1847, A BOAT APPROACHED THE *STONINGTON*. UNLIKE recent visits, this one was coming not from the *Congress* but from the USS *Portsmouth*, a sloop-of-war that had arrived at San Diego on December 9, the same day that Lieutenant Beale had arrived from San Pasqual, and while the *Stonington* was still making its way north to All Saints Bay. Its commander was John B. Montgomery, who nearly six months ago had sailed the *Portsmouth* into the harbor of what was then Yerba Buena, later to become San Francisco, and on July 9 had replaced the bear flag with that of the United States, thus bringing to a close the Bear Flag Republic.

"I wish to speak with your captain," called a sailor from the boat.

"You are speaking with him," replied Alanson Fournier, who had been standing at the rail watching the boat approach.

"I have an order for you from Commander Montgomery, now also governor of San Diego," said the sailor.

"And what might that be?"

"You are to send twenty of your men to town to provide for its defense."

"Will that be all?"

"All for today, sir."

"Sounds as though you'll be back."

"That'll depend on the commander," said the sailor, giving Fournier a salute as his boat began its return to the *Portsmouth*.[1]

Fournier gave Montgomery's order some thought. He understood that it was his duty to comply, but he did not want to cause his ship to be shorthanded. After careful consideration, he made his decision, and at four p.m., two boats left the *Stonington* and delivered eight men each at La Playa.

The following day, another boat from the *Portsmouth* approached the *Stonington*.

Fournier steeled himself in preparation to defend his decision to send sixteen instead of twenty men.

"Good morning, Captain," called the same sailor that had delivered Montgomery's order the day before.

"So far, so good," said Fournier, holding himself straight and tall. "What brings you back so soon?"

"Commander Montgomery, sir. He wants you to send two of your guns and fifty-one round shot to the town."

"Anything else?"

"That'll be all for today."

"I'll organize that shipment straight away," said Fournier with a wave.

"Much obliged, sir," said the sailor, waving back.

As the boat rowed away, Fournier breathed a quiet sigh of relief and went to coordinate the delivery of the guns and ammunition.[2]

Two days later, on Monday, January 4, yet another boat was on its way to the *Stonington*, but this time it was coming from shore.

"Mr. Fournier," called Gardner Jaques, "there's a boat comin', and unless my eyes are deceivin' me, I believe I'm seein' Captain Hamley in it."

Fournier went to the rail and pulled out his spyglass. "You can trust your eyes, Jaques," he said. "That's the captain, all right."

The boat pulled up alongside and Hamley climbed up to the deck.

"Welcome back, Captain," said Fournier.

"Yes, Fournier, I'm back, but not to stay. Commodore Stockton has sent me on a mission to deliver a dispatch to Colonel Frémont." Hamley continued talking as he made his way to his cabin, and Fournier followed along, listening intently.

"We were in our camp at San Luis Rey two days ago when the commodore learned that Frémont had left Santa Barbara and was marching toward Los Angeles, and that the Californios were on their way from that same town to attack him. Fastest way to get the message to Frémont is by ship. Stockton sent me down here yesterday from Las Flores. Told me to sail aboard the *Malek Adhel* and to bring that customs collector, Carrillo, with me." Hamley gathered some clothing as he continued. "I found him in town when I rode in. He's on his way to that ship. That's all I've got time to tell you."

Hamley made his way hurriedly back up on deck and climbed down to his awaiting boat.

"You've got command of the ship for a while longer, Fournier. I'll expect it to be in good shape when I return."

"Aye, sir," called Fournier as the boat rowed away. "Fair seas and following winds!"

He watched the boat make its way to the *Malek Adhel*, and also saw the boat coming from shore carrying Pedro Carrillo, the customs collector for San Diego. Carrillo was a friend of Frémont's whom Stockton knew would be helpful to Hamley in making his way through the countryside and finding Frémont.[3]

CHAPTER 44

The Pathfinder

SAILING NORTHWARD FOR APPROXIMATELY ONE HUNDRED EIGHTY miles, the *Malek Adhel* arrived at San Buenaventura on Friday, January 8. Hamley and Carrillo left the ship and, under cover of darkness, made their way inland for thirty-six miles, passing stealthily through the Californios' lines.

The next morning, they reached Frémont and his battalion near Rancho San Francisco, a portion of which had actually been under Carrillo's ownership for a brief time, in 1843. As they approached the sentries, Carrillo identified himself.

"Good morning, gentlemen. I am Don Pedro Carrillo, a friend of Colonel Frémont," he said to the men guarding the camp. "This is Captain George Hamley of the ship *Stonington*. He has a dispatch from Commodore Stockton for Colonel Frémont. Would you be so kind as to bring us to the colonel so that the captain may deliver his message to him?"

The sentries led the two men into the camp, where they saw a group of men milling about, some in discussion with one another. The men were dressed in buckskins, with knives or pistols hanging at their waists.

As the two visitors approached, some of the men looked toward them questioningly. One walked toward the visitors with an outstretched hand. He was of medium height, slender, with dark, curly hair that was parted in the middle and hung loosely over his ears and the back of his neck. His full beard was as dark as the hair on his head, and his piercing blue eyes looked out over a long, straight nose.

"Don Pedro!" the man exclaimed. "It's good to see you again."

"It is good to see you as well, my friend," said Carrillo as they shook hands. "Please allow me to introduce Captain George Hamley. Captain Hamley, this is Colonel John Frémont."

Hamley extended his hand amid surprise and, to some extent, disbelief. Although he had been at sea since the year immediately following Frémont's first expedition in 1842, he had still heard tales of the man people called "The Pathfinder." Now he was face-to-face and shaking hands with Frémont, who, despite his fame and rank, was dressed no differently than any of the other men in the camp.

"Pleased to meet you, Captain," said Frémont. "To what do I owe the honor of this visit?"

"I have a dispatch for you from Commodore Stockton," replied Hamley, handing the packet to Frémont.

"I see," said Frémont in a serious tone. He opened and read Stockton's message:

Camp at San Louis Rey

January 3, 1847

My Dear Colonel:

We arrived here last night from San Diego, and leave to-day on our march for the City of the Angels, where I hope to be in five or six days. I learn this morning that you are at Santa Barbara, and send this dispatch by way of San Diego, in the hope that it may reach you in time. If there is one single chance against you, you had better not fight the rebels until I get up to aid you, or you can join me on the road to the Pueblo.

These fellows are well prepared, and Mervine's and Kearny's defeat have given them a deal more confidence and courage. If you do fight before I see you, keep your forces in close order. Do not allow them to be separated, or even unnecessarily extended. They will probably try to deceive you by a sudden retreat, or pretended runaway, and then unexpectedly return to the charge after your men get in disorder in the chase. My advice is to allow them to do all the charging and running and let your rifles do the rest.

In the art of horsemanship, of dodging, and running, it is in vain to attempt to compete with them.

In haste, very truly, your friend and obedt. servt.,

R. F. Stockton

P.S. I understand that it is probable they will try to avoid me and fight you separately.

Frémont muttered to himself as he read the message, then looked up at Hamley and Carrillo. "And this was brought to you in San Diego?"

"No, sir," replied Hamley, "the commodore sent it with me from the camp near San Luis Rey. Don Pedro and I sailed from San Diego to San Buenaventura and then made our way to you."

"So you are a captain in Stockton's force?" Frémont asked Hamley.

"I marched with the force, sir, but I'm the captain of the whaleship *Stonington* that's in San Diego, in the service of the government."

"Ah," said Frémont admiringly, "I've heard much about the usefulness of your ship."

"Yes, sir."

"Well, Captain, Don Pedro," Frémont said to his two visitors, "you are welcome to join us on our march to Los Angeles. Be advised that there'll likely be some action with the Californios along the way."

Hamley looked at Carrillo resolutely.

Carrillo said to Frémont, "I believe I speak for both of us, my friend, when I say that we will be honored to march with you."

"Good," said Frémont. "We'll break camp presently and be on our way."

Frémont and his California Battalion of over four hundred men that now included Hamley and Carrillo marched eastward that morning of Saturday, January 9, for about twelve miles along the Santa Clara River before setting up camp at a rancho owned by an elderly Californian. As they marched that day, they occasionally spotted a few Californio lookouts atop the hills to the south.

The following morning, January 10, they set out in a more southeasterly direction, still keeping the hills to their right. After about ten miles of marching, they set up camp at the entrance of a canyon that led southward through the hills. They saw Californios atop the hills again, but there were now nearly fifty of them. Frémont, recalling Stockton's advice in the dispatch brought by Hamley, kept his battalion encamped but at the ready.[1]

On Monday, January 11, Frémont organized his force into two groups before setting off into the canyon. The majority of the men would march through the hills, keeping the canyon below them to their left. The supplies, artillery, and livestock, guarded by a smaller group of men, would follow the main trail through the canyon. Thus configured, Frémont and his men would be prepared should the Californios decide to attack. The battalion made its way cautiously, fully expecting that at any moment the enemy would descend upon them. They reached the crest of the hills, and as they looked out over the large plain ahead, there was no enemy to be seen.

While the main group made its way down from the hills to the southern end of the canyon to rejoin the rest of the battalion, two riders galloped toward the smaller group and, after identifying themselves as friendly, asked that they be allowed to deliver a message to Colonel Frémont. Men of the battalion escorted them, and the messengers delivered their news to Frémont.[2]

CHAPTER 45

Two Battles

THE NEWS THAT JOHN C. FRÉMONT RECEIVED FROM THE TWO MESSEN-
gers explained the surprising absence of enemy forces as he and the California Battalion entered the San Fernando Valley on Monday, January 11,
1847. General José María Flores, commander of the Californios aligned
with Mexico against the United States, had been preparing to send his
troops to engage in battle with the California Battalion after learning in
the first few days of January that Frémont and his forces were on their
way from Santa Barbara to Los Angeles. Flores changed his plans within
days, however, upon learning that a large number of troops headed by
Commodore Stockton and General Kearny was nearing Los Angeles
from the south. He recalled General Andrés Pico and his force from the
engagement with Frémont and ordered them south to the San Gabriel
River, where they joined with the Californios led by Captain José Antonio Carrillo, the officer who had defeated Captain Mervine in the Battle
of the Old Woman's Gun at Dominguez Rancho the previous October.[1]

The Americans under the command of Stockton and Kearny had
approached the San Gabriel River on the morning of January 8, the
thirty-second anniversary of the Battle of New Orleans that had made
Andrew Jackson a national hero and propelled him to the office of president of the United States. In the distance, they saw arrayed before them
on the northern bank the lancers and artillery under the command of Pico
and Carrillo. Kearny sent a group of men to scout the situation. Leading
them was Samuel Hensley, the man who, with some of the very same
men, had sailed on the *Stonington* far south of San Diego to round up

horses and cattle for the march in which they were now engaged. Kearny, to whom Stockton had deferred regarding the land movement of their forces, ordered the troops to advance. The Californios fired their guns persistently but ineffectually as the Americans began crossing the river. They then mounted a charge, but the Americans held their positions with bayonets and pikes angled against the oncoming horses and with musket fire from their rear. Charges continued from different approaches but were ultimately unsuccessful, and the Californios eventually rode back up to the top of the ridge that fronted the riverbank. Hensley and his Osos pursued them and drove them from their previous positions, then the rest of the American forces joined them and secured the ridge.[2]

The ridge that the Americans now occupied was the outer edge of a large mesa that stretched before them. General Flores and his lancers positioned themselves several miles northeast of the American forces. Both sides spent the night watching uneasily for a potential attack from their opponents. There were no attacks, but a courier did arrive in the American camp to inform Commodore Stockton that John C. Frémont and his battalion were in the San Fernando Valley.

The next morning, January 9, the Americans resumed their march to Los Angeles. Flores was determined to halt their advance. He opened fire with his artillery, and at the sound of the guns, the Americans did as Stockton had ordered and lay flat on the ground until they were certain the projectiles had passed over them. The Californios' celebration of what they assumed to be their deadly accurate shots dissipated quickly when they saw the Americans rise and renew their forward movement. Flores then decided to attack the enemy from all sides. As the Californios deployed themselves in a horseshoe shape, the Americans formed their standard square, which the sailors among them called a "Yankee corral," placing the livestock and wagons in the center of ranks and files of men on all four sides. The Americans then deployed their artillery with lethal accuracy. The Californios attempted repeatedly to penetrate the square but relented eventually and withdrew to safety.

Kearny and Stockton led their forces westward for about six miles and established their camp within sight of Los Angeles. After two days of fierce fighting in which each side suffered minimal casualties, the town was on the verge of changing hands yet again.[3]

The Americans broke camp on Sunday morning, January 10, but before they began their march into Los Angeles, three emissaries from General Flores arrived carrying a flag of truce. Their message was that Flores was willing to surrender the town if Stockton and Kearny would keep their forces from doing any harm to its inhabitants or their property. The parties agreed to those terms, but the Americans suspected there would be resistance, so they made their way into town with great caution. Many townspeople, some carrying weapons, jeered the Americans as they arrived. After some minor disturbances, the American forces positioned themselves, and Captain Archibald Gillespie, whose harsh rule of the town had led to his earlier defeat by the Californios, raised the US flag, the same one that he had had to lower just a few months ago.[4]

CHAPTER 46

The Treaty of Cahuenga

Captain George W. Hamley had arrived in Colonel John C. Frémont's camp on Saturday, January 9, the same day as the Battle of San Gabriel. Frémont, unaware of what was occurring fifty-five miles away to the southeast, had continued his advance to Los Angeles. When he entered the San Fernando Valley two days later, on January 11, Frémont received news of the two battles and the retaking of Los Angeles.

The California Battalion arrived at the San Fernando Mission that afternoon and camped in the buildings. Frémont sent Don José de Jesús Pico—a cousin of former governor Pío Pico and General Andrés Pico, who had been traveling with the battalion for over a month—to a nearby rancho to suggest to the Californios that they should engage in treaty negotiations. General Flores, who had just surrendered Los Angeles the day before, could not bring himself to admit total defeat. Instead, he relinquished his command to General Pico, then he and General Manuel Castro set off for Mexico.[1]

The next morning, Jesús Pico escorted Captain José Carrillo and Captain Agustín Olvera to the mission to meet and discuss terms with Frémont. The meeting was not conclusive, but it did produce a basic framework for the capitulation of the Californios, as well as an agreement to a cease-fire until they completed the terms. The negotiations ended in the afternoon with assurances that both sides would continue their talks the next day.

On Wednesday morning, January 13, the Californio forces moved eastward to Rancho Tujunga, which overlooked the valley, while the battalion headed to the southern end of the valley near the mouth of Cahuenga Pass. Soon after, General Andrés Pico, along with captains Carrillo and Olvera, arrived to finalize negotiations with Frémont, who was accompanied by three battalion officers, as well as Don Pedro Carrillo, who served as Frémont's interpreter. They met at an adobe building owned by Eulogio de Celis, a citizen of Spain who owned most of the land in the valley. Within a matter of hours, the two sides came to an agreement over the resulting seven Articles of Capitulation. Pico and his captains and Frémont and his officers signed what would become known as the Treaty of Cahuenga, thus bringing an end to the Mexican-American War in California.[2]

Pico had approved and signed the treaty as the sole commander of the Californios. Frémont, however, was but a junior officer to Commodore Stockton and General Kearny, whom he knew were only about twenty miles away in Los Angeles, yet he had taken it upon himself to negotiate and sign the treaty as the "Military Commandant of California." He sent Colonel William Russell, one of the negotiators and signers, to Los Angeles to deliver the treaty to Stockton and Kearny, both of whom were somewhat taken aback by Frémont's actions, but eventually accepted what he had accomplished.

On Thursday, January 14, amid a heavy rainfall, Frémont led the battalion through Cahuenga Pass and into Los Angeles. Very few Californio residents had remained in the town. The majority of the inhabitants were now the combined US forces, most of whom would need to return to San Diego.

Kearny and his dragoons marched out on January 18. Stockton took thirty men with him the following day after having put Captain Gillespie in charge of the battalion that would continue to occupy Los Angeles. The remaining force of over five hundred sailors and marines marched to San Pedro, where they would embark on a ship that was making its way to them from San Diego.[3]

CHAPTER 47

A Change of Command

ALANSON FOURNIER HAD BEEN SERVING AS THE TEMPORARY CAPTAIN of the *Stonington* since December 29, the day that George Hamley left to march with Stockton and Kearny. The ship had remained in San Diego harbor from that point on. Some of the crew, as ordered by commander and acting governor John B. Montgomery, had gone into town to help provide for its defense. The rest had stayed aboard doing regular ship's duty.

All of that was about to change.

"Mr. Fournier," called out one of the crew on Tuesday, January 12, "we've got boats comin'."

Fournier went to the starboard rail and saw several boats approaching, some from shore, others from the warships moored in the harbor. Two of them were being rowed by the men that had gone ashore to defend the town. One boat was carrying a man in a naval officer's uniform, and as that boat drew nearer, Fournier could see that the officer was young and a bit haggard-looking.

"May I speak with the officer in charge, please?" asked the uniformed man in a weakened voice.

"That would be me, sir," replied Fournier.

"I am Lieutenant Beale, United States Navy," stated the officer. "I have orders from Commander Montgomery to take charge of this ship and sail to San Pedro."

"I see," said Fournier, a bit crestfallen that his time as acting captain was apparently coming to an end. "Well, then," he continued, "you'd best come aboard."

Beale rose unsteadily and slowly made his way up the rope ladder and onto the deck. It had been just over a month since he had made the torturous trek through the desert from San Pasqual to San Diego, and he had not yet recovered fully from the ordeal.

"Welcome aboard, sir," said Fournier as he saluted Beale. "Let me show you to your quarters."

Beale nodded and followed Fournier toward the companionway. Meanwhile, the returning crew members hoisted themselves and their boats onto the deck, then stowed the boats on the roof of the amidships shelter that served as a boat bearer. The rest of the crew busied themselves hauling onto the deck the provisions and ammunition that Montgomery had sent along, provided by the *Congress*, *Portsmouth*, and *Cyane*, according to the orders that Stockton had written and sent on January 7.

"This sure is a lot of food," exclaimed Martin Larkins as he hefted yet another barrel of pork to be stowed in the hold. "Looks like we're gettin' ready to feed an army."

"Or a navy," said Peter McDonnald, who was a few steps ahead of Larkins and carrying a barrel of beans.

"What makes you say that?" asked Larkins.

"Oh, just a hunch," replied McDonnald.

Unbeknownst to both of them, that was precisely the purpose of all those provisions.[1]

"We will be sailing to San Pedro in the morning," explained Lieutenant Beale to Alanson Fournier when they got to the captain's quarters. "There, we will make ourselves available to take aboard the sailors and marines that marched to Los Angeles with Commodore Stockton. There are over five hundred of them, so if we do take them on board, this ship will be a bit crowded."

"It certainly will, sir," said Fournier, "but I'm sure we'll find room for them. We had similar circumstances when we first arrived here in San

Diego and had to provide shelter for all the people in town that were being run out by the Californios."

"Yes, I've heard tell of that," responded Beale. "You performed an important service."

"We did what we could, sir," replied Fournier, "but no more important a service than what you accomplished by making it through that desert."

Beale closed his eyes and nodded in silent acknowledgment.

"Will you be needing me for anything else, sir?" asked Fournier.

"Not at the moment."

"Well, then, I'll take my leave and see how things are progressing up top," said Fournier as he saluted and made his way to the deck.

Upon his arrival there, Fournier observed the coordinated movements of the crew as they finished loading the cargo that Montgomery had sent. He made special note of the two extra boats stowed on the amidships shelter as he looked around at the entire deck, then pictured in his mind the ship's hold.

I'd say "a bit crowded" is an understatement, he thought, reflecting on what Lieutenant Beale had told him.[2]

The *Stonington* left San Diego on the morning of January 13, the same day that Colonel Frémont and General Pico would sign the Treaty of Cahuenga. The weather was fair but there was no wind, so Fournier ordered a boat lowered to tow the ship out to Point Loma. Once they rounded the Point, there was enough of a breeze to set sail, and they set their course for San Pedro. The crew was in good spirits, having received a portion of the pork, beef, beans, and bread from the provisions that had arrived the previous day.

"Milnor," said Fournier to the ship's carpenter, upon finding him in his quarters, "I want you to inspect all of our boats and make any necessary repairs. They may see a good deal of use at San Pedro."

"Right, sir. What sort of use, if I may ask?"

"We may be embarking the naval forces that marched to retake Los Angeles."

"Sounds as though it might get a bit crowded around here."

"Certainly seems that way," said Fournier with a knowing chuckle. "I'll leave you to your work, then."

As Fournier left Milnor's quarters, he remembered there was an old sail on board that had come from the *Congress*. The first men he saw when he got up on deck were Joseph Miller and John Williams. He approached them and said, "I've got a special mission for you two."

They looked at him with a hint of suspicion, and Miller asked, "What might that be, sir?"

"You're going to help this ship go faster," Fournier answered.

"You want us to lower a boat and start towing?" asked Williams half-jokingly.

"No, nothing as strenuous as that," replied Fournier. "I want you to take that old sail we got from the *Congress*, make a spanker out of it, then bend it to the rigging. With an extra sail at our stern, we should be able to catch more wind and shorten our trip to San Pedro. Of course," he continued, "if you think you'll need more than just the two of you to handle the job . . ."

The two crewmen looked at each other, then Miller said, "No need for that, sir. We can handle this just fine."

"I knew I chose the right men," said Fournier. "I look forward to admiring your work," he said, leaving the two men and heading toward the bow.[3]

There was one more task that Fournier needed to assign, and he knew just the men for the job.

"Well, gentlemen," he said, as he approached Davis, Jaques, Peters, and Harry, "it's good to find you all here together."

Aaron Peters smirked at the other three crewmen. "I'm thinking he wants to hear us sing again."

"You've got a talent for reading minds, Peters," said Fournier. "We're about to head up to San Pedro, fellas, and we don't want to be carrying any more weight than we have to. Last time you pumped the bilge was about a month ago. You got three hundred strokes then. Care to guess how many you'll get this time? I'll see to it that the man with the closest number gets an extra serving from the cook."

"I'll say two hundred," responded Jaques, "on account of we've just been here in the harbor for weeks."

"Three hundred again," said Harry, "no more, no less."

"Four hundred fifty," said Peters, and the other three shook their heads at him as if he were crazy. "I like big numbers," he added with a wink, to which they all chuckled.

"I'll bring us back to reason," said Davis. "Two hundred fifty."

"Time to put those numbers to the test," said Fournier. "I'll keep an ear open for your counting."

The four men headed toward the mainmast, positioned themselves at the pumps, and began:

They *say* life has its *ups* and downs
That *really* now is *quite* profound
I'd *like* to push the *cap*stan 'round
But it's *pump* me boys be*fore* we drown.

Pump me boys, *pump* 'er dry
Down to hell and *up* to the sky
Bend your back and *break* your bones
We're *just* a thousand *miles* from home . . .

Fournier made his rounds, checking on Milnor and then Miller and Williams, all the while listening to the rising count from the bilge-pump quartet.

"The four boats that are ours are in good shape," reported Milnor. "Now I've got to check those two stored on the boat bearer."

"All right," said Fournier. "Let me know about those two when you've finished with them."

He then went to the place where the tryworks used to be, between the fore- and mainmasts, to see how the spanker was coming along.

"Just one more side to go, sir," said Miller, "then it'll be ready for bending."

"Good work, men," said Fournier, looking carefully at their trim work, "and just in time, too, if my weather sense is accurate. Feels as though we've got a change coming that'll fill that sail properly."

Fournier then turned toward the quartet as the water from the pumps continued to flow onto the deck and out through the scuppers. The count continued to rise, and there was a surprised look on all their faces as they passed the four-hundred-and-fifty mark that Peters had predicted. The water finally came to a full stop at five hundred.

Fournier approached and said, "Well, Peters, I hope you're feeling hungry," to which Peters grinned and said, "I am, sir, I certainly am!"[4]

CHAPTER 48

Hurry Up and Wait

FOURNIER'S WEATHER SENSE PROVED TO BE ACCURATE. AS JANUARY 14 arrived and progressed, the breezes went from small to strong and the fog became rain. By nightfall, the *Stonington* was in the midst of squalls, but despite the weather, the visibility was good enough that Fournier heard one of the crew cry, "Land ahead!" He took out his spyglass to get a better look and saw the point of San Pedro in the distance, about five miles off the larboard bow.

He made his way aft, saying "Hold your course steady, Comstock" as he passed the helmsman.

Mark Comstock nodded as Fournier went down the companionway.

"Lieutenant Beale, sir?" Fournier said, after knocking on the cabin door.

"What is it, Fournier?" asked Beale, as he sat resting on the cushioned bench below the stern windows.

"San Pedro's in sight, sir. Should be there by morning."

"We've made good time, then, haven't we?" Beale said, rising slowly from his seat. "Once we're anchored off the point, fire a salute from one of the guns to announce our arrival. We don't know the situation in Los Angeles, but they'll at least know that we're here."

Fair weather returned on Friday morning, January 15, making it possible to see clearly the shoreline of San Pedro, as well as the northern point of Santa Catalina Island, to the south by southwest.

"It doesn't look as though our men have made it to the coast yet," Lieutenant Beale said to Alanson Fournier as they stood at the starboard bow. "May I use your spyglass?"

"Certainly, sir," answered Fournier, handing the glass to Beale.

Beale scanned the coastline but saw no troops. "We'd best keep ourselves a safe distance from shore until we've got a better notion of the situation. Once we're secured, fire that salute and let me know the response."

"Aye, sir," replied Fournier, and Beale headed back to his quarters.

Fournier had one of the crew check the depth, and when the answer came back as ten fathoms, he gave the order to drop anchor. "Set that cable ready for slipping, men. We'll be moving in closer fairly soon." He called out, "Single reef the topsails!" and crewmen at each of the three masts climbed the ratlines up to the second and third spars, where they shortened and fastened the sails.

When that work was completed and the men had returned to the deck, Fournier approached James Rice and said, "You're good with a musket, Rice. Let's see how you are with a gun."

Rice looked at him with a mixture of surprise and concern.

"No," explained Fournier, "we're not attacking—we're signaling our troops to let them know we're here. I just need you to fire a blank."

Rice, visibly relieved, said, "Aye, sir." He loaded one of the starboard guns with a charge, yelled "All clear!" and then fired the gun. The loud, booming sound carried across the water and through the air inland. Fournier marked the time as four p.m. and searched the shore with his spyglass at regular intervals. After doing so for a couple of hours and seeing no response, he went to Lieutenant Beale to report the results.

"Thank you, Fournier," said Beale. "Tomorrow we'll pull ourselves a bit closer to the land and give them another salute."[1]

The next morning, January 16, Fournier followed Beale's orders. The crew completed the anchoring adjustments, and James Rice fired a second salute in the evening. Fournier again scoured the shore for any signs of response, but saw none.

"We'll hold our position," said Beale after Fournier made his report, "and stand ready to take those men on board when they arrive."

The waiting dragged on into the next few days.

On Tuesday, January 19, there was a break in the monotony.

"Thar she blows!" cried the young harpooner Edwin Arthur.

"Where away?" called Fournier.

"Out to larboard," replied Arthur, "a great many of 'em."

All eyes focused on an area a couple hundred feet southwest of the ship where a large pod of whales was swimming toward the bay.

"They seem so gentle-like," said Thomas Folger, another harpooner.

"Not when we get to them, they aren't," replied Arthur.

"Of course not," responded Fournier, "we go out to kill them. Perfectly natural response for them to get angry."

"I s'pose so," said Folger, as he and the rest of the crew watched the huge creatures move gracefully through the water. The men thought about how different the activity aboard the ship would have been just a few months ago upon hearing Arthur's "Thar she blows," and they wondered when, if ever, they would get back to what they had signed on to do, which was to hunt whales.[2]

CHAPTER 49

A Bit Crowded

TWO DAYS LATER, ON THURSDAY, JANUARY 21, A LOOKOUT CALLED DOWN to the deck, "Troops on the way!"

Alanson Fournier went to the bow and, using his spyglass, saw many men in blue and white uniforms marching toward the shore. He alerted Lieutenant Beale, who followed him back onto the deck. Beale looked through the spyglass and said, "Finally!" in a thankful and relieved tone. "Those are our men, all right, Mr. Fournier. Bring us within a mile of the shore and then start sending the boats."

"Time for the ship to get a bit crowded, Lieutenant?" asked Fournier with a slight grin.

"It is indeed, Mr. Fournier," answered Beale.

At four o'clock that afternoon, having secured the *Stonington* one mile from shore, Fournier ordered the boats to be lowered, and the embarkation began. Each boat set out with a crew of three in order to leave room for the sailors and marines. Fournier stood at the starboard rail and waited for the first few boats to return, watching for an officer so that he could coordinate with him the placement of the passengers. He spotted a marine officer coming on deck and introduced himself. "Welcome aboard, sir. I am Second Officer Alanson Fournier. And you are?"

"I am Second Lieutenant Henry Watson," said the officer with a gentle Southern drawl, "in charge of the marine guard on the USS *Portsmouth*."

"Pleased to meet you, Lieutenant Watson. I trust that all is well in Los Angeles?"

"Yes, sir, the town is ours once again," replied Watson. "We had two encounters with the Californians along the way, both of which ended in our favor, and then we eventually marched in and occupied the town. We heard your salutes, but we were obliged to put things in order before we were able to leave, hence our delay in arriving to you."

"The good news is worth the wait, Lieutenant, and all with minimal casualties, I hope."

"We fared well, Mr. Fournier—better than the Californians."

"Well, sir, now that you've made it here safely, allow me to explain where you and the rest of the men may find room to stay while on board the *Stonington*."

"By all means, do proceed."

"The largest open spaces available are here on the deck and in the lower deck. In the 'tween deck, there's the main cabin that you and the other officers are welcome to use, and there's also the blubber room. The remainder of spaces in that deck are the small cabins with bunks for mates, harpooners, the carpenter, the cooper, and others with specific jobs, and then there's the fo'c'sle with bunks for the regular crewmen."

"I appreciate your hospitality, sir," said Watson. "You have listed quite a few options. I do believe, however, that given the number of men that will be coming aboard, the ship will inevitably become a bit crowded."

"Yes, sir," responded Fournier with a straight face, "that would be an accurate description of the situation. We'll do our best to sail to San Diego as quickly as possible."

"Well, Mr. Fournier, let us hope that the weather proves to be as accommodating as you are. Now, please excuse me while I direct the men to their places."

"Of course, sir," said Fournier. "I'll assist you as well."

For the next few hours, a steady stream of boats went from the *Stonington* to shore and returned with groups of sailors and marines who, following the directions of Watson and Fournier, found spaces for themselves aboard the ship. Each boat made about five round-trips, and by late evening, two hundred fifty men along with their equipment had come aboard.

"We've taken all aboard that were onshore, sir," reported Fournier to Lieutenant Beale in the captain's cabin. "The rest of them will be along tomorrow morning. We should be ready to leave for San Diego sometime in the afternoon."

"Thank you, Fournier," said Beale. "I trust you've found room for everyone so far?"

"So far, sir, but the real test will come tomorrow."

"Yes, well, see to it that they're as comfortable as possible, and be sure they get some food and water," said Beale as he went back to his seat.

"Aye, sir, will that be all?"

"That will do for now."

Fournier nodded and left to find Alexander Anthony, who, as steward, would be responsible for apportioning the meals for the officers, after which he would direct David Redding, the cook, to take care of the rest of the men.[1]

The embarkation continued the following day, January 22, with more men than had arrived the previous day. By one o'clock in the afternoon, the *Stonington* had taken on a total of five hundred thirty men and their gear. They crammed themselves into the spaces that Fournier had designated. Two hundred of them were in the lower deck, where light and air were at a minimum due to the fact that its intended use was to store casks of whale oil, not to provide living quarters for people. In the 'tween deck, one hundred men filled the blubber room, as well as the carpenter's and cooper's workspace before it. Thirty-nine officers crowded into the ten-foot-square main cabin. The remainder of the men, numbering nearly two hundred, had to find places on the upper deck where they could stay without being in the way of the *Stonington*'s crew when they went about the business of sailing the ship.

"All the passengers and their equipment are situated, sir," Fournier reported to Lieutenant Beale in the captain's cabin.

"Right, then, Fournier. Time to weigh anchor and get this ship back to San Diego."

"Aye, sir."

As Fournier left and headed toward the companionway, he heard a cacophony of voices flooding the 'tween deck with more volume than he had ever heard in the ship before. He felt a sense of relief when he emerged into the openness of the upper deck. There were many voices here as well, but unlike in the enclosed space below, which caused the sounds to resonate into a steady roar, the voices on deck dispersed freely into the air.

Fournier made his way forward, and when he was near the fo'c'sle, called out, "All hands! Haul anchor and set sail!" Some of the passengers came to attention at hearing the order but then relaxed when they realized that they were just that—passengers. They watched with a certain amount of admiration as the *Stonington*'s crew went about their work with fluid precision. The ship got under way at four p.m. under fair skies, and with a small northwest breeze that by evening had shifted and was coming from the south.[2]

The passengers on the upper deck were crowded and somewhat uncomfortable, but glad to be in the open air. Those below were in even more crowded conditions, and were beginning to deal with an additional discomfort in their stuffy confines. At first a few, then several, and then many of the men were scratching themselves, no matter where in the ship they happened to be.

Henry Watson looked at his fellow officers in the main cabin and, in the midst of his own scratching, said one word: "Fleas." The insects had been generally dormant within the ship, but the warmth and humidity from so many men packed together had drawn them out of their cocoons, and they were now feasting on the multiple sources of blood. All those bodies so close together were like a banquet for the tiny biting insects.

In order to keep their minds off of the incessant itching, the men resorted to taking turns telling stories and jokes. Another distraction occurred when Alexander Anthony and David Redding began distributing bread and salted meat from the provisions that Commodore Stockton had ordered to be loaded onto the ship back in San Diego. Whether complaining about the quality of the food or simply eating it, the passengers' minds were focused on something other than their own physical discomfort.

By Saturday, January 23, the weather had become stormy, with rain and wind blowing from the southeast. The nearly two hundred passengers on the upper deck scrambled for whatever bits of shelter they could find. Some of them packed themselves under the boat bearer, while most of them huddled around the hatches and any other structure that provided even the slightest amount of protection from the wind that was quickly becoming a gale. There was no getting away from the heavy, pelting rain, though, and as the waves grew larger, the seawater that splashed onto the deck combined with the rainfall to create streams that ran beneath the men wherever they sat or stood. The sight of the crew working in the rigging provided some distraction from their miserable plight, even though they could lift their faces upward only briefly before having to shield themselves again from the driving rain.

The crewmen worked persistently throughout the night as Fournier ordered them to reduce the surface area of one course of sails after another, maneuvering in the dark in harsh conditions that at any moment could result in their falling from their perches. Finally, at two a.m. on the 24th, the wind began to decrease and shifted to westward. By noon, the weather was once again fair, and Point Loma was within sight.

"Drop anchor a half-mile southeast of the Point, Mr. Fournier," said Lieutenant Beale when Fournier had come to his cabin to report that they would be there before midnight. "We'll wait until morning to make our way into the harbor."

"Aye, sir," replied Fournier. "I'll look in on the passengers to see how they've fared and let them know our position."

"That's a fine idea, Fournier. Be on your way."

"Yes, sir."

Fournier's first stop was the main cabin. Looking in, he spotted a familiar face.

"Lieutenant Watson," he called out over the heads of the other officers, "our journey is coming to a close. We should be at Point Loma sometime this evening."

"That, my good sir, is most welcome news," said Watson emphatically. "Your ship rides well in rough seas, Mr. Fournier, but I believe I speak for the majority of my men when I say that I have never experienced such a miserable time as I have had these past two days."

"I'm sorry to hear that, Lieutenant."

"We were accosted by an army of fleas. Amid the constant slapping and scratching, there was no sleep to be had."

"Well, you'll soon be free of the little devils. For now, I'll make my way through the ship to let the rest of your men know our position."

"I thank you for that, Mr. Fournier."[3]

Fournier went down to the lower deck, where the pungent odors from two hundred men crowded into a space with minimal ventilation for two days led him to make his announcement brief so that he could exit quickly.

He then made his way to the one hundred men in the blubber room, where the smells were not quite as bad, resulting in his lingering long enough after his announcement to hear from one ordinary seaman, who identified himself as Joseph T. Downey, about the food.

"The bread was passable," Downey said, "but the uncooked salted beef and pork was difficult to stomach."

"Well, you'll be in port soon and back on your own ship, where you can put all of this behind you."

"I'm looking forward to the putting behind, sir," replied Downey with a half grin.

Fournier nodded to Downey and the others, then turned and went up the companionway to the main deck.

"Listen up, men," he called out. "As you've probably already noticed, we're coming close to Point Loma. We'll be anchoring just outside of the harbor for the night. By tomorrow morning—"

"By tomorrow morning," interrupted one of the sailors, "maybe our clothes'll be dry!"

To which his fellow passengers responded with a mixture of groans and laughter.

"There's not much we could do about the weather, men," responded Fournier, "but we did get you back safely."

"Aye, there's that," called out another sailor. "This old tub did serve its purpose. I suppose we do owe you a bit of thanks."

"Aye," said most of them as they nodded their heads in agreement.

"We've done what we could," said Fournier modestly.[4]

At ten p.m. Sunday, January 24, the *Stonington* anchored a half-mile off Point Loma. Boats from the three warships began arriving to transfer the men and their equipment.

After most of the men had disembarked, the load was now light enough for safe passage over the bar. Lieutenant Beale gave the order to heave up the anchor and tow the ship into the harbor. The crew dropped the starboard anchor at two a.m., and at seven o'clock that morning, the remaining passengers disembarked with their arms, ammunition, and provisions.

The *Stonington* and its crew had successfully completed their mission, retrieving the sailors and marines that had participated in the retaking of Los Angeles and returning them to San Diego, a town that was now at peace as a result of the Treaty of Cahuenga.[5]

Alanson Fournier went to the captain's cabin to deliver his report to Lieutenant Beale. When he entered, he saw the lieutenant gathering his belongings.

"We've disembarked the last of the passengers, sir," said Fournier.

"Not quite, Fournier," said Beale. "You've got one more to go." He stood still and looked straight at Fournier, who by now realized that the final passenger was Beale himself. "Now, if you'd be so kind as to escort me to a boat," said Beale, "I'll be on my way."

"Of course, sir," responded Fournier, and the two men went to the upper deck.

Fournier called a crew to one of the boats and said, "Bring Lieutenant Beale to where he needs to go," then turned to Beale. "It's been an honor to serve with you, sir."

"You're a fine second officer, Mr. Fournier," replied Beale earnestly. "You've got a good way with your men. In my opinion, you're ready to be captain of a ship, and I hope that happens for you soon."

"Thank you, sir, much obliged," said Fournier. He saluted Beale, who returned the salute, then climbed into the boat and was on his way.

On Monday morning, January 25, John Spun Yarn, a crewman from the Sandwich Islands, called out to Alanson Fournier, "Boat comin', Mr. Fournier. Look like Captain Hamley in it."

Fournier lifted his spyglass. "Good eye, Spun Yarn."

The boat came alongside the *Stonington*, and George Hamley climbed up onto the deck.

"Welcome back, Captain," said Fournier. "You look as though you've had quite the adventure." Hamley's hair and beard had grown longer, his skin was a shade darker, and his clothes were torn in several places.

"Yes, Fournier," he replied, "I've had a time of it—finding Colonel Frémont, then traveling with him and his men through mountains and valleys to Los Angeles, and then marching back here as part of Commodore Stockton's forces. I'll be happy to finally return to my cabin and get some rest."

"Aye, sir. You go right ahead. I'll mind the ship."

"Thank you, Fournier," said Hamley as he headed to the companionway, and then down to his cabin. Within seconds of his descent, there was a loud cry of "Fournier!"

Alanson Fournier proceeded quickly down the companionway.

"What in damnation is this god-awful stench?" yelled Hamley.

Fournier explained the trip to Los Angeles and the five hundred thirty passengers.

"I want this ship cleaned properly, Fournier," said Hamley angrily. "Get the men working immediately!"

"Aye, sir."

He was halfway up the companionway when he heard another "Fournier!"

He returned to the doorway of Hamley's cabin.

"What's the meaning of this?" Hamley demanded.

"I'm not sure I—"

"Using my cabin while I was away!"

"It wasn't me, sir, it was Lieutenant Beale."

Hamley stopped and stared at Fournier. "Beale?" he asked incredulously.

"Yes, sir."

Hamley collected himself and then said flatly, "Well, I see we've had a bit of a celebrity on board. Some of General Kearny's men told me about his journey through the desert." His tone shifted back to annoyance. "All right, get Anthony in here to set the place a-right, and get the men to work on cleaning."

"Aye, sir," replied Fournier.[6]

CHAPTER 50

Discharged

On Tuesday morning, January 26, the crew of the *Stonington* was finishing the unpleasant task of emptying buckets and swabbing decks to remove all traces of the bodily fluids and solids that had accumulated in the spaces occupied by hundreds of passengers for just over two days.

"This is the second time I've been on this sort of cleaning detail," complained William Elliot while working in the lower deck. "I thought sheep in the boats was foul, but men in the ship is worse by far."

"Your next duty is another familiar one."

Elliot spun around to see Alanson Fournier, who had made his way to the lower deck to see how the work was progressing.

"Not another mess, sir, please," said Elliot.

"No, Elliot. We've received orders to collect water for the *Cyane.* You'll be out in the fresh air."

"That's a relief for certain, sir."

"I thought it might be more to your liking. Make your way up top as soon as you're finished here."

"Aye, sir," said Elliot enthusiastically, returning to his cleaning at a slightly faster pace.

Boats went out from the *Stonington* that Tuesday, towing rafts of empty casks that the crews filled with freshwater and then delivered to the sloop-of-war *Cyane.* The following Wednesday, the boats went out again, this time delivering water to the other warships moored in the harbor.

On Thursday, it was a boat coming from the USS *Congress* that caught Alanson Fournier's eye. As it drew closer, a familiar voice rang out.

"Good to see you made it back, sir," said the sailor.

"And it's good to be back—so far. What brings you here on this fine San Diego morning?"

"Well, sir, Lieutenant Livingston, he's been in charge of the ship since the commodore's been gone. Now that you're back, he'd like you to return an item that belongs to the *Congress*."

"What item is that?"

"That would be the anchor that we sent aboard the day you came back from your trip south and threw a gun overboard to hold your ship in place," replied the sailor with a grin.

"Ah," exclaimed Fournier, "that."

"Yes, sir."

"Tell the lieutenant I'll send a boat with the anchor presently."

"Right, sir. Good day to you."

"It's a day," Fournier replied as the boat rowed away.

He went to Hamley's cabin to inform him of Livingston's orders, then arranged for a crew to deliver the anchor.[1]

The next day, Friday, January 29, 1847, as Fournier was looking out over the sunny harbor from the starboard rail of the *Stonington*, he saw the boat from the *Congress* heading his way. When the boat was close enough, he could see that it was the familiar sailor.

"We've only one anchor left, good man," Fournier called out.

"Ah, sir," responded the sailor, "today I've something for you and all aboard your ship."

"Well, I don't see an anchor, so it can't be that Lieutenant Livingston doesn't want it after all."

"I believe it best if you would allow me to come aboard and present it to you directly, sir."

"Now you've got my curiosity," replied Fournier. "Climb on up."

When the sailor came onto the deck, he stood at attention and handed a folded piece of paper to Fournier.

"Shall I open this?"

"I believe so, yes, sir."

Fournier's jaw dropped when he unfolded the paper and saw the words "Honorably Discharged," printed in large letters. When he had regained his composure, he looked at the sailor and said, "I suppose this means our meetings are coming to an end."

"It seems so, sir. It's clear that congratulations are in order for you, your captain, and the crew. This ship has provided a wide range of services for the country. You've done yourselves proud."

"Thank you. I hope that you, too, are soon bound for home."

"Aye, sir."

Fournier extended his right hand, and the two men shook hands heartily. The sailor climbed down into his boat, waved, and headed back to the *Congress*. Alanson Fournier returned the wave and smiled as he walked toward the companionway to deliver the news to Captain Hamley.[2]

"So, we're finally heading home again, eh, Fournier!" exclaimed Hamley after reading the discharge paper. "Time to see to it that the ship is ready for the voyage. Call all hands to the deck. I'll give them the news and then you can put them to work."

"Aye, sir."

Fournier walked the length of the 'tween deck, calling out "All hands on deck" a few times. When he climbed the fo'c'sle companionway and stepped onto the upper deck, he called it once more, and then headed toward the mainmast where Hamley stood waiting for all to gather.

"Men," Hamley called out as he raised his right hand, "I hold in my hand our discharge from service to the US Navy. We're going home!"

Cheers broke out among the crew. Henry Thompson, the blacksmith, and Thomas Milnor, the carpenter, clapped each other on the back. The bilge-pump quartet of Davis, Jaques, Peters, and Harry shook each other's hands. The Comstock brothers looked each other in the eye and grinned as they rested their hands on each other's shoulders. Peter McDonnald turned to James Rice and said with a smile, "Well, Rice, this long shortcut of yours is finally moving in your direction."

"It's been a long four months, McDonnald," said Rice as he breathed a sigh of relief.

"We've got a lengthy voyage ahead of us," continued Hamley after motioning for quiet, "and part of it around the Horn, so I want this ship in top shape. Mr. Fournier will give you your duties. We'll sail when your work is done."

With that said, Hamley returned to his cabin, and Fournier began assigning tasks.

CHAPTER 51

Preparing for Sea

FOR THE NEXT WEEK OR SO, THE CREW OF THE *STONINGTON*, AS DIRECTED by Second Officer Fournier, worked through every aspect of the ship in order to ensure its seaworthiness. They checked all of the sails and all of the rigging on the three masts and the jibboom, making repairs where needed. They also checked the ship's machinery, such as the windlass and the steering linkage, to be sure they were in proper working order. On Sunday, January 31, in the midst of their ship's duty, the men got a preview of sorts. The sloop-of-war *Cyane* passed by on its way through the harbor and out to sea. *That'll be us, soon*, thought James Rice as he worked on a sail.[1]

While the work on board continued, Fournier sent men ashore on various tasks. Some gathered freshwater and provisions, including a bullock. Others returned a cable to the hide houses and then retrieved the ship's guns that had been used to fortify the town.

On Monday evening, February 8, Fournier made his report to Captain Hamley.

"Ship is all ready for sea, sir," he said, standing at the door of the captain's cabin.

"That's welcome news, Fournier."

"Aye, sir, welcome news indeed."

"You may take us out of the harbor tomorrow. We'll make for Callao as our first main port, with some stops along the way for provisions to last us until we get there."

"Aye, sir. Will that be all?"

"All for now," answered Hamley.

Fournier nodded and went to his quarters to lie down in his bunk and get some sleep, although the anticipation of what was in store the next day kept sleep at bay for a while.

On Tuesday morning, February 9, 1847, one hundred thirty-four days after first arriving in San Diego, Alanson Fournier called out, "All hands, heave short and set sail!"

The men sprang to their various stations, and as the *Stonington* made its way out of the harbor, they took a final look at what had for so long been their unexpected home port. Much had happened during that time, particularly their participation in a war that was now over in California but still raged on in Mexico. They watched as the town receded in the distance while they moved past the low, flat spaces of Coronado Island to larboard and the towering, steep cliffs of Point Loma to starboard.

By one p.m., they were six miles south of the Point and on their way to the Peruvian port of Callao, about four thousand miles to the southeast. They hoped there would be no more major interruptions to their voyage home.[2]

PART VIII

CHAPTER 52

Heading South

THE *STONINGTON* MADE ITS FIRST STOP FOR PROVISIONS ABOUT SEVENTY miles south of San Diego at Ensenada in All Saints Bay, a place with which the men were all too familiar, having delivered sailors, marines, and battalion members there to round up horses and cattle for the march to Los Angeles. Captain Hamley took two boats with minimal crews ashore on Wednesday, February 10, to see about getting wheat or corn as well as some meat. Second Officer Fournier and the rest of the crew waited on board, anchored in the bay.

When night fell without any sign of the captain or the others, Fournier became a bit concerned. He posted men on deck as lookouts and told them to alert him to any movement onshore. It was nearly two o'clock on Thursday afternoon when he received word that Hamley and the others were on their way back.

As the boats drew alongside the ship, Hamley shouted, "Haul this wheat aboard. We've got to head back to shore for a couple of bullocks."

The men on board hoisted the sacks of wheat that filled each boat and then the boats left to retrieve the meat. By the time they returned, the winds had picked up, making it difficult to hoist the boats and unload the butchered animals onto the ship. The gale abated around midnight, but by Friday morning it was again strong and accompanied by squalls. At one o'clock that afternoon, Hamley gave the order to heave anchor and make sail, and the ship continued on its way southward through weather that alternated from moderate to squally to dead calm. The unsettled weather, coupled with the captain's prolonged stay onshore, gave Fournier an uneasy feeling that caused him to pause for a moment before carrying on with his work.[1]

Several days later, on Wednesday, February 17, still unable to dismiss that uneasy feeling, Fournier went to Thomas Milnor's quarters.

"Milnor," he said to the ship's carpenter, "I want you to check the guns, make sure they're secure in their carriages, and that the carriage tackle is in good order. Take Miller and Desantos with you. Since they helped you with the installation, the three of you will know how the gear should be and will be able to put it a-right if it isn't."

"Aye, Mr. Fournier, we'll take care of 'em. Expectin' some sort of trouble, are ya?"

"I just want us to be ready if it does come."

"Aye, sir," said Milnor, and he headed off to find his helpers and get to work.

The *Stonington* was now about three-quarters of the way down the Baja peninsula, just past Punta Santo Domingo. Fournier decided it would be good to check the bilge, as it had been about a month since they had last done it. He put the regular quartet to the task, and at the end of their pumping and singing, they had gotten four hundred seventy strokes of water out of the ship, just a bit less than the five hundred that had resulted in Aaron Peters winning his wager on January 13. Fournier thanked the men for their work and went to make his report to the captain.

"That's a fair amount of water, Fournier," said Hamley. "Let's not wait as long for the next time," he said, a hint of reprimand in his voice.

"Aye, sir, I'll see to that."

"We're coming to the tip of the peninsula, and we'll be at San José in a matter of days," said Hamley, changing the subject. "I want to bring the ship in there for watering and provisions."

"Aye, sir. Anything else, sir?"

"No, Fournier, that's all for now. You may go."

Fournier exited and went to his own cabin, where he looked at his charts and plotted the course to San José del Cabo.[2]

Early Saturday evening, February 20, Fournier sighted San José about four miles in the distance, and at eleven p.m. he anchored the ship about a mile offshore.

The following morning, Hamley summoned Fournier to his cabin.

"I want you to heave short and bring the ship closer to shore, then send a raft of casks ashore for water. I'll be going ashore to see about bullocks and other provisions. Give the crew liberty after they've completed their work, and have them back by sundown."

"Aye, sir," said Fournier. He went up to the deck and called, "All hands!" He relayed the captain's orders, and the men reacted enthusiastically to the portion about liberty. Some of them worked quickly to assemble the raft while others tended to repositioning the ship, and in about an hour a boat was on its way to shore with the raft in tow.

"Give it all you've got, men," called Peter McDonnald as he pulled on his oar. "The sooner we get these casks filled and back to the ship, the sooner we get liberty for us and our fellows still aboard."

They reached the shore and met a local inhabitant who directed them to an estuary that was fed by a river that flowed fresh and clean from the nearby mountains. Ships had been using the estuary as a watering source for many years. McDonnald thanked the man and then said, "Let's go, boys." The boat forged ahead, and when it reached the proper spot, the men began the work of filling the casks.

Not long after the boat with the casks had left the ship, Captain Hamley set out for town in another boat with a small crew, including Antone Rogers as boatsteerer. Rogers accompanied Hamley into town while the others remained with the boat. In a little over an hour, the two men returned to the boat, and Hamley ordered his crew to row back to the ship.

"Fournier," said Hamley after getting aboard, "you'll need to send four boats to shore tomorrow. One of them is to get the provisions that I've arranged for, and another will get more water. The other two will transport eight passengers and their baggage."

"Aye, sir," said Fournier, a bit puzzled. "Passengers, sir?" he asked.

"Yes," replied Hamley impatiently. "We'll be landing them at San Blas or some other convenient place on the west coast of Mexico."

"Yes, sir," said Fournier, and he went to organize crews for the boats.

As he was speaking to men on deck about the next day's duties, he saw the cask-towing boat returning to the ship.

"All right, enough about tomorrow," he said. "You men get those casks stowed so you can get on with your liberty."

They responded with an almost simultaneous chorus of "Aye, sir!" and then got to work.

When they were finished, they joined the others on deck who were busy preparing to lower the boats.

"Listen here, men," called out Fournier. "You have the rest of the daylight to enjoy yourselves onshore. Mind, I expect you back on the ship at sundown."

The men nodded and raised their hands in acknowledgment, then got in their boats and headed off for a mixture of relaxation and merrymaking.[3]

Fournier watched the large orange ball that was the sun slide gradually downward to touch the long line of the horizon that separated the bright blue of the sky and the darker blue of the ocean. In the multicolored afterglow of the sunset, standing all by himself on the deck of the *Stonington*, he listened to the distinct sounds of the ship as it rocked to and fro on a gentle sea. The higher pitches of the tautening then loosening ropes, the lower tones of the spars and masts rubbing against each other, and the deep thrumming of the hull in the water combined to form a nautical orchestra improvising its own unique composition. Although his life as a whaleman was often stressful, uncomfortable, and dangerous, Fournier knew that this was where he wanted to be—this was where he was *meant* to be.

His soothing, contemplative moment could have lasted longer if not for the raucous sounds now coming from the returning boats. He watched over the rail as they approached and performed a silent roll call as the men stepped onto the deck. After the last boat had emptied, there was still one man he hadn't seen: ship's carpenter Thomas Milnor.

"Has anyone seen Milnor?" he asked.

The men shook their heads silently and made their way to their quarters.

Fournier went down to steerage to see if Milnor had already climbed into his bunk, but he was not there, either. Fournier knew it was important to maintain discipline, but he did not want to see the man flogged, which is what the captain was likely to demand in this case, considering the drunken incident back in December that had resulted in Milnor being put in chains. He decided to give the carpenter the benefit of the doubt and wait until the next day to see what would develop.

On Monday morning, February 22, Fournier dispatched four boats according to Captain Hamley's orders. The first one, to return with sacks of provisions and the meat of a slaughtered bullock; the last one back towed the raft of casks filled with freshwater. In between those arrivals came the two boats carrying what appeared to be nine passengers rather than the eight that Hamley had said would be coming aboard. Taking a closer look, Fournier could see that the ninth passenger was none other than the prodigal Thomas Milnor.

Fournier watched as Milnor came on deck and then proceeded to graciously assist each passenger out of the boat with their baggage, chatting pleasantly with each one. He did the same for the second group of four, before turning toward Fournier.

"Good mornin', sir," said Milnor cheerfully.

"Morning it is," replied Fournier, looking at the carpenter warily. "I'll speak with you after I get these passengers situated."

"Yes, sir," said Milnor with an emphatic nod.[4]

Fournier showed the eight men to the blubber room and explained that they could bunk there until the ship reached San Blas. Then he went aft to steerage, found Milnor in his bunk, and told him to meet him on deck.

"Milnor," began Fournier sternly, "there had better be a good explanation for you overstaying your liberty, because if there isn't, you're in for a certain flogging from the captain."

"Yes, sir," said Milnor. "You see, toward the end of the day, after a friendly encounter with a fair *señorita*, I just needed a little shut-eye before headin' back to the boats. Next thing I knew, roosters was crowin' and the sun was comin' up. I jumped out of that bed lickety-split and ran straight down to the shore, not knowin' if there'd be a boat for me to catch, and there they were, these eight people just standin' there, starin' out at the water and jabberin' with each other, their baggage all 'round 'em on the sand."

He continued in what seemed to Fournier to be an exaggeratedly earnest tone.

"I could see that they surely needed some assistance, so I walked up to 'em and asked if I could help. I was surprised to find that they were waitin' to come onto our ship, but weren't certain if they were in the right place or if they should go to a different location, and I decided that I would give 'em all the help that they might need," he said. "I saw the boats a-comin' and I let 'em know that they were ours. They relaxed, then, and we had a fine time of it. The boats pulled up and I helped 'em in. The other fellas helped, too, and after we got 'em all settled with their baggage, we shoved off, rowed to the ship, and you saw the rest. God's honest truth, sir, no disrespect meant, and my apologies for bein' late, but I think that it all turned out right in the end."

Fournier looked at Milnor skeptically, unsure if what he had just heard was a yarn meant to prevent harsh punishment or an honest account of genuine helpfulness. After pondering through a silence that was uncomfortably long for Milnor, Fournier decided that the truth was likely somewhere in the middle.

"Your explanation is good enough to avoid a flogging, Milnor, but don't push your luck."

"Yes, sir, thank you sir," said Milnor, and the two went off to their quarters, one hoping he had been believed, the other wondering if he had just been outmaneuvered.

By early Wednesday afternoon, February 24, the crew had finished loading provisions from shore.

"Haul anchor and set sail!" came the call from Alanson Fournier, and the canvas began to billow in the fresh breeze as the *Stonington* got under way for what would prove to be a most fateful stop at San Blas, about three hundred twenty-five miles southeast of San José del Cabo.[5]

CHAPTER 53

Fournier's Dilemma

THE *STONINGTON* PASSED BY THE ISLAS MARÍAS ARCHIPELAGO FRIDAY afternoon, February 26, and on Saturday afternoon, February 27, anchored off San Blas, a port that during the Spanish colonial era had served an important role in shipbuilding and as a point of departure for ships supplying goods to California.

After the crew had moored the ship securely, Fournier headed below, and on the way to his quarters, he heard Hamley call him to the captain's cabin.

"Yes, sir?" asked Fournier.

"Get a boat ready for me, Fournier. Don Pedro, one of the passengers, and I are going ashore."

"Begging your pardon, sir," responded Fournier with a concerned look, "but from what we know, it's only California where the war has ended. This part of Mexico is still enemy territory."

"Confound it, Fournier, I didn't ask for your analysis of the situation," Hamley shot back indignantly. "I ordered you to get me a boat!"

"Yes, sir," replied Fournier, a bit dejectedly.

"Put Rogers as boatsteerer, and give him four men that'll row with him. Don Pedro and I will be up presently, so get on with it," demanded Hamley.

"Aye, sir," replied Fournier, an uneasy feeling creeping into his gut.[1]

Hamley and Don Pedro came on deck and strode to the larboard boat where Antone Rogers was standing along with Joe Miller, Joe Catone,

John Williams, and an Italian, whose name Fournier did not know, that had come aboard before the ship left San Diego and was working his passage.

Rogers steadied the boat as the captain and Don Pedro climbed in, then he and his crew boarded, lowered the boat, and began the trip to shore. Fournier watched as the boat skirted to the left of where tall waves maintained their crests for what seemed an interminable distance before finally breaking fifty to one hundred feet beyond the white sands of the coast. The boat landed, and the crew dragged it onto the beach beyond the high-tide line. Fournier lost sight of them as Hamley led Don Pedro and the others into town.

Darkness eventually fell, with no sign of Hamley and those that had gone ashore with him. Thinking it imprudent to lay at anchor so close to enemy territory, Fournier decided to move the ship farther out into deeper water. There was an English frigate moored nearby, and Fournier thought he might be able to learn something from it regarding the state of affairs at San Blas. He arranged for a boat to take him to the frigate, and after identifying himself, he received permission to come aboard and speak with the ship's captain. Even though he had had his own misgivings about Hamley and the others going ashore, the news that he heard still stunned him. Upon entering the town, the captain and all those with him were arrested and immediately taken to prison by the Mexican authorities. Fournier expressed his appreciation for the information and then returned to the *Stonington*, went to his quarters, and pondered what to do next.[2]

At five a.m. Sunday morning, Alanson Fournier gave orders to haul anchor and set enough sail to patrol the waters off San Blas and watch for Captain Hamley and the others.

"Something's not right," said Peter McDonnald to James Rice as they stood on deck.

"What do you mean?" asked Rice.

"We'd normally just rest at anchor and wait for a boat to come back from shore. Instead, we've been tacking back and forth for hours now, as if there's some reason for not staying still."

"Any idea what that might be?"

"I'm not quite sure, but I have a feeling those two boats heading toward us from that English ship might give us a clue."

Rice looked out toward the frigate and saw two boats approaching the *Stonington*.

As they came alongside, Alanson Fournier stood at the rail to greet them. "What ho?" he called.

"Orders from shore, sir," said an officer in one of the boats. "The authorities demand that you hand over the other passengers. We are here to transport them. You've done well to get yourself under way as you have. The Mexicans are fitting up four gunboats for the express purpose of capturing your ship, so it would be best if you put some distance between yourself and this coast after we take those passengers."

Despite the many thoughts crowding his mind at the moment, Fournier focused and said to the officer, "Aye, sir, we'll have those passengers to you presently." He turned to find someone to send to the blubber room. "McDonnald," he called.

"Aye, sir."

"You and Rice fetch the passengers from below. Tell them to bring their belongings. Get them here quickly."

"Yes, sir," the two men responded.

"I guess that answers the question, McDonnald," said Rice as they hurried toward the companionway and the blubber room.

"Yes, but it creates even more questions—like what do we do about the captain? And what about our shipmates that went with him?"

"Fournier's in a tough spot."

"Toughest yet, I'd say," replied McDonnald.[3]

The two men reached the blubber room and told the seven remaining passengers to gather their belongings and follow them to the upper deck, where they led them to Fournier, who explained they were to board the awaiting boats. When some of them began to question him, Fournier responded firmly that the ship was in danger, and they were to follow his orders.

Once the boats were loaded, the officer looked at Fournier and said, "Godspeed."

"Thank you, sir," said Fournier in solemn response, and the boats rowed away toward shore.

Fournier gave orders to bring the ship farther away from shore, and then went to his quarters to consider his dilemma—whether to save the captain and the four crewmen with him, or save the ship.

Within an hour, he returned to the deck and called, "All hands!"

After the crew had gathered at the mainmast, Fournier spoke.

"Men, I have something of the utmost importance to say to you. Taking everything into consideration, including the danger of lying on an enemy's coast nearly unarmed, the imminent approach of their gunships, and the uncertainty of seeing an American man-of-war come to our aid, I have resolved that we should bear away for the port of Callao, as that was the port that Captain Hamley had intended to stop at. I regret leaving him and the men behind, but the safety of the ship and all of you renders such a proceeding necessary."

The men stood silently for a moment—although it seemed much longer to Fournier.

Then a strong voice broke the silence. It was Peter McDonnald. "Aye, sir," he said firmly, "you're in charge now."

Fournier stood tall and looked him straight in the eyes, then looked at the others. Taking a deep breath, he said, "Set sail for Callao, men."

The crew went briskly to their stations.

I am now the captain of these men, thought Alanson Fournier humbly, *and I pledge to get them home safely.*[4]

CHAPTER 54

Toward Callao

THE WEATHER ON MARCH 1 WAS CALM AS ALANSON FOURNIER BEGAN adjusting to his responsibilities as the lead officer of the *Stonington*. One of his first actions was to secure the belongings of the men that had been captured in San Blas. He gathered George Hamley's clothing and other possessions and, seeing there was no lock on Hamley's trunk, opened it to store the items. When he did, he saw Hamley's papers regarding ship's business and decided to separate them from the personal articles with the intent of delivering them to Williams & Barns, the New London firm that owned the ship. Fournier then had the other men's chests brought aft for safekeeping.[1]

For the next several weeks on the way to Callao, often through squally weather, the crew spent their time on various ship's duties, such as mending sails and repairing rigging. They also managed to do some fishing to add to the ship's provisions, and on one particularly productive day near the end of March, they caught forty albacore tuna.

There was one chore that a certain group of men was attending to with increasing frequency—pumping the bilge. The amount of water that the quartet was getting out of the ship each time they performed their task was causing Fournier's concern to grow. After making an inspection during the middle of April and determining that it was the decks that were leaking, he assigned work details to remedy the situation. One group picked oakum, which was the tedious, hand- and finger-wearying task of taking sections of old rope, separating each into individual strands, then rolling and twisting the strands together into wadded lengths that would be used as caulking. The other group used mallets and irons to tap the lengths of oakum into the seams between the planks. The men caulked as much as they could, knowing they would have to wait until they arrived in port at Callao to do a more thorough job. For now, though, they had to stop as much of the leaking as possible in order to keep the ship afloat and prevent water from damaging any items stored in the hold.[2]

Fournier called to Samuel Comstock, the younger of the two brothers.

"Comstock, take a group of men down to the hold and bring the bone up on deck to dry. We can't afford to lose what's left of our whale hunts."

"Aye, sir," replied Comstock, who soon had five men following him. Within fifteen minutes, they were passing long, dark slats up from the hold, through the main hatch, and onto the deck. The slats were five to six inches wide and less than half an inch thick, hairy on their edges, and they varied in length from five to eight feet. This "bone" was the baleen that had hung, one slat next to the other, from the upper jaws of the toothless whales they had caught. The baleen, made of the same substance as human fingernails and hair, was the feeding filtration system for those whales. They would collect enormous amounts of seawater in their mouths and then force it out through the baleen, leaving krill and other small creatures in their mouths to then swallow and digest.

The load of baleen was the only potentially profitable whaling material that remained aboard after emptying the ship of the whale oil when it had first arrived in San Diego. It was a valuable commodity to humans, prized for its strength and flexibility, utilized to make corset stays, buggy whips, parasol ribs, backscratchers, and many other items that in later centuries would be made from plastic. If the "bone" was going to be worth anything at all upon arrival in New London, it would have to be free of rot, so the men set about unbundling it and spreading it out on deck for drying and inspection. After discarding the slats that had rotted due to moisture, they carefully stored the dried pieces back in the hold.[3]

While dealing with too much sea- and stormwater coming into the ship, Fournier had to also confront the issue of not having enough freshwater on board.

He summoned the steward, Alexander Anthony, to the main cabin.

"I've checked, and we're down to about twenty-eight barrels of water on board. I want you to regulate each man's coffee allowance to one quart per day."

"Aye, sir," replied Anthony, who paused and then asked, "or should I say, 'Aye, Captain'?"

"No, Anthony, not yet. For now, 'Mr. Fournier' will be fine."

Anthony made his way to the cook's galley. On the way, he passed by the second officer's quarters, and could see that Fournier was still using that bunk, rather than occupying the captain's cabin. He nodded in approval, and went up the companionway.[4]

CHAPTER 55

A Closer Port

THE ADVERSE WINDS AND STRONG OCEAN CURRENTS OF THE PAST TWO months had made it difficult for Fournier to maintain a steady course toward Callao. As April drew to a close, water and other provisions were running low, and the ship was in need of repair. Taking all of that into account, Fournier recalculated the *Stonington*'s position and saw that the nearest port was now Valparaíso, about halfway down the coast of Chile. He went to the helmsman and gave him the new heading.

The weather seemed to agree with that change of course, as it was mostly fair for the next several days. Fournier took advantage of the mild conditions and gave orders to set full sail. He also had men bring the baleen on deck Saturday, May 1, for further drying, after which they bundled it and stowed it between decks.[1]

As the *Stonington* approached the Juan Fernandez Islands on May 8, about four hundred fifty miles west of Valparaíso, the welcome sight of two ships appeared on the horizon. It had been two months since the crew had seen anyone other than themselves, and they were eager to make some contact with at least one of the vessels. Fortunately for them, the *Mary*, out of Edgartown, Massachusetts, drew near enough for the crews to salute each other and for the officers to speak with one another. Fournier learned from Captain Pease that the *Mary* had been at sea for just over two years and had taken fourteen whales.

As the ships sailed apart from each other, the crew of the *Stonington* realized that although the US Navy had interrupted their pre-charted course, the time they had spent in and around San Diego had afforded them far more interaction with other people than they would have experienced had they simply continued on their regular, whaling way.[2]

Two days later, the weather began to change for the worse, and by nightfall on Tuesday, May 11, gale-force winds were blowing. Fournier shouted orders to the crew in order to be heard over the raging winds.

"Hand the main course! Close reef the mizzen topsail! Clew up the fore topsail and furl it! Clew up the main topsail and furl it! Furl the foresail and the mizzen topsail!"

The winds intensified through the night, and by six a.m. Wednesday it had become a heavy gale. Around eleven a.m. the winds moderated, and Fournier ordered the crew to set a double-reefed main topsail, which partially opened the canvas to the wind. The weather turned fierce in the afternoon, however, and at nine-thirty that evening, accompanied by thunder and lightning, the heavy gales were so powerful that they snapped the lines holding the main topsail and shredded the canvas to pieces. The sea was running in multiple directions, creating a jumble of crashing waves, and without sails to steady it, the ship was at its mercy. At eleven p.m. the weather finally abated, and the crew was able to set some sails to stabilize the ship.[3]

The situation with the ship's food supply continued to worsen. Alexander Anthony had already opened the last bag of flour, and upon inspecting the wheat supply, he found that it was too wet to grind into additional flour. Considering the leaking deck, the damaged rigging, and the dwindling supply of food and water, Alanson Fournier was growing more concerned about the *Stonington*'s circumstances.

On Thursday morning, May 13, however, his spirits rose. There had been a ship in the distance on the day that the storm began, and it had been heading in the same direction as the *Stonington*. That ship was now drawing close enough for Fournier to speak with its commander, and as it neared, it became clear that this was a most familiar ship—the USS *Congress*.

When the two ships were close enough to each other, Fournier called over for permission to come aboard. With that request granted, he had a boat bring him to the side of the *Congress*. Just as he was about to climb up to the deck, he heard a familiar voice say, "Well, sir, this is a switch, isn't it, you coming to my ship?" He looked above and saw that it was the sailor that had brought him so many messages in San Diego harbor, including the *Stonington's* discharge papers.

"As I live and breathe," exclaimed Fournier. "I thought I'd seen the last of you months ago."

"Ah, there's no escaping me, sir! I gather you're here to see the captain."

"Insightful as always."

"One of my many gifts, sir. Allow me to escort you to the captain's cabin," he said, and Fournier followed him.[4]

The sailor knocked on the cabin door.

"Yes, what is it?"

"Visitor from the nearby ship, sir," answered the sailor.

"Very well, show him in."

Fournier stepped into the cabin and saluted the tall, uniformed man with brown wavy hair that stood before him.

"Good day to you, sir," he said in an authoritative voice. "I am Elie Lavallette, captain of this ship. With whom do I have the pleasure?" he asked with a slight Southern drawl.

"Good morning, Captain. I am Alanson Fournier, second officer of the ship *Stonington*."

"Second officer? Why am I not speaking with your captain?"

"Captain Hamley was captured by the Mexicans at San Blas two months ago, sir. I am now the acting commander of the ship." It was the first time that Fournier had identified himself as such.

Lavallette put his hand to his chin. "Ah, yes, I remember hearing of that episode from an officer aboard the *Savannah*. Very unfortunate. What brings you here?"

"We've been through a tough stretch, sir, and are on our way to Valparaíso for repairs and provisions. We find ourselves in need of some supplies to hold us over until we arrive there."

After a brief discussion, Captain Lavallette agreed to sell one hundred pounds of bread and one pound of sail twine to Fournier, with the understanding that the Williams & Barns firm would make payment when they received the bill.

As the two men parted, Lavallette said, "I'll have some of my crew bring those supplies to your boat. Good luck to you in your voyages, sir, and in your new position as captain. It's a weighty responsibility, but you seem well suited to it."

"Thank you, Captain. Fair seas and following winds to you as well," said Fournier.

The sailor met Fournier outside the captain's cabin and brought him topside. As the bread and twine were being loaded into the boat, Fournier turned to the sailor and said, "Thank you for your hospitality, sir."

"A pleasure to have you aboard, sir."

Fournier climbed down to the boat and he and the sailor waved to one another as the boat returned to the *Stonington* with the much-needed supplies.

As the two ships sailed away from each other, Fournier and his crew hoped they would soon be safely anchored at Valparaíso.

Unfortunately, the weather caused yet another change of plans.[5]

CHAPTER 56

"Thundering Sky"

Fresh winds were blowing on May 14, and Alanson Fournier ordered all sails to be set to take advantage of the breezes. As the day progressed, however, so did the winds, until by early evening the ship was once again in the midst of a gale that continued into the next several days, bringing with it heavy rain, squalls, lightning, and very large waves. The crew shortened sails accordingly, but the sails were getting so worn and damaged that there were not enough of them in proper shape to hold the ship to windward. Over the past few weeks, the prevailing winds and currents had drawn the *Stonington* off course. Fournier decided to shift his heading and sail for Talcahuano, a Chilean port in the Bay of Concepcíon, two hundred seventy-five miles south of Valparaíso. If he had known that Talcahuano was an Indigenous word meaning "thundering sky," he might have had second thoughts about his decision.[1]

On May 19, the gale winds eased in the early afternoon, and by four p.m. the weather was clear enough that the cry of "Land, ho!" came from the lookouts. Fournier calculated that they were near the Itata River and set his course southward.

At seven o'clock the next morning, he stood on the deck and saw, eleven miles distant, Quiriquina, the island at the entrance to the Bay of Concepcíon.

"We're almost there, men. Make for the bay," Fournier called out.

At nine p.m. he gave the order to drop anchor. "We'll stay here for the night, then tomorrow morning we'll stand in closer to town," he said to his helmsman, Mark Comstock.

At five a.m. the next morning, Fournier called, "Haul anchor and set sail." He was anxious to reach Talcahuano, nestled at the western side of the bottom of the U-shaped bay. The weather, however, was still frustrating his efforts, now to the other extreme. Instead of fierce blowing winds, there was dead calm. It wasn't until five p.m., after the winds had reappeared, that Fournier was able to bring the ship within two thousand feet of shore and drop anchor in six fathoms of water.

It was Friday, May 21, 1847, and the *Stonington* was finally in safe harbor.

The custom house officer paid his visit, and then Fournier took a boat to shore to get some provisions. Before he left, he went to the ship's carpenter.

"Milnor," he said, "now that we're in port, I want to do a complete survey of the ship, and the first thing I want to take a look at is the rudder. I need you to unship it and hoist it onto the deck. Gather some men to help you. I'm heading into town for some provisions. I'll check on your progress when I return."

"Aye, sir," replied Milnor, "I'll see to it."[2]

The relief that Fournier felt upon reaching the safety of Talcahuano did not last as long as he would have liked. "Milnor," he called to the carpenter after directing the storage of the provisions that he had brought back from town, "how's that rudder?"

"I'll know better in tomorrow mornin's daylight, sir," Milnor answered. "From what I could see, the gudgeons are firm on the stern-post, but the pintles don't have much to hang on to. That rudder seems quite worn."

"All right, then," said Fournier. "I'll make a closer inspection in the morning when I begin my survey."

On Saturday, May 22, Fournier called "All hands!" and waited for the crew to assemble.

"Men," he began, once everyone had gathered at the mainmast, "I've completed my survey of this ship and have found it to be completely unseaworthy. The work that we did before leaving San Diego served us well for a time, but the rough weather we've had for the past few months has taken its toll. Some of the work will have to be redone, and there are some other repairs that we'll need to see to, such as rebuilding the rudder, before this ship is ready to go back to sea. This may take some time to accomplish, but I take it as my solemn duty, now that I am your captain, to get all of us back safely to our homes and families, and with your help, that is what I will do."

The men nodded in acknowledgment, and then Fournier continued.

"Knowing that we will be here in Talcahuano for a good number of days, and knowing that tomorrow is Sunday, I have decided that it will be a day of liberty. I'll need a few of the shipkeepers to remain on board with me, but they'll have their chance for liberty, too, eventually. You'll have from sunup to sundown, and I'll expect you to be ready to get to work first thing Monday morning. Is that clear?"

"Aye, sir," was the general response, with some of the men saying, "Aye, Captain" to Fournier for the first time. He dismissed them and went to his quarters to begin planning the work to be done.[3]

CHAPTER 57

Seaworthy

Alanson Fournier spent a good deal of time Sunday, May 23, formulating the work details that he would assign on Monday: rebuild the rudder; mend old sails and acquire new ones; obtain rigging chains and another anchor; caulk the decks; paint the ship; clean and coal-tar the ship's bends; repair the sheathing on the hull; fix the truss on the foremast; repair the quarter blocks and sling on the main yard. It was an extensive list, he knew, but all of it was necessary if they were to make their way around Cape Horn and then northward along South, Central, and North America to their home port in Connecticut.[1]

The next day, the men set about their tasks; all the men, that is, except for one—ship's carpenter Thomas Milnor. Fournier waited impatiently through Monday; then on Tuesday, while the work continued, he had a few men row him to shore in one of the boats. Not wanting to repeat the demoralizing effects that had resulted from bringing crewmen with him to retrieve Henry Thompson in San Francisco, he left the men to wait in the boat while he went to the local police station, where he explained the situation, gave a description of Milnor, and asked the police to bring him to the beach. Once they got him there, they would place him in a boat that Fournier would hire to bring him back to the ship. After providing the police with some monetary incentive to complete the task, he went back to the waterfront and hired the boat, then returned to his own boat, which brought him back to the ship. There he waited until, early that afternoon, a boat approached the *Stonington* carrying a lone passenger.[2]

Thomas Milnor stepped onto the deck, and before Fournier had a chance to say anything to him, Milnor said excitedly, "They've got it right, Captain, and it's gonna be just fine!"

"What the devil are you talking about, Milnor?"

"Why, the rudder, sir."

Fournier looked askance at him and asked, "What about the rudder?"

"Well, sir, when I woke up Monday mornin'—and I apologize mightily for havin' overslept again, sir—I skedaddled out of that house I was in and went straight to shore to catch a boat, but as I passed by the workplaces near the docks, I spotted what looked to be our rudder. I went over there and took a closer look, and sure enough, it was. I asked around 'til I got to the head of the crew and asked if I could see what they was plannin' to do for the rebuild. Darn good thing I did, too, 'cause it woulda been a complete mess if they'd continued with their second-rate ideas."

Fournier stood stiffly with his arms crossed, listening skeptically.

"I sat down with those fellas and went about settin' 'em straight. It took a while to convince 'em—into the night, in fact—but I finally got 'em to where they'll be doin' the work just as you'd want 'em to. Mornin' broke, and before I had the chance to get goin,' some police came along, brought me to the shore, put me on a boat, and here I am," concluded Milnor.

Fournier looked at him with a blank stare and then said coldly, "Get caulking."

"Aye, Captain," replied Milnor, "and like I said, that rudder's gonna be just fine."

The sounds of work filled the air for the next three weeks as the crew of the *Stonington* prepared the ship for sea, the most prominent being the constant tapping of mallets on irons from the men that were caulking the decks.

When Sunday, May 30, arrived, Fournier saw there was still much work to be done, so instead of granting liberty to the entire crew at the same time, he decided to allow one watch per day to go ashore, thereby ensuring that the work would continue at a steady pace.

By Wednesday, all of the men had spent a day off the ship—all, that is, except Thomas Milnor, whom Fournier had kept on board as both a precautionary and a disciplinary measure.

The following Saturday, June 5, when he granted another series of liberty, Fournier decided to give Milnor a chance to redeem himself and allowed him to go ashore with that day's group. When they returned to the ship that evening, Milnor was not among them. Fournier had his eye on the next group when they returned from their liberty on Sunday evening, but still no Milnor. He finally came back to the ship with the watch that had liberty on Monday, June 7.

The weather that evening was as stormy as Fournier's mood as he stood at the starboard rail and watched the men come aboard. Milnor stepped onto the deck, and before he had a chance to open his mouth to speak, Fournier let loose on him.

"This is the final straw, Milnor! You've no consideration for your fellow crewmen. The hours of lost work from you piles up on them, but you don't give that a thought. You focus too readily on your personal pleasure instead of pitching in with the rest of us to get this ship ready for sea. The crew shouldn't have to put up with that, and I won't stand for it. Hear me now and hear me well—you'll be waiting a long while before I even think of granting you another liberty!"

Milnor was about to reply with some of his cleverness, but Fournier's glare made him reconsider. Instead, he simply said "Aye, sir," in a subdued tone.

"Head to your quarters and be ready for a full day of work tomorrow," said Fournier sternly.[3]

The structural maintenance was nearly done, and it would soon be time to install the repaired rudder, fasten the newly made sails, and bring on board the provisions that would sustain the crew on the next portion of their journey back home.

There was one task to perform, however, before attending to all of that. Early on the morning of Thursday, June 10, it was time to "smoke out" the ship.

In order to eliminate the rats, fleas, and other unwelcome creatures that had found their way on board, the crew set contained fires in various spots within the ship, fueled by charcoal and laced with arsenic. After ensuring that all the men were outside on deck, they then closed off all hatches and entryways into the ship's interior. For the next several hours, the smoke from the fires permeated all areas belowdecks.

That evening, after the fires had burned themselves out, crew members reopened the ship, allowing the smoke and fumes to escape before going below to clear out the remains of the unwanted pests. They were now ready to take on the fresh supplies and prepare to go to sea—although they would end up taking on more than just supplies.[4]

The next day, three new men signed on for duty: Samuel Slocum and Samuel Ayling joined as seamen, and a Mr. Johnson joined as second mate. The following day, two more men came on board as passengers bound for New London, an arrangement that had been negotiated between Fournier and Mr. William Crosby, the American consul to Chile. All the while, the crew had been hard at work in the rigging, attaching sails and lines. They had also been transporting water, wood, and other provisions, as well as installing the rebuilt rudder.

It was time to inspect the ship.

On Tuesday, June 15, twenty-four days after he had found it unfit to sail, Alanson Fournier declared the *Stonington* to be seaworthy in all respects.

Two days later, he and his crew sailed their ship out from Talcahuano to continue their journey home. To get there, they would have to make their way around Cape Horn at the southern tip of South America, through what many considered the most treacherous waters in the world.[5]

PART IX

CHAPTER 58

Around the Horn

As the *STONINGTON* MADE ITS WAY SOUTHWARD ALONG THE COAST OF Chile in mid-June, 1847, the weather turned from calm to squally within a few days. It also grew significantly colder, with temperatures gradually nearing the freezing mark. They were heading toward Drake Passage, the point at which the South Pacific Ocean squeezes its way into the South Atlantic Ocean through a six-hundred-mile strait between South America and Antarctica. That width may have seemed somewhat large in other circumstances, but it was minuscule when dealing with the collision of the two largest oceans on the planet.

In addition to high winds and low temperatures, the turbulent sea currents combined to make this stretch of water a nautical nightmare. Captain Fournier and his crew were certainly glad they had seen to the repair of the rudder along with all the other work they had accomplished during their layover in Talcahuano. Without a properly functioning rudder, the *Stonington* would have been unable to maintain a steady course through the Passage, and it could have fallen victim to any number of catastrophes, from smashing against rocky outcroppings to capsizing amid pounding waves.[1]

About halfway between Talcahuano and Drake Passage, as the winds increased to gale force, one of the lookouts spotted what looked like sails on the horizon. It proved to be an English ship heading northward. The heaving sea caused the two ships' captains to avoid bringing their vessels close to one another, and the distance between them coupled with the howling wind prevented their having an extended conversation. As they exchanged basic greetings and details about their destinations, their ships gradually sailed away from each other, one of them having made it through the fierce challenge the other was heading straight into.[2]

For the next three weeks, the weather grew increasingly harsh. Squalls were relentless and eventually turned from rain to snow as the *Stonington* drew steadily closer to Cape Horn.

On Monday, July 5, the men could see the Diego Ramírez Islands, just eight miles to the east–southeast. This meant that the ship was only about seventy miles away from Cape Horn. Rather than worsen, however, the weather took an unexpected turn the next day and became calm, with a gently falling rain. The respite turned out to be a brief tease by Mother Nature, though, as the squalls returned the following day, the rain quickly turning to snow. Gale-force winds lashed at the rigging and raging waves pounded the hull. The crew went about their work in clothing that was drenched and had no chance to dry. They were pushing their bodies to the limit, working persistently in freezing temperatures. In the same manner, the tumultuous weather and the turbulent currents were pushing the *Stonington* to its limits, putting to the test all of the work that the crew had done in Talcahuano. The men wondered, hoped, trusted that they had done enough to make it through the Passage and around the Horn.[3]

The days of formidable weather wore into a third week. Monday, July 12, brought with it a ferocious snow squall. Earlier that day, the crew had spotted a ship off to the north–northwest. The sight had provided a bit of reassurance, a sense that they were not alone in this dangerous place. The blinding fury of the storm soon enveloped them, however, and they lost track of their momentary companion.

After six more days of continuously stormy weather, the beleaguered crew of the *Stonington* saw an even more reassuring sight—George Island and Porpoise Point, the southern portion of the Falkland Islands. Captain Fournier had brought them around the Horn. The entire crew had survived the ordeal without suffering any casualties or significant injuries. The ship was intact, the only damage being a torn sail that was now repaired.

Fresh breezes and fine weather were the favorable conditions that greeted the *Stonington* on Monday, July 19. Captain Fournier welcomed the improved situation by ordering additional sails to be set, and the crew went about their work with a certain lightness in knowing they were bringing themselves closer to home.[4]

The weather remained favorable into the following day, but as Tuesday drew to a close, so did those pleasant conditions. Over the next five days, the winds grew stronger and eventually became gales. Clear skies gave way to clouds that brought with them rains that intensified from gentle showers to pelting downpours. Waves that had provided a rolling cushion for the ship to glide upon soon developed into ever-higher obstacles to be mounted.[5]

CHAPTER 59

Struck

P ETER M C D ONNALD WAS HIGH IN THE RIGGING WHEN THE LIGHTNING struck. It was Monday, July 26, and fierce winds of up to sixty miles an hour were churning the South Atlantic Ocean one thousand miles northeast of the Falkland Islands, pushing the wooden whaleship mercilessly through skin-stinging rain squalls, up the sides of enormous waves that threatened to swallow the ship, only to send it charging down the steep back side of each towering wall of water before shoving it up the next. Thunderclaps boomed and echoed so often and intensely that it seemed as though the entire night sky was about to break apart and collapse on the heaving ship. Although every man's ears were pounding under the assault of the noise, there was no mistaking the sound they heard at McDonnald's position.

The singularity of the sound was so startlingly loud and concentrated, so forceful and commanding, that it overpowered everything else that was flooding the crew's hearing and made them look immediately toward the spot where it had happened—the sling on the mainmast that was nearly sixty-five feet above the deck of the ship. Peter McDonnald had been standing next to that spot. His feet had been positioned on an arc of rope suspended three feet or so under the yard from which was hanging the main topsail, a broad expanse of canvas measuring nearly six hundred square feet. As the ship continued its violent undulations amid the raging storm, McDonnald, James Rice, and three others were perched precariously at the yard, their feet on the rope, their arms over the rounded wooden beam, their hands beginning the strenuous task of gathering up the sail to prevent it from filling with wind and hurtling their ship uncontrollably through the sea.

Then it happened—a blinding bright light, a piercing explosive sound, and McDonnald began to fall.

Rice yelled "McDonnald!" and grabbed hold of him to keep him from plunging overboard into the dark, roiling sea that was nearly eighty feet below them.

Captain Fournier reacted quickly to the perilous scene above him as he stood on the deck.

"Get a rope around him!" he shouted. "You in the rigging, get in place to guide him down, keep him from swinging out!"

Rice held on tightly to his unconscious friend, saying to him repeatedly "I've got you, I've got you" as the men repositioned themselves. One of them made his way over and fastened a rope around McDonnald.

"Easy, now," Fournier called out as they began lowering the limp body of their crewmate. At each level of the rigging, men reached out and held McDonnald steady, focused on keeping him centered over the deck despite the pitch and yaw of the ship in the turbulent sea. A small group of men stood on deck looking upward, waiting for the still-unconscious McDonnald to come within reach. As he did, they cradled him to the deck.

"Take off that rope and bring him to the cabin," said Fournier, "and be gentle. He looks to be hurt badly."

The men eased McDonnald onto the table in the cabin. Even in the dimness of the lantern light, it was clear that the lightning strike had caused severe and life-threatening injuries. Thomas Milnor and Alexander Anthony positioned themselves at McDonnald's head and feet in order to protect him from falling onto the floor or being jostled too much by the movement of the ship. Alanson Fournier began the delicate process of removing McDonnald's charred, wet clothing and examining the damage to his body. What they saw made them wince and recoil. McDonnald's head and torso were covered with terrible burns, ranging in color from bright pink to deep, dark red. Most of them were massive blotches, while others actually had a defined look about them that resembled the patterns of snowflakes. The burns extended down his left leg and beyond the top of his boot. When Fournier removed the boot, he saw two small round holes—one in the bottom of the boot, the other in the ball of McDonnald's left foot. They could now see the full and fierce passage that the lightning had made through his body from head to toe.

Fournier turned to Joseph Frank and David Redding, the other men that had helped Milnor and Anthony carry McDonnald, and said, "You two check the bed in this cabin and make sure it's ready for him. He's going to need all the comfort he can get."

"Aye, sir," they responded, and when they entered the bedroom, they were surprised by the condition of the bed. They returned to the group, and Redding said, "You must be a light sleeper, Captain. That bed looks like it hasn't been slept in at all."

"You're right," said Fournier, "it hasn't," as he began applying salve and bandages to McDonnald's burns. "I've been keeping to my old quarters. Just didn't seem right to move in here."

The four men looked at Fournier, then at each other, nodding in silent admiration.

"Let's get him into that bed, shall we," said Fournier, when he was finished dressing the wounds.

They lifted McDonnald gingerly, and as they laid him on the bed, he began to moan. They gazed down at their shipmate, then into each other's eyes. Without needing to speak a word, they bowed their heads and, in their own individual ways, joined together in silent prayer that this man might somehow recover from his awful calamity, or at the very least, that he would not have to suffer long.[1]

CHAPTER 60

The Vigil

JAMES RICE MADE HIS WAY BELOW AS SOON AS THE NEXT WATCH CAME on duty. He went straight to the captain's cabin and knocked on the open door. Fournier emerged from the bedroom and motioned for him to come in.

"Where's McDonnald, sir?" asked Rice.

Fournier gestured for Rice to speak softly. "In here," he said quietly.

Rice walked in slowly and stood at the side of the bed where his friend lay half-conscious and writhing in pain. He looked at the extent of the wounds, and his eyes welled with tears. Standing behind him, Fournier could see his shoulders shaking as he sobbed silently. Fournier waited, and when Rice was still, he said solemnly, "The next several days will be critical for him. He'll need someone to—"

"I'll be here," said Rice, wiping his face.

"You're a good friend, Rice."

"And he's my good friend, sir."

"All right, then," said Fournier, "I'll be going to my quarters. You can find me there if you need me."

"Your quarters, sir?"

"Yes, right across the way."

Rice looked at him for a moment, then said, "Aye, sir. Thank you, sir."

For the next three days the weather continued to be severe, as did Peter McDonnald's condition. James Rice stationed himself at his friend's bedside throughout most of each day. During the moments when

McDonnald was somewhat lucid, Rice would lift his head with one hand and put a cup of water to his mouth with the other. McDonnald would take a few sips and then lapse back into semiconsciousness.

Alanson Fournier checked on McDonnald's condition each day, and was growing increasingly concerned. Late Friday afternoon, July 30, he spoke with Rice in the main room of the cabin. "His wounds smell very bad, and he's had no passage through him since he was struck. I'd like your help in changing his dressings, and then I'll give him a bit of medicine, perhaps some powdered rhubarb, to stimulate his bowels."

"Aye, sir," said Rice, and the two men got to work. Fournier peeled away the old dressings and dropped them in a bucket, then applied salve before taking the fresh bandages from Rice and laying them over the wounds. They grimaced at the sight and stench of the burned skin, and as they worked, their manipulations drew McDonnald into consciousness.

"What are you doing? Where am I?" said McDonnald groggily as he winced in pain.

"It's all right, McDonnald," replied Rice, happy to hear his friend speak again. "We're helping you."

"It hurts," said McDonnald.

"I'm sure it does," said Fournier. "That lightning hit you hard."

"That what?" said McDonnald. "What do you mean?"

"You were hit by lightning," answered Rice.

"When?" asked McDonnald incredulously.

"Three days ago," replied Fournier.

While McDonnald stared at them in disbelief, the two men finished re-dressing the wounds while they explained what had happened.

"These burns will take some time to heal," said Fournier, "but we've got to get your systems moving before you start eating again. I've got a mixture I want you to drink that ought to help." He put the cup to McDonnald's mouth. After he drank it down, McDonnald said, "I feel cold, in here," pointing to his chest, "and in my feet."

"I'll get you some more covers," responded Rice. He returned with more blankets, laid them over his friend, and said, "It's good to have you back."

"I don't know where I was," replied McDonnald, "but I'm glad I'm here—I think."

"I'll look in on you again tomorrow," said Fournier. "Rice will be here if you need any assistance." Then he went to his quarters.

Rice stayed in the bedroom for a few minutes, and after making sure that McDonnald was as comfortable as possible, said, "You rest up, now. I'll be in the other room. Call me if you need anything." McDonnald nodded and was about to close his eyes when he said, "Rice?"

"What is it?"

McDonnald looked straight at him and held his gaze for a moment. "Thank you," he said in a most sincere tone.

"Of course."

McDonnald closed his eyes, and Rice went to the couch in the main room where he had been sleeping for the past few nights. He sat down, and offered up a prayer for his friend's recovery.[1]

When Fournier checked on him the next evening, McDonnald had still not passed anything through his bowels.

"I'm going to give you a dose of calomel and jalap, see if that'll help move things along," said Fournier.

"Aye, Captain," replied McDonnald, "whatever you think's best."

Fournier gave him a spoonful of each laxative. "If you feel the start of any rumblings, there's a bucket here for you to use," he told him. "Don't fret if you can't get there in time. The extra linens underneath you are there for that purpose. I'll check on you again tomorrow to see if there's been any progress."

"Thank you, sir," said McDonnald, and Fournier left to go topside, concerns building in his mind over McDonnald's condition, and the fact that his body might be shutting down. When he reached the deck, he could feel the gentle breezes and light air, and hoped the improved weather was a good sign for McDonnald.[2]

The weather on Sunday, August 1, continued mild, with light, fresh breezes. The crew went about tending to ship's duty, but in the backs of their minds, their thoughts were of their crewmate, hoping that he would somehow pull through. Each time Fournier passed by them, they asked questions like "How's McDonnald?—How's he doing today?—Any better, sir?" to which Fournier would calmly reply, "He's holding steady."

Later that day, Fournier went to the cabin to see if the laxatives had spurred any action.

"Anything?" he said to James Rice as he entered the cabin.

"No, sir, not a thing."

Fournier entered the bedroom. "The medicine I've given you hasn't done what I had hoped it would," he told McDonnald, "and your recovery depends on regular, smooth passage."

"Like the ship, I suppose?" asked McDonnald wryly.

"You might say so, yes," replied Fournier, happy to see that McDonnald's sense of humor was still intact. "Since the medicine entering through your mouth doesn't appear to be working," he continued, "I'm going to shift to the other end of your system."

McDonnald's eyes widened, and Fournier quickly said, "Don't worry, it won't hurt; it's just a clyster. I'll pump some fluids into your rear end and see if we can get them to flush you out."

"If you think it'll help," said McDonnald tentatively.

"That's the goal, McDonnald," said Fournier reassuringly, "that's the goal."

Fournier administered the clyster, and told McDonnald that Rice would be nearby if he needed him. "I'll be back soon to check on your progress."

"Aye, sir," said McDonnald as he lay on his side and waited.[3]

Fournier returned to the cabin in a little over an hour, and as he entered, he detected a different but familiar odor. He looked into the bedroom and saw McDonnald lying on his back and Rice kneeling on the floor next to him.

"Praying, Rice?" Fournier asked hesitantly.

"No, sir," said Rice, turning his head slightly to face Fournier, "I've done quite a bit of that already. This time, it's cleaning."

"I thought I recognized that smell," replied Fournier. "Good work, McDonnald!" he said encouragingly.

"A bit of smooth sailing, eh, Captain?" said McDonnald with a smile.

"Yes," said Fournier. "Now let's take a look at those dressings, get them changed out."

Rice finished cleaning and then made room for Fournier, who began gently peeling the old bandages while Rice fetched new ones.

"McDonnald," said Fournier as he continued, "your body's cooperating in more ways than one. These wounds are healing fast."

"Happy to hear it," said McDonnald, flinching a bit as Fournier removed a dressing.

"Rice," said Fournier, "go find Anthony. Have him prepare some broth for our patient. I believe he's ready to start eating again. What do you say to that?"

"Yes, sir—I'm hungry, indeed," answered McDonnald.

Rice left, and when he returned, Alexander Anthony, the steward, was with him, carrying a bowl of warm broth.

Fournier had just finished dressing the wounds, and made room for Anthony to enter.

"You've got a visitor, McDonnald," said Fournier.

Anthony stepped into the bedroom and said, "It's good to see you, mate."

"It's good to be seen."

Rice helped McDonnald sit up a bit, then he took the bowl from Anthony. "Best I help you with this," he said, bringing a spoonful to McDonnald's mouth.

"Mmm," said McDonnald, enjoying his first bit of food since being struck. "Thank you," he said to Anthony.

"My pleasure," replied the steward. "The crew's been asking about you since you've been down here. They'll be happy to hear you're improving."

McDonnald nodded as Anthony left.

Fournier looked into the bedroom and said, "Enjoy your banquet, and keep resting."

"Aye, Captain," said McDonnald between spoonfuls.

Fournier went to his quarters with a sense of relief and optimism. He, too, was happy to see that McDonnald, who had been so near death, had made a turn for the better.[4]

CHAPTER 61

Toward the Equator

THROUGHOUT THE FIRST TWO WEEKS OF AUGUST, PETER MCDONNALD continued to improve remarkably, and by Saturday, August 14, his recovery was nearly complete.

"You're a lucky man, McDonnald," said Alanson Fournier when he looked in on him that day, "and a tough one at that. You could have easily ended up in the deep if Rice here hadn't latched onto you so quick. You're a fast healer, too. From the look of these wounds, you might even be ready for some light duty by the time we reach the equator."

"Well, Captain," said McDonnald, "getting the royal treatment from you and Rice sure helped move things along in the right direction."

Fournier chuckled, and then said, "Rice, you've done a fine job of nursing your friend back to health. I believe he's well enough for you to resume your duties. I'll still depend on you to keep an eye on him, though, and see to it that he doesn't get himself into any trouble."

"I'm ready to oblige on both counts, Captain," replied Rice.

"All right, then," said Fournier. "I believe it's time for the two of us to head up top. McDonnald, I'll have Anthony bring you some grub."

"Thank you, sir."

"I'll see you later, McDonnald," said Rice.

"Is that a threat or a promise?" asked McDonnald.

"Both!" answered Rice as he left the cabin.[1]

As Peter McDonnald was making progress, so, too, was the *Stonington*. The ship had made its way into the trade winds that were now propelling it in a north–northwesterly direction. The crew had continued to repair the damage done to the sails by squalls and storms, including the one that had stricken McDonnald. The weather had settled into a stretch of clear skies and bright sunshine, and other ships were visible to the north and south.

On Thursday, August 19, came the cry of "Land, ho!" and the next day the crew could see a lighthouse about fifteen miles to their north-west. The ship was off the coast of Pernambuco at the westernmost tip of Brazil. In just over five hundred miles they would be at the equator. On Saturday, August 21, they saw more signs of life other than themselves in the form of several catamarans and a schooner. While these conditions and sightings lifted the spirits of the men, what gave them the greatest lift was when they saw a familiar figure they hadn't seen for nearly a month walk onto the deck.

"McDonnald!" shouted William Fisher. "You finally done with your beauty rest?"

"Just about. You think it helped?"

"Not much," yelled Nelson Davis.

"You're still ugly as ever," cried Joseph Frank.

"Ah," said McDonnald with a smile, "it's good to be back among friends!"

The crew watched him doing light tasks as they went about their work. They could see that his movements were slower and a bit stiff, but when they considered the severity of his injuries, their admiration for him increased substantially. They felt a sense of relief and a renewed determination to complete their voyage home.[2]

CHAPTER 62

Heated

As the ship drew nearer to the equator, the combined rise in temperature and increase in humidity created uncomfortable conditions for the crew. To be belowdecks provided a chance to avoid the direct rays of the sun, but the cramped quarters and stillness of the air were oppressively stifling. When on deck, the exertion involved in even the slightest task resulted in great amounts of sweat and fatigue. At night, the sun was out of the sky, but its effects had little chance to dissipate before it rose again the next morning.

The *Stonington* crossed the equator during the night of Monday, August 23. The sweltering weather persisted, and tempers were on edge as the men tried in vain to escape the effects of the heat.

On Friday afternoon, August 27, the air became violent, and so did one member of the crew.

A squall arose at four p.m., and its fierce winds coming directly out of the northwest began to fill the sails at their fronts, with the potential to take the ship hard aback. This was a dangerous situation that could ultimately cause serious damage to the ship, including ripped sails, broken yardarms, and even snapped masts. More immediately, it meant that the ship would lose steerage way because it was not moving forward fast enough for the forces on the rudder to have any effect. The *Stonington* would essentially be out of control.[1]

Captain Fournier responded quickly and decisively, shouting, "Brace around the yards!"

The crew began moving into position to haul on the lines that would turn the sails away from the wind.

Fournier noticed one man who hadn't followed the order. It was George Hopkins, who had been a reliable member of the crew since the voyage began just over four years ago. On this day, however, the accumulated stresses of his duties combined with the intense, prolonged heat had taken their toll. He was about to snap.

"Hopkins," yelled Fournier, "turn to!"

"No," answered Hopkins bluntly as he walked aft, past Fournier.

"Bear a hand, Hopkins!" shouted Fournier.

Hopkins stopped, turned, said emphatically, "No!" and then continued walking away.

The rest of the crew was struggling to maintain control of the ship, and they needed every man to do his part. Fournier strode up behind Hopkins to stop him, grabbing him by the back of his collar.

Hopkins spun around and, with both hands, latched onto the front of Fournier's shirt and began trying to throw him down onto the deck, tearing his shirt in the process.

Antone Joseph, the mate, stepped in and pulled the two grunting men apart.

"I'll flog you for this!" yelled Fournier.

"Go ahead!" Hopkins retorted.

"Don't do that to him!" cried some of the men.

"Knock off duty," Fournier said angrily to Hopkins, and pointed aft.

Hopkins stood breathing heavily, then turned in the opposite direction and went into the fo'c'sle.

Joseph went to the companionway and called down, "Hopkins, you come up!"

"I won't," replied Hopkins.

Fournier came behind Joseph and also called below. "Hopkins, come up on deck."

"I can't," answered Hopkins.

By this time, the squall had abated and the crew had secured control of the ship. Fournier called, "All hands, aft!" and the men gathered between the main- and mizzenmasts.

"Listen carefully, men," began Fournier. "There's one thing I take more seriously than anything else, and that's the safety of this crew. It is my responsibility to see to it that each of you pulls your weight for the sake of all of us. If one person decides not to do their job, it means there's much more of a chance for something to go wrong. We've all had short tempers lately, and I lost mine when Hopkins refused my order. However, I cannot and will not excuse behavior such as his, and that is why I will punish him with a flogging."

A small group of men responded immediately with statements such as "No, Captain, do not flog him!" and "Not that—you can't!," the same ones who had spoken out after Antone Joseph had broken up the fight and Fournier had threatened to flog Hopkins.

Fournier looked at them sternly and was about to reprimand them when he paused and detected a particular earnestness in their pleas.

"What makes you say so?" he asked.

Henry Thompson, the blacksmith, answered plainly. "He's just not right, Captain."

Samuel Ayling and Samuel Slocum, who since signing on in Talca-huano had become friendly with Hopkins, joined in.

"Something's wrong with him, sir," said Ayling.

"His constitution is off-kilter," said Slocum, "and I fear a flogging might actually kill him."

What those men said made Fournier pause. He was, as he had said, genuinely concerned with the well-being of his crew, and if, as these men were saying, Hopkins was suffering from some malady, then he believed it was his responsibility to address it appropriately. After thinking a bit longer, Fournier said to the now-quieted crew, "I appreciate what you've told me, and I will take it into consideration when making my decision on this matter. For the moment, Thompson, I want you to check on Hopkins and bring him some water. He may very well be in need of it. The rest of you, head back to your duty, and be on the lookout for any further squalls."

"Aye, sir," responded the men, and they returned to work as Fournier left and went to his quarters.

Alanson Fournier was by nature disinclined to use harsh means of discipline, and he was well aware of the tense and threatening atmosphere that a flogging could create among a crew. He had heard the stories about ship's captains that had seen it as their responsibility to employ severe corporal punishment to enforce discipline, only to find that it resulted in a crew that grew steadily more uncooperative and prone to mutiny.

As he sat in his room and pondered the situation, he knew he had to do something to address what had amounted to a physical assault on the captain. If he let it go unanswered, then he might project a weakness that could lead to more such incidents. If what the men had said about Hopkins was true, however, then he had to accept that Hopkins's actions were the result of his condition and not intentionally mutinous.

He decided he needed to see Hopkins himself before reaching any conclusions, and so he made his way forward to speak with him.

When he reached the fo'c'sle, Fournier saw Henry Thompson speaking with George Hopkins, who was lying in his bunk.

"Thank you, Thompson," said Fournier. "I'd like to speak with Hopkins alone, please."

"Aye, sir," replied the blacksmith. "Rest easy, now, Hopkins," he said as he left, to which Hopkins nodded.

"How are you feeling, Hopkins?" asked Fournier.

"Better, sir. Captain?"

"Yes?"

"I want to apologize, sir. I was wrong to act the way I did. I'm ashamed of it, and I know there's got to be some punishment that comes from it. Whatever it is, I'll take it like a man."

Fournier looked at him for a moment, then said thoughtfully, "I accept your apology, Hopkins. The way you acted was not like your normal self. I understand that. What you did was not only to me, however. You put the safety of all the men in jeopardy, and I believe you owe some sort of apology to your crewmates as well. Perhaps not so much in words as in actions. I want you to give some thought as to what form that will take.

"For now, you are to remain here in your quarters until further notice. I'll instruct one of your crewmates to bring food to you, and they'll keep you watered as well." He paused and then asked, "Have I made myself clear?"

"Yes, sir."

"I'll leave you to your thoughts," said Fournier, and he made his way back to his room.

By the end of that tumultuous day, word of Fournier's decision had reached the entire crew, and they reacted with a mixture of relief and respect. Peter McDonnald, who a month after being struck so savagely by lightning was now back to his usual quarters in the fo'c'sle, summed it up best as he spoke with a large group of men gathered there that evening.

"That was a tough one," he said in his deep, contemplative voice. "There are some that would have taken the route of saving face—make an example of Hopkins and just flog him—and end up making matters worse. Not Fournier. He sees the whole picture. Sees long term. Cares about more than just himself. Not many captains like him. Wish there were more of 'em."

The men nodded and grunted their agreement.

George Hopkins, still in his bunk, lay quietly and gave serious thought to what Fournier had said about an apology to the crew.[2]

CHAPTER 63

Forward Movement

AFTER A FEW DAYS OF UNSETTLED WEATHER THAT BROUGHT A MIX-
ture of sun and squalls to the *Stonington*, August 31 began with clear
skies, and remained that way.

Captain Fournier took advantage of the pleasant conditions.

"Men," he called to the watch on duty that Tuesday, "let's bring the
whalebone out of the hold. It's been a few months since we last checked
it, and we'll need it to be in good shape if we're to get anything for it in
New London."

The men brought the baleen onto the deck, loosened the bundles,
and spread them out to receive the sunlight.

"How does it look, Larkins?" Fournier asked one of the men.

"Good, sir. I don't see any pieces with rot."

"Let's give it a good long dry to keep it that way."

"Aye, Captain," replied Larkins, and the baleen remained on deck for
several hours until the next watch came on duty, bundled it, and returned
it to the hold.

On Thursday, September 2, the *Stonington* was eight hundred fifty miles
due east of the Caribbean island of Barbados, with New England just two
thousand miles away to the northwest. If all went well, the ship could be
sailing into New London harbor within a few weeks.

"All hands!" called Alanson Fournier, and the crew assembled at the
mainmast.

George Hopkins, who was still confined to his quarters, remained in his bunk.

"Men," said Fournier, "we're drawing closer to home. This ship has seen some special duty during this voyage, and it ought to look special when it sails into the river. Let's get started today on a fresh coat of paint. Once that's done, we'll coal-tar the boats and give them some new paint, too. Milnor, you take a careful look all around, and if you see anything that needs patching or repair, get some men to help you tend to it before it gets painted. That's all for now. Time to get to work!"[1]

The men dispersed and settled into their tasks.

Two days later, on Friday, September 3, George Hopkins rejoined the crew on deck after his weeklong confinement to quarters. His shipmates welcomed him back without any mention of the incident that had caused his confinement, and he fell right in to the daily routine.

As the days progressed and the work continued, however, the crew noticed something different about Hopkins. Each time his watch duty ended, he would stay on and continue working for a while with the next group. He would also join in on the work that was happening well before his own watch was due to begin. The crew weren't the only ones that noticed Hopkins's new habits. Alanson Fournier had spotted them as well, and understood them precisely.

One particular day, as Hopkins was heading to work with the watch before his own, he saw Fournier standing nearby. He stopped, looked calmly at Fournier, and said, "Captain." Fournier returned his gaze and said just as calmly, "Hopkins." It was a simple acknowledgment that both men understood keenly, and without either of them needing to say anything further, Hopkins continued walking and went on duty before his watch began.

Several days of clear weather, interrupted briefly at times by some small midday squalls, enabled the crew to make significant progress in their tasks.

"Fine work, men," said Fournier as he made his rounds one day. "The ship looks near brand new."

On Friday morning, September 10, about six hundred miles northeast of Puerto Rico, as they were preparing to tar the starboard boat, the crew saw a sail to the north. Drawing nearer, they could see that it was an English barque, the *Carmelus*. The captains spoke with each other once the ships were close enough, and they were amused to learn that one of them was heading to London, and the other, to New London.

On the following day, another sail appeared, this time to the east. Fournier maintained his course, however, rather than make contact with this ship, and it was well that he did. The waters were becoming busy, and unfortunately, so was the weather.[2] It was the middle of the Atlantic hurricane season, and knowing a significant storm could destroy the ship and all those aboard, Fournier realized he had to get the *Stonington* north of the Caribbean region as soon as possible.

Within two days, the weather turned rough. Late Monday, September 13, the winds that had been coming from the east throughout the day grew stronger, eventually bringing with them a severe rain squall that included thunder and lightning. The situation was eerily similar to that fateful day nearly two months ago that had almost cost the life of Peter McDonnald. Fournier was determined to do all he could to take them safely through this and any other storms that might come their way.

Squalls continued to swirl intermittently around the *Stonington* for more than a week as Fournier guided the ship northward between the island of Bermuda and the Atlantic coast of the United States. Every other day, as they passed by Florida, Georgia, the Carolinas, and Virginia, the crew could see at least one other ship in the distance to the south, journeying in the same general direction in which they were headed.[3]

CHAPTER 64

Home Port

ON SATURDAY, SEPTEMBER 25, THE CREW OF THE *STONINGTON* COULD sense a change in the behavior of the ship. For the past few days, beginning about three hundred miles off the coast and moving through the latitude of North Carolina into that of Virginia, it had seemed as though no matter how they set the sails to catch the wind, it was the water that was controlling their direction. When they moved into the latitude of New Jersey, however, there was a feeling of release, of having broken free from some restraint. The *Stonington* had just made its way out of the grip of the Gulf Stream, a very strong warm-water current originating in the Gulf of Mexico that could have led the ship toward Europe if Captain Fournier had not maintained his northward course. Now that they were clear of that obstacle, the route to New London would be fairly straightforward, as long as the weather held out.[1]

Early Sunday morning, September 26, in the midst of strong winds and thick clouds, Captain Fournier calculated that the ship was getting close to Long Island, New York.

"Jennings," he called to one of the crew, "give us a sounding."

John Jennings grabbed a line with a large lead weight attached at one end. Giving himself clearance, he held the coiled line with one hand while using the other hand to hurl the weighted end out into the water. The lead sank quickly and pulled the line down with it until it hit the bottom, at which point the line went slack and Jennings began hauling it back up, noting the marks that were in the line at every fathom, or six feet, along the way. When the line tightened, he knew that he had found the depth and called out, "Mark fifty-five!" The ship was now in three hundred thirty feet of water.

"We'll do another sounding in a few hours, see what we've got then."

"Aye, Captain," replied Jennings.

Four hours later, at six a.m., Fournier gave the order, and Jennings flung the lead weight up and over the side. As before, the indentation at the end of the weight was packed with wax. When the weight struck bottom, some of the seabed would stick to the wax, and upon inspecting it after hauling in the line, one could tell the composition of the ocean floor in that area.

The line slackened, and Jennings began hauling it in. When it tightened, he called out, "Mark forty-five!" The water was sixty feet shallower.

"Bottom?" asked Fournier.

"Sandy," answered Jennings, looking at the end of the weight.

"We're nearing Montauk Point, Jennings," said Fournier. "Almost home."

As close as they were, though, the weather was not about to let it be an easy ride. Monday, September 27, continued with the strong gales and thick weather of the previous day, although the direction of the wind had shifted. Whereas on Sunday it was coming advantageously from the south, now it was blowing from the northeast, effectively pushing the *Stonington* in the opposite direction of where Captain Fournier and his crew wanted to go.

"I don't care which direction the wind decides to blow from," said Fournier to Mark Comstock, who was tending the helm. "We'll tack this ship as many times as we have to in order to get ourselves into the Thames River."

"Aye, Captain," replied Comstock. "After what we've been through, and close as we are."

As the ship went through its maneuvers, the crew saw several vessels plying the waters. At two p.m., a lookout called, "Land ahead!"

Stretching out before them in the distance was the southeast coast of Long Island. The next morning the ship was seven miles from shore, and Fournier recognized immediately the beaches of Southampton. About twenty miles inland was his hometown of Greenport.

By noon that Tuesday, the ship was abreast of Montauk Lighthouse at the easternmost tip of the island. Wednesday, September 29, 1847, exactly one year since arriving in San Diego, brought even more welcomed sights—Little Gull Island Lighthouse, Fisher's Island, and finally, after four years at sea, the mouth of the Thames River.[2]

At five p.m. the weather lightened up, and Alanson Fournier decided to take advantage of the relative calm.

"All hands!" he called, and the crew gathered between the main- and mizzenmasts, with Mark Comstock nearby at the helm, keeping the ship steady.

"Men," began Fournier, "we're about to head into the river and up to our mooring. Before all of that hustle and bustle occurs, I want to say a few words to you." The crew focused on him, not knowing what to expect. "It's been a long four years," he continued. "We did our fair share of whaling and collected a sizable amount of oil that would have turned a pretty profit. But, as you know, life had other plans for that cargo, for us, and for this ship. You took on a duty like no other whalemen before you—perhaps none after you, either—and you performed it admirably. You should be proud of yourselves. I'm proud to have served with you, and although the way it happened was unfortunate, it's an honor to have become your captain."

He paused, checked his emotions, and then went on to a more practical matter.

"The profits from the oil that we collected would have been the basis of your pay for this voyage. The whalebone may fetch a good price, but it will be far less than what the oil could have brought. As soon as we've got the ship secure at the mooring, I will go to Mr. Williams and Mr. Barns and explain to them why we have no oil. They will likely contact the United States government for compensation, and I will personally vouch for each and every one of you that was with us in San Diego, and for the services you rendered. To my understanding, government is a slow-moving machine, so it may be a while before any of us gets our money, but in the meantime, we certainly do have some stories to tell, don't we?"

"Aye, Captain," a voice rang out, "that we do!"

All eyes turned to see that it was Peter McDonnald who had spoken, and as they thought of all that he had been through, they began to recall the many adventures they themselves had experienced on this most unusual of voyages.

McDonnald began to sing what the men recognized as "Roll the Old Chariot." He was giving it some new lyrics that the men followed with ease:

Oh, a *drop* of Fournier's *blood* wouldn't *do* us any *harm*,
Oh, a *drop* of Fournier's *blood* wouldn't *do* us any *harm*,
Oh, a *drop* of Fournier's *blood* wouldn't *do* us any *harm*,
And we'll *all* hang *on* be-*hind*!

And we'll *roll* the *old* chariot a-*long*,
We'll *roll* the *old* chariot a-*long*,
We'll *roll* the *old* chariot a-*long*,
And we'll *all* hang *on* be-*hind*!

Oh, the *sheep* in the *boats* wouldn't *do* us any *harm*,
Oh, the *sheep* in the *boats* wouldn't *do* us any *harm*,
Oh, the *sheep* in the *boats* wouldn't *do* us any *harm*,
And we'll *all* hang *on* be-*hind*!

And we'll *roll* the *old* chariot a-*long*,
We'll *roll* the *old* chariot a-*long*,
We'll *roll* the *old* chariot a-*long*,
And we'll *all* hang *on* be-*hind*!

They continued through several more verses, with Fournier joining in, and after the final chorus, they cheered loudly.

Then Fournier said, "All right, men, let's bring this ship home!"

The crew went to their positions and sailed the *Stonington* into the river. To its larboard was the ninety-foot-tall Harbor Light, gleaming white in the early evening sky. As the ship made its way upriver, the sandy beaches along the western shore eventually gave way to the maritime businesses that lined the waterfront. About three miles from the light-house, they reached the mooring area behind the Williams & Barns whaling firm.

"Drop anchor!" called Fournier, and as the chain clanked and the anchor fell to the bottom, the men of the *Stonington* breathed deep sighs of relief. They had made it back safely to their home port.

As they secured the ship and gathered their belongings, they spoke with each other about what they would do next.[3]

"Sam and I are headed for Uxbridge, just over the line into Massachusetts," said Mark Comstock, "let the family know we're alive and well. Might head down to New Bedford after that, see about signing on to a whaler in our own state."

"I'll be signing on to another ship somewhere," said Aaron Peters. "Whaling's one of the only places where a Black man like me gets treated by the quality of their work, not the color of their skin."

"Truth in that," said George Hopkins in agreement.

"I'm going straight across that river to Groton and see my girl," said James Rice enthusiastically.

"If she was fool enough to wait for you, that is," said Martin Larkins with a grin.

"There's a grog shop right up the road that's waitin' for me!" added Thomas Milnor, raising a chorus of laughter.

"I've been thinking of maybe having a saloon of my own here in town," said Alexander Anthony. "Be my own boss for a change."

"I'll be your best customer!" shouted Milnor, to even more laughs.

The banter continued as the men made their way to the boats.

Alanson Fournier stood near the mainmast and exchanged farewells with them.

"Stay out of trouble, Milnor," he said to the happy-go-lucky carpenter.

"Why bother?" Milnor replied, with his trademark *hee-hee* giggle.

"Thanks for not throwing me overboard when you found me, Captain," called out James Rice.

"Good luck finding your girl," said Fournier with a smile.

George Hopkins paused to say, "Thank you, Captain," and Fournier said, "Be well, Hopkins."

Peter McDonnald walked up to Fournier with his right hand outstretched. As the two men shook hands, McDonnald said, "Captain, you saw me through a rough time and stuck with me until I got better. You did the same with this ship and the rest of the crew. Fair winds and following seas, sir."

"Thank you, McDonnald," replied Fournier. "You take care of yourself."

Alanson Fournier stood on the deck of the *Stonington* after the last of the men had gone ashore and took advantage of this moment of calm and relative silence before the customs officer of New London and the agent for Williams & Barns came aboard to conduct their business. He listened to the wind whistling gently through the rigging and the ship creaking quietly as it rocked in the river, and as he listened, he heard the echoes of all that had happened to the ship and its crew during the past few years, especially this most recent year, the one that had changed the course of their lives.

The sound of an approaching boat interrupted his contemplation.

"Captain Hamley, I am the customs officer for this port," began one of the men who had come aboard. "I will need to see your cargo, especially your oil."

"Excuse me, sir, but I am not Captain Hamley," said Fournier, "and we have no oil."

"What do you mean, no oil?" said the other man incredulously. "As the agent for Williams & Barns, I demand to speak with Captain Hamley."

"Captain Hamley is not here," replied Fournier. "I have been in charge of this ship since he was captured in Mexico."

"Who are you?" demanded the agent.

"What is the meaning of all this?" shouted the officer.

"Well, gentlemen," Fournier began, "it's a long story."

Aft Words

Whatever Became of . . . ?

Edward F. Beale—brought the first samples of gold from California to Washington, DC, in 1848. Became first superintendent of Indian Affairs in California, 1852. Led a wagon road expedition with a combination of horses, mules, and camels through New Mexico Territory in 1858–1859. Portions of the road became the transcontinental railroad and Route 66. Purchased Decatur House in Washington, DC, in 1871, where he and his wife hosted parties for the Washington elite. Appointed ambassador to Austria-Hungary in 1876. Became close friend of Ulysses S. Grant and delivered the eulogy at his funeral. Died April 22, 1893.[1]

John Bidwell—elected state senator in first California legislature, 1849. Appointed by Governor Stanford as commander of Fifth Brigade California Militia, 1863–1865. Delegate to 1864 National Republican Convention, member of delegation that informed Abraham Lincoln of his renomination. Thrice nominated (1867, 1875, 1890) for governor of California. Nominated for president of United States by National Prohibition Party, 1892. Died April 4, 1900.[2]

Pedro C. Carrillo—held municipal positions, including *alcalde* of Santa Barbara and justice of the peace in Los Angeles. Died May 28, 1888, in Los Angeles. Grandson Leo Carrillo became a successful actor, best known for his role as Pancho in the early television series *The Cisco Kid*.[3]

Miguel de Pedrorena—succeeded Pedro Carrillo as San Diego customs collector, 1847–1848. Participated in California's Constitutional Convention of 1849. Partnered with four other men to develop a new site for the town of San Diego. Died March 21, 1850.[4]

Robert C. Duvall—commanded gunboat *Beaufort* for North Carolina navy and Confederate States Navy after secession in 1861. Left military service due to ill health, subsequently died in 1863.[5]

Henry D. Fitch—remained the leading trader in San Diego until his death in 1849. Last person to be buried on Presidio Hill in San Diego.[6]

Alanson Fournier—married Martha Robinson at Southampton, New York, on November 9, 1848. Made one more voyage in 1849 as captain of the whaleship *Vesper*. Died on April 16, 1853, and is buried in Green Hill Cemetery, Greenport, New York.[7]

John C. Frémont—returned to Washington, DC, with Stephen W. Kearny to face court-martial for insubordination. After being convicted, he resigned his commission and moved to California, where he bought the expansive and gold-rich Rancho Las Mariposas. Was elected one of the first two US senators from California, and was the first presidential candidate of the newly formed Republican Party in 1856. Died July 13, 1890.[8]

Archibald Gillespie—narrowly avoided two courts-martial regarding his dishonesty, one in 1854 as marine officer aboard a US Navy warship, the other in 1863 as a major in the Union Army. Died August 16, 1873, in San Francisco.[9]

George Hamley—got out of Mexico and returned to California on September 20, 1847. Eventually put his affairs in order and recovered financially, then acquired Rancho Guejito, a tract of 13,298.59 acres, and retained it throughout a series of legal challenges during the 1850s and 1860s. The rancho eventually passed through several owners. Rancho

Guejito, just over a mile from the San Pasqual Battlefield, is the only remaining rancho that still has its original boundaries, and it is now a successful vineyard and cattle ranch.[10]

Stephen W. Kearny—engaged with Robert F. Stockton and John C. Frémont in controversy over leadership of California after US victory. Became military governor of California Territory and then Veracruz, where he caught yellow fever. Died October 31, 1848.[11]

Ezekiel Merritt—worked mining gold with a partner, left to bring two hundred pounds of gold to San Francisco, never returned, and died just months after the Mexican-American War ended.[12]

Panto—after guiding Beale and Carson through the desert from San Pasqual to San Diego, continued to aid the American cause, lending horses and oxen to Stockton for his march to Los Angeles. Persisted as an advocate for the Kumeyaay and fought against encroachment on their land by settlers. Following his death at San Pasqual, April 27, 1874, settlers eventually took over the land and scattered the tribe.[13]

Andrés Pico—allied himself with the Americans after the war. Acquired significant amount of land. Elected state representative and later state senator in the California government. Obtained commission as brigadier general in California militia. Died February 14, 1876.[14]

Pío Pico—returned from Mexico to Los Angeles, acquired property and wealth, then lost it through various causes, including his own generosity. Died poor in 1894.[15]

Albert Smith—became a municipal official in San Diego, executed the sale of Rancho Guejito after a lawsuit judgment ruled against George W. Hamley. Acquired a sizable amount of land and wealth, then lost it. Died April 11, 1867.[16]

Robert F. Stockton—left US Navy in 1850, then was elected US senator from New Jersey and sponsored bill to abolish flogging. Participated in Peace Conference of 1861 that sought to prevent secession. Commanded New Jersey militia during Civil War. Died October 7, 1866.[17]

Serbulo Varela—quick temper led to three separate incarcerations at Los Angeles jails, 1854–1860, two of them on assault charges. Soon after 1860 release, died from stab wounds by an unknown assailant.[18]

NOTES

CHAPTER 1:

1. Alanson Fournier, "Logbook, 1846, February 28–1847, September 29," *Collections & Research*, https://research.mysticseaport.org/item/l031976/, 52.

2. Thomas W. Williams, "Bill Sale 1/32 part Ship *Stonington*," VFM 1688 - Twelve bills of sale [manuscript], 1824–1862 (Mystic: Mystic Seaport Museum, 1998); John F. Leavitt, *The Charles W. Morgan* (Mystic, CT: Mystic Seaport Museum, 1998), Scale Drawings; Connecticut General Assembly. "Jonathan Law," *The Governors of Connecticut*, https://www.cga.ct.gov/hco/speakers/bios/Jon_Law_Gov.pdf.

3. Ibid.

4. Fournier, op. cit., 43–47.

CHAPTER 2:

1. Ibid., 44, 11–12; New Bedford Whaling Museum and Mystic Seaport Museum, "Stonington: 1843–1847," American Crew List, https://whalinghistory.org/?s =AC134881; Martha's Vineyard Museum, "Meet the Crew—Captain," *Laura Jernegan: Girl on a Whaleship*, girlonawhaleship.org.

2. Fournier, op. cit., 44; Library of Congress, Bosqui Eng. & Print. Co., *View of San Francisco, formerly Yerba Buena, in -7 before the discovery of gold* [San Francisco?, 1884] Map. https://www.loc.gov/item/74693207/.

3. Fournier, op. cit., 44; Henry Bulls Watson, "The Journals of Marine Second Lieutenant Henry Bulls Watson 1845–1848," *Electronic Library Display*, https://www .marines.mil/News/Publications/MCPEL/Electronic-Library-Display/Article/899914/ the-journals-of-marine-second-lieutenant-henry-bulls-watson-1845-1848/, 213.

4. Fournier, op. cit., 45.

CHAPTER 3:

1. Amy S. Greenberg, *A Wicked War: Polk, Clay, Lincoln, and the 1846 U.S. Invasion of Mexico* (New York: Vintage Books, 2012), 56–58; John S. D. Eisenhower, *So Far from God: The U.S. War with Mexico, 1846–1848* (Norman: University of Oklahoma Press, 1989), 199–204; Robert W. Merry, *A Country of Vast Designs: James K. Polk, the Mexican*

War, and the Conquest of the American Continent (New York: Simon & Schuster Paperbacks, 2009), 165–69.

2. Ibid., 181–87.

3. Dale L. Walker, *Bear Flag Rising: The Conquest of California, 1846* (New York: Tom Doherty Associates, LLC, 1999), 29; Sean Wilentz, *The Rise of American Democracy: Jefferson to Lincoln* (New York: W. W. Norton & Company, 2005), 562–63.

CHAPTER 4:

1. Fournier, op. cit., 47; Traditional, "Haul Away Joe" (United States Navy Band), https://www.youtube.com/watch?v=-emxN-PEKiA; New Bedford Whaling Museum and Mystic Seaport Museum, op. cit.

2. Fournier, op. cit., 47; Leavitt, op. cit., 45; William Taylor, interview by author, November 18, 2021.

3. Fournier, op. cit., 48; Nelson Cole Haley, *Whale Hunt: The Narrative of a Voyage by Nelson Cole Haley, Harpooner in the Ship* Charles W. Morgan, *1849–1853* (Mystic, CT: Mystic Seaport Museum, Inc., 2002), 56–57.

CHAPTER 5:

1. Fournier, op. cit., 48.

2. Ibid., 49; James P. Baughman, *The Mallorys of Mystic: Six Generations in American Maritime Enterprise* (Middletown, CT: Wesleyan University Press, 1972), 46–47, 71, 404.

CHAPTER 6:

1. Fournier, op. cit., 47, 49.

2. Daniel Walker Howe, *What Hath God Wrought: The Transformation of America, 1815–1848* (New York: Oxford University Press, 2007), 520–23; John Quincy Adams to Roger Sherman Baldwin, 9 March 1841, Baldwin Papers, Yale University Library.

3. Fournier, op. cit., 50.

CHAPTER 7:

1. Ibid.

2. Eric Duvall, "A Page from History: Bouncing along the Old La Playa Trail," *Point Loma and OB Monthly*, https://www.pointlomaobmonthly.com/news/story/2021-07-18/a-page-from-history-bouncing-along-the-old-la-playa-trail.

CHAPTER 8:

1. John Adam Hussey, "The Origin of the Gillespie Mission," *California Historical Society Quarterly*, https://www.militarymuseum.org/OriginGillespieMission.pdf), 44–45; Gabrielle M. Neufeld Santelli, *Marines in the Mexican War* (Washington, DC: History and Museums Division Headquarters, US Marine Corps, 1991), 8; Mary M. Bowman, "Deposition of Archibald H. Gillespie Concerning Mission San Diego," *Annual Publication of the Historical Society of Southern California*, vol. 10, no. 3 (1917), 79–81, University

of California Press on behalf of the Historical Society of Southern California, https://www.jstor.org/stable/41168748, 80.

2. Santelli, op. cit., 8; Neal Harlow, *California Conquered: War and Peace on the Pacific, 1846–1850* (Berkeley: University of California Press, 1982), 78–79.

3. Steve Inskeep, *Imperfect Union: How Jessie and John Frémont Mapped the West, Invented Celebrity, and Helped Cause the Civil War* (New York: Penguin Press, 2020), 134–35; Sally Denton, *Passion and Principle: John and Jessie Frémont, the Couple Whose Power, Politics, and Love Shaped Nineteenth-Century America* (New York: Bloomsbury USA, 2007), 122–25; John Bidwell, "Frémont in the Conquest of California," *Museum of the City of San Francisco*, http://www.sfmuseum.org/hist6/fremont.html), 29.

4. Walker, op. cit., 91–92.

CHAPTER 9:

1. Harlow, op. cit., 97..

2. Ibid., 98–99.

3. Walker, op. cit., 88; Bidwell, op. cit., 7.

CHAPTER 10:

1. Harlow, op. cit., 106, 111–12; Bidwell, op. cit., 29, 25; Marcus Benjamin, *John Bidwell, Pioneer: A Sketch of His Career* (Washington, DC: [s.n.], 1907), https://babel.hathitrust.org/cgi/pt?id=loc.ark:/13960/t1hh6t656&view=2up&seq=5, 29.

2. Walker, op. cit., 140–43, 110–14.

3. Ibid., 144, 151; Harlow, op. cit., 139; Stephen C. Rowan, "Recollections of the Mexican War," *Proceedings*, vol. 14/3/46 (July 1888), https://www.usni.org/magazines/proceedings/1888/july/recollections-mexican-war.

4. Harlow, op. cit., 148–50.

CHAPTER 11:

1. Fournier, op. cit. 50; Harlow, op. cit., 159–71.

2. James R. Mills, *San Diego: Where California Began* (San Diego: The Journal of San Diego History, 1960), Part 4: Yankees Move In; Hannah Clayborn, "A San Diego Landlord: Captain Henry Delano Fitch," *Hannah Clayborn's History of Healdsburg*, http://www.sonic.net/janosko/ourhealdsburg.com/history/fitch.htm; Ronald L. Miller, "A California Romance in Perspective," *San Diego Historical Society Quarterly*, vol. 19, no. 2 (Spring 1973), https://sandiegohistory.org/journal/1973/april/fitch-2/.

CHAPTER 12:

1. Walker, op. cit., 196; Harlow, op. cit., 162, 171–72; Bidwell, op. cit., 39.

2. Harlow, op. cit., 162–68; Walker, op. cit., 196–200; *Savannah* (ship, 1842), Wikimedia Commons, https://commons.wikimedia.org/wiki/Category:Savannah_(ship,_1842); Les Driver, "Carrillo's Flying Artillery: The Battle of San Pedro," *California Historical Society Quarterly*, December 1969, https://www.militarymuseum.org/Cabbrillo.pdf.

3. William E. Smythe, *History of San Diego: 1542–1907* (San Diego: The History Company, 1907), 202.

CHAPTER 13:
1. Fournier, op. cit., 51; Smythe, op. cit., 202.
2. Fournier, op. cit., 51.
3. Ibid.; New Bedford Whaling Museum and Mystic Seaport Museum, "Stonington: 1843–1847," American Crew List.
4. Fournier, op. cit., 51; Sharon Heinz, ed., *Saddleback Ancestors: Rancho Families of Orange County California*, rev. ed. (Orange, CA: Orange County California Genealogical Society, 1998, https://occgs.com/projects/saddleback/saddleback.html), 216; Richard Griswold del Castillo, "The U.S.–Mexican War in San Diego, 1846–1847," *San Diego Historical Society Quarterly*, vol. 49, no. 1 (Winter 2003), https://sandiegohistory.org/journal/2003/january/war-2/.
5. Fournier, op. cit., 51.
6. Fournier, op. cit., 51–52.

CHAPTER 14:
1. Curtis Winkle, "A Short History of Oil: 1700–1870," *Trainings & Demos*, https://kimray.com/training/short-history-oil-1700-1870#:~:text=1846%3A%20Kerosene%20in%20Canada&text=This%20new%20discovery%20burned%20more,per%20gallon%20for%20whale%20oil; Ian Webster, "$1 in 1846 ⊠ 2023 | Inflation Calculator," *Official Inflation Data, Alioth Finance*, https://www.officialdata.org/us/inflation/1846?amount=1; Greenberg, op. cit., 198–99.
2. Haley, op. cit., 56–57.

CHAPTER 15:
1. Robert Carson Duvall, "Log of the U.S. Frigate *Savannah* Kept by Robert Carson Duvall," *The Mexican War and California*, https://militarymuseum.org/History%20Mex%20War.html, 119; National Park Service, "Estudillo House, San Diego, California," *American Latino Heritage*, https://www.nps.gov/nr/travel/american_latino_heritage/estudillo_house.html.
2. Fournier, op. cit. 52.
3. Ibid.; Smythe, op. cit., 98.
4. Martha's Vineyard Museum, "Explore the Ship—Try Pot," *Laura Jernegan: Girl on a Whaleship*, girlonawhaleship.org.
5. Fournier, op. cit., 11–12, 52.
6. Fournier, op. cit., 52.
7. Ken Simon, *The Mark of Uncas* (SimonPure Media, 2002), https://www.youtube.com/watch?v=ohDSVulkCWY.

CHAPTER 16:
1. Fournier, op. cit., 52; Smythe, op. cit., 203.
2. Fournier, op. cit., 52; GlobalSecurity.org., "Sailing Ship Armament," https://www
.globalsecurity.org/military/systems/ship/sail-armament.htm.
3. Fournier, op. cit., 52.

CHAPTER 17:
1. Fournier, op. cit., 53.
2. Ibid.

CHAPTER 18:
1. Richard F. Pourade, *History of San Diego, Volume 3: The Silver Dons, 1833–1865*, San
Diego History Center, https://sandiegohistory.org/archives/books/dons/ch5/.
2. Grace Monfort, "Few Celebrate Where Many Once Feted San Diego Hero Who
Spiked Guns," *San Diego Sun*, 1938, http://albertbsmith.blogspot.com/.
3. Ibid.; Smith Official DNA & One Name Study, "Albert Benjamin Smith," https://
www.smithsworldwide.org/tng/getperson.php?personID=I91998&tree=tree1.
4. Montfort, op. cit.

CHAPTER 19:
1. Fournier, op. cit. 53.
2. Pourade, op. cit.
3. Victor Walsh, "The Machado Sisters: The Californianas of Old Town, San Diego,"
CA.GOV, https://www.parks.ca.gov/pages/663/files/MachadoSistersOfOldTown_ADA
-Compliant_20191204.pdf, 1; Rosemary Masterson, "The Machado-Silvas Family," *San
Diego Historical Society Quarterly*, vol. 15, no. 1 (Winter 1969), https://sandiegohistory.org
/journal/1969/january/part4-2/.
4. Rita Larkin, ed., "Historic Landmarks of San Diego County," *San Diego Historical
Society Quarterly*, vol. 14, no. 3 (July 1968), https://sandiegohistory.org/journal/1968/july
/landmarks/; Masterson, op. cit.

CHAPTER 20:
1. University of Southern California Libraries and California Historical Society,
"Portrait of Don Miguel de Pedrorena," https://digitallibrary.usc.edu/asset-management
/2A3BF1I77RR?FR_=1&W=1280&H=625; C-SPAN, "La Plaza Mexican-American
Cultural Center," *American History TV-American Artifacts*, https://www.c-span.org/video
/?302512-1/la-plaza-mexican-american-cultural-center&event=302512&playEvent;
Smythe, op. cit., 202, 172–73; Fournier, op. cit., 53; National Park Service, "Estudillo
House, San Diego, California," *American Latino Heritage*, https://www.nps.gov/nr/travel/
american_latino_heritage/estudillo_house.html.

CHAPTER 21:

1. National Park Service, "San Diego Mission Church (San Diego de Alcala)," *Early History of the California Coast*, https://www.nps.gov/nr/travel/ca/ca3.htm#:~:text=The %20mission%20was%20founded%20in,fourth%20constructed%20at%20the%20site.
2. Smythe, op. cit., 204.
3. Fournier, op. cit., 53.
4. Clayborn, op. cit., "Old Town San Diego 1852 (above) and 1854 (below)."
5. Museums of History NSW, "Loading and Firing the Flintlock Musket," https:// www.youtube.com/watch?v=lfGOLqxcbIg.

CHAPTER 22:

1. Fournier, op. cit., 54; Naval History and Heritage Command, "Uniforms of the U.S. Navy, 1830–1841," *Heritage—Uniforms*, https://www.history.navy.mil/browse-by -topic/heritage/uniforms-and-personal-equipment/uniforms-1830-1841.html.
2. Center for Living History, Inc., "Captain Mervine," *Pictures*, http://www.cyane.org /pictures.
3. Duvall, op. cit., 119.
4. Fournier, op. cit., 54.
5. Ibid.; Clayborn, "A San Diego Landlord: Captain Henry Delano Fitch."
6. Fournier, op. cit., 54.

CHAPTER 23:

1. Ibid.
2. New Bedford Whaling Museum and Mystic Seaport Museum, "Magnolia: 1845–1848," *American Voyage*, https://whalinghistory.org/?s=AV08768.
3. Duvall, op. cit., 119.
4. Duvall, op. cit., 120.
5. Mike Emett, "Fort Guijarros and the Battle of San Diego," *Clio: Your Guide to History*, April 3, 2017, https://www.theclio.com/entry/35766.

CHAPTER 24:

1. Jay G. Forst, "Coronado: A Beginning," *Coronado Journal*, vol. 75, no. 14 (Thursday, April 3, 1986), https://cdnc.ucr.edu/?a=d&d=CJ19860403&e=-------en--20--1--txt -txIN-coronado+journal+april+3%2c+1986-------; Coronado Historical Association and Coronado Museum, "A Timeline of Coronado History," *Coronado History*, https:// coronadohistory.org/historic-coronado/a-timeline-of-coronado-history/.

CHAPTER 25:

1. Fournier, op. cit., 54; Duvall, op. cit., 119–20.
2. Fournier, op. cit., 55; Rowan, op. cit.
3. Fournier, op. cit., 55.
4. Ibid.

CHAPTER 26:

1. W. B. Campbell and J. R. Moriarty, "The Struggle Over Secularization of the Missions on the Alta California Frontier," *San Diego Historical Society Quarterly*, vol. 15, no. 4 (Fall 1969), https://sandiegohistory.org/journal/1969/october/struggle/.

2. Damian Bacich, "Native Americans of Southern California: The Kumeyaay," *The California Frontier Project*, https://www.californiafrontier.net/the-kumeyaay/#Kumeyaay _and_Missions; Duvall, op. cit., 120.

3. Duvall, op. cit., 120.

CHAPTER 27:

1. Fournier, op. cit., 56.

2. Duvall, op. cit., 120.

3. Fournier, op. cit., 56; Off Grid with Doug & Stacy, "Lamb Birth from Start to Finish: Off-Grid Homesteading," https://www.youtube.com/watch?v=s5GTuLJgr0k.

4. Fournier, op. cit., 56.

CHAPTER 28:

1. Fournier, op. cit., 56.

2. Naval History and Heritage Command, "*Congress IV* (Frigate)," *Boats–Ships–Frigate: Ship History*, https://www.history.navy.mil/research/histories/ship-histories/danfs/c/congress-iv.html; Samuel J. Bayard, *A Sketch of the Life of Commodore Robert F. Stockton; with an Appendix Comprising His Correspondence with the Navy Department Respecting His Conquest of California* (New York: Derby & Jackson, 1856), 10–11; Naval History and Heritage Command, "Stockton, Robert F.," *Photography-US People-S*, https://www.history.navy.mil/content/history/nhhc/our-collections/photography/us-people/s/stockton-robert-f.html.

3. Rowan, op. cit.; Bayard, op. cit., Appendix A, 19–24.

CHAPTER 29:

1. Bayard, op. cit., Appendix A, 25.

2. Pourade, op. cit.

3. Fournier, op. cit., 56; Naval History and Heritage Command, "*Malek Adhel*," *DANFS-M.*, https://www.history.navy.mil/content/history/nhhc/research/histories/ship -histories/danfs/m/malek-adhel.html; Bayard, op. cit., Appendix A, 24.

CHAPTER 30:

1. Fournier, op. cit., 56.

2. Fournier, op. cit., 57; Duvall, op. cit., 120–21.

3. Fournier, op. cit., 57.

4. Fournier, op. cit., 57–58.

CHAPTER 31:

1. Fournier, op. cit., 58; Bayard, op. cit., Appendix A, 25.
2. Bayard, op. cit., Appendix A, 25.
3. Ibid.
4. Duvall, op. cit., 121.

CHAPTER 32:

1. Fournier, op. cit., 59.

CHAPTER 33:

1. Fournier, op. cit., 59.
2. Fournier, op. cit., 132; New Bedford Whaling Museum, "Life Aboard," *Learn-Whaling History*, https://www.whalingmuseum.org/learn/research-topics/whaling-history/life -aboard/.
3. Fournier, op. cit., 59; Duvall, op. cit., 122.
4. Duvall, op. cit., 122.

CHAPTER 34:

1. Fournier, op. cit., 60.
2. Duvall, op. cit., 122; Mills, op. cit.
3. Fournier, op. cit., 60.
4. Ibid.; Bayard, op. cit., Appendix A, 25; SJPL California Room Collections, "1850 Portrait of Major Samuel J. Hensley," *Historic Photograph Collection* (SJPL California Room), https://digitalcollections.sjlibrary.org/digital/collection/arbuckle/id/368; Walker, op. cit., 88; Edwin Bryant, *What I Saw in California* (Lincoln: University of Nebraska Press, 1985), 367; Smythe, op. cit., 206.
5. Fournier, op. cit., 61; Mary Lee Spence and Donald Jackson, eds., *The Expeditions of John Charles Frémont, Volume 2: The Bear Flag Revolt and the Court-Martial* (Urbana: University of Illinois Press, 1973), 210; Walker, op. cit., 198; Harlow, op. cit., 95–96.
6. Fournier, op. cit., 61.

CHAPTER 35:

1. Fournier, op. cit., 61.
2. Fournier, op. cit., 61–62.
3. Fournier, op. cit., 62–63.
4. Fournier, op. cit., 64.
5. Ibid.; Sheringham Shantymen, "Pump Shanty," *Songs for Seafarers*, https://www .youtube.com/watch?v=oK6uruj2ab0.

CHAPTER 36:

1. Fournier, op. cit., 64; Bayard, op. cit., 25.
2. Fournier, op. cit., 64.

3. Ibid.

CHAPTER 37:
1. San Pasqual Battlefield State Historic Park, "The Battle of San Pasqual," *San Pasqual Battlefield State Historic Park: Virtual Battle Day Event 2020*, https://youtu.be /ijsOf1kmFVU; Smythe, op. cit., 207–09; del Castillo, op. cit; Huntington Library, Art Museum, and Botanical Garden, "General Andrés Pico," *Photographs*, https://hdl .huntington.org/digital/collection/p15150coll2/id/8071; Walker, op. cit., 197; Lt. Col. W. H. Emory, *Notes of a Military Reconnoissance [sic] from Fort Leavenworth, in Missouri, to San Diego, in California* (Washington, DC: Wendell and Van Benthuysen, Printers, 1848), 53; Harlow, op. cit., 175–76; Spence and Jackson, op. cit., xxiv.
2. Col. J. J. Warner, "Reminiscences of Early California from 1831 to 1846," *Annual Publications of the Historical Society of Southern California 1907–1908* (Los Angeles: J. B. Walters, Printer, 1909), 176; Walker, op. cit., 210–12; H. D. Barrows, "Memorial Sketch of Col. J. J. Warner," *Annual Publication of the Historical Society of Southern California* (Los Angeles: 1895), 23.
3. Emory, op. cit., 107–08; Walker, op. cit., 219.
4. Harlow, op. cit., 188–90.
5. Harlow, op. cit., 190; Emory, op. cit., 112–13.

CHAPTER 38:
1. Fournier, op. cit., 65.
2. Ibid.
3. New Bedford Whaling Museum and Mystic Seaport Museum, op. cit.

CHAPTER 39:
1. Bryant, op. cit., 305, 310.

CHAPTER 40:
1. Richard Henry Dana Jr., *Two Years Before the Mast* (New York: Viking Penguin, Inc., 1981), 170.
2. Phillip Colla, "Aerial Photo of Kelp Forests at Cabrillo SMR, #30643," *Natural History Photography-Galleries*, http://www.oceanlight.com/spotlight.php?img=30643; DiveViz, "Point Loma," *Boat Dives and Trips*, https://chris-cheezem-799y.squarespace .com/point-loma; Todd Miller, "Point Loma Kelp Dive," https://www.youtube.com/watch ?v=Z0QfTDVH4XE; Wikimedia Commons contributors, "File:1857 U.S.C.S. Map of San Diego Bay, California-Geographicus-SanDiegoBay-uscs-1857.jpg," *Wikimedia Commons,* https://commons.wikimedia.org/w/index.php?title=File:1857_U.S.C.S. _Map_of_San_Diego_Bay,_California_-_Geographicus_-_SanDiegoBay-uscs-1857.jpg &oldid=745852967.

Chapter 41:
1. Fournier, op. cit., 65–66.

Chapter 42:
1. Bayard, op. cit., Appendix A, 25.
2. Fournier, op. cit., 66.
3. Naval History and Heritage Command, "*Cyane II* (Sloop)," *DANFS-M*, https://www.history.navy.mil/research/histories/ship-histories/danfs/c/cyane-sloop-ii.html.
4. Ibid.; Fournier, op. cit., 66.
5. Bayard, op. cit., Appendix A, 8, 12–13; Pourade, op. cit., https://sandiegohistory.org/archives/books/dons/ch7/; Joseph T. Downey, *The Cruise of the Portsmouth, 1845–1847: A Sailor's View of the Naval Conquest of California*, ed. Howard Lamar (New Haven: Yale University Press, 1958),, 186; Watson, op. cit., 259–61.

Chapter 43:
1. Fournier, op. cit., 67; Watson, op. cit., 160.
2. Fournier, op. cit., 67.
3. Ibid.; Spence, op. cit., 238.

Chapter 44:
1. Arthur B. Perkins, "Rancho San Francisco: A Study of a California Land Grant," *The Historical Society of Southern California Quarterly* (June 1957), https://scvhistory.com/scvhistory/perkins-rsf-1957.htm; Spence, op. cit., 238; Bryant, op. cit., 366; Utah State Historical Society, "John Charles Fremont," *History to Go*, https://historytogo.utah.gov/fremont-john/; Denton, op. cit., 9; Spence, op. cit., 249–50; Harlow, op cit., 230; Bryant, op. cit., 389–90.
2. Bryant, op. cit., 390.

Chapter 45:
1. Harlow, op cit., 209–11.
2. Harry L. Watson, *Andrew Jackson vs. Henry Clay: Democracy and Development in Antebellum America* (Boston: Bedford/St. Martin's, 1998), 37; Harlow, op cit., 209–13.
3. Harlow, op cit., 214–15; Emory, op. cit., 119; Henry Bulls Watson, op. cit., 276–80.
4. Harlow, op cit., 217.

Chapter 46:
1. Bryant, op. cit., 390–91; Hubert Howe Bancroft, *History of California, Volume V, 1846–1848* (San Francisco: The History Company, 1886), 402.
2. Bryant, op. cit., 391–93; John M. Foster, Leonard Pitt, Edna E. Kimbro, *Second Addendum Report: Archaeological and Historic Investigations at Campo de Cahuenga, CA-LAN-1945H* (Pacific Palisades, CA: Greenwood and Associates, 2000), 22; Harlow, op cit., 231–32.

3. Bancroft, *History of California, Volume V, 1846–1848*, 404; Bryant, op. cit., 393–94, 413–14.

CHAPTER 47:
1. Fournier, op. cit., 68.
2. Ibid.
3. Fournier, op. cit., 69.
4. Ibid.; Sheringham Shantymen, op. cit.

CHAPTER 48:
1. Fournier, op. cit., 69.
2. Fournier, op. cit., 70.

CHAPTER 49:
1. Fournier, op. cit., 71; Henry Bulls Watson, op. cit., 285.
2. Fournier, op. cit., 71; Martha's Vineyard Museum, op. cit.
3. Fournier, op. cit., 71; Henry Bulls Watson, op. cit., 286; Hilary Granson, "How to Control Fleas in Your Pet," *TexVetPets.org*, https://www.texvetpets.org/article/fleas-never-ending-itch/.
4. Downey, op. cit., 233–35.
5. Fournier, op. cit., 71–72.
6. Fournier, op. cit., 72.

CHAPTER 50:
1. Fournier, op. cit., 72.
2. Fournier, op. cit., 73.

CHAPTER 51:
1. Fournier, op. cit., 73.
2. Fournier, op. cit., 74.

CHAPTER 52:
1. Fournier, op. cit., 75.
2. Fournier, op. cit., 76.
3. Fournier, op. cit., 77.
4. Fournier, op. cit., 78.
5. Ibid.

CHAPTER 53:
1. Fournier, op. cit., 79.
2. Ibid.; Henry Bulls Watson, op. cit., 303.

3. Ibid.
4. Ibid.

CHAPTER 54:

1. Fournier, op. cit., 80.
2. Fournier, op. cit., 80–89.
3. Fournier, op. cit., 90; New Bedford Whaling Museum, "Whales and Hunting," *Learn-Whaling History*, https://www.whalingmuseum.org/learn/research-topics/whaling -history/whales-and-hunting/.
4. Fournier, op. cit., 90.

CHAPTER 55:

1. Fournier, op. cit., 91.
2. Fournier, op. cit., 92.
3. Fournier, op. cit., 95.
4. Fournier, op. cit., 96.
5. Naval History and Heritage Command, "*Congress IV* (Frigate)," op. cit.; Destroyer History Foundation, "RADM. LA VALLETTE," *Find a Ship-Selected Ships G-L-USS La Vallette DD 448*, https://destroyerhistory.org/fletcherclass/ns_lavallette/index.asp?r =44800&pid=44801.

CHAPTER 56:

1. Fournier, op. cit., 96–97; Wander, "Travel to Talcahuano," *Destinations-Talcahuano*, https://www.wander.am/travel/talcahuano-82031.
2. Fournier, op. cit., 98–99.
3. Fournier, op. cit., 99.

CHAPTER 57:

1. Fournier, op. cit., 99–102.
2. Fournier, op. cit., 100.
3. Fournier, op. cit., 100–02.
4. Fournier, op. cit., 102; Robert White Stevens, *On the Stowage of Ships and Their Cargoes* (Plymouth, England: Stevens, 1858), 158.
5. Fournier, op. cit., 102–03.

CHAPTER 58:

1. Fournier, op. cit., 103–04; Oceanwide Expeditions, "What to Expect When Crossing the Drake Passage," *Resources-Stories-Blog*, https://oceanwide-expeditions.com/blog/ the-wild-drake-passage.
2. Fournier, op. cit., 105.
3. Fournier, op. cit., 105–08.
4. Fournier, op. cit., 109–10.

5. Fournier, op. cit., 110–11.

Chapter 59:

1. Fournier, op. cit., 111–12; Stephanie A. Eyerly-Webb, et al., "Lightning Burns and Electrical Trauma in a Couple Simultaneously Struck by Lightning," *NIH National Library of Medicine-National Center for Biotechnology Information*, https://www.ncbi.nlm.nih.gov/pmc/articles/PMC5965181/.

Chapter 60:

1. Fournier, op. cit., 112; Wellcome Collection, "Mahogany Medicine Chest, England, 1801–1900," *Science Museum, London, Attribution 4.0 International (CC BY 4.0)*, https://wellcomecollection.org/works/ysz9yw4d; The Day, "Kevin Crandall describes surviving a lightning strike," https://www.youtube.com/watch?v=iZh0QAUuUIs.
2. Fournier, op. cit., 113; Wellcome Collection, op. cit.
3. Fournier, op. cit., 113.
4. Ibid.

Chapter 61:

1. Fournier, op. cit., 113–15.
2. Fournier, op. cit., 115–16.

Chapter 62:

1. Fournier, op. cit., 116; William Taylor, interview by author, April 25, 2023.
2. Fournier, op. cit., 116–17.

Chapter 63:

1. Fournier, op. cit., 118.
2. Fournier, op. cit., 119.
3. Fournier, op. cit., 119–20.

Chapter 64:

1. Fournier, op. cit., 121; Joanna Gyory et al., "The Gulf Stream," *Ocean Surface Currents-Atlantic*, https://oceancurrents.rsmas.miami.edu/atlantic/gulf-stream.html; National Environmental Satellite, Data, and Information Service, "The Gulf Stream Seen through Sea Surface Temperature," https://www.nesdis.noaa.gov/news/the-gulf-stream-seen-through-sea-surface-temperature.
2. Fournier, op. cit., 121; Oliver Hazard Perry Rhode Island, "ASK US ANYTHING: Finding Water Depth! Soundings, Lead, Lines, Fathoms, and More!," https://www.youtube.com/watch?v=gCSQCuGnpYY; Curiosity Show, "Swinging the Lead: What Does That Mean, and Why?," https://www.youtube.com/watch?v=_73VunCxE1U.

3. Fournier, op. cit., 121; David Coffin, "Roll the Old Chariot," https://www.youtube .com/watch?v=49FWp7WLYKw&t=4s; Harlan Hamilton, *Lights & Legends: A Historical Guide to Lighthouses of Long Island Sound, Fishers Island Sound and Block Island Sound* (Stamford, CT: Westcott Cove Publishing Company, 1987), 179–82.

AFT WORDS:

1. Gerald Thompson, *Edward Beale & The American West* (Albuquerque: University of New Mexico Press, 1983), 30–31, 49, 88, 103–06, 194–96, 199–201, 211, 226, 236–37; History.com Editors, "Route 66 Decertified, Highway Signs Removed," *History-A&E Television Networks*, https://www.history.com/this-day-in-history/route-66 -decertified.

2. Rockwell D. Hunt, "John Bidwell: A Prince Among Pioneers," *Annual Publication of the Historical Society of Southern California* 10, no. 3 (1917): 48–56, https://doi.org/10 .2307/41168744.

3. Marcy Bandy and Maurice Bandy, *Saddleback Ancestors: Rancho Families of Orange County, California*, rev. ed. (Orange, CA: Orange County California Genealogical Society, 1998), 216, 219; Rancho Carrillo Community, "Leo Carrillo," *More-History-Leo Carrillo*, https://www.ranchocarrillo.com/history/leo-carrillo.

4. Smythe, op. cit., 173; William Heath Davis, *Sixty Years in California: A History of Events and Life in California* (San Francisco: A. J. Leary, 1889), 367.

5. Online Archive of California, "R.C. Duvall Journal and Log of U.S. Frigate *Savannah*: And Other Material, 1845–1847," https://oac.cdlib.org/search?group=Items;idT =UCb182960870.

6. Smythe, op. cit., 274.

7. Find a Grave, "Capt. Alanson Fournier," https://www.findagrave.com/memorial /34554183/alanson-fournier; "Whaling Crew List Database," *List View-168*, https:// www.whalingmuseum.org/online_exhibits/crewlist/listview.php?reverse=ASC&order_by =name&term=&page=168.

8. Harlow, op. cit., 275; Utah State Historical Society, op. cit.

9. Dick Camp, "Archibald H. Gillespie, USMC: Presidential Secret Agent," *Leatherneck*, December 2013; 96, 12; *Marine Corps Gazette & Leatherneck Magazine of the Marines*, 12, https://mca-marines.org/wp-content/uploads/Archibald-Gillespie-San-Pasqual.pdf, 15.

10. George W. Hamley, "Letter to H. D. Fitch, Oct. 5, 1847," BANC MSS C-B 55, folder 454, Berkeley: The Bancroft Library; California Digital Newspaper Collection, "Elisor's Sale," *San Diego Herald*, vol. 5, no. 5 (May 19, 1855), p. 3, advertisements column 1, https://cdnc.ucr.edu/?a=d&d=SDH18550519.2.10.1&srpos=3&e=------185-en --20--1--txt-txIN-hamley----1855—; H. I. Willey, "Report of the Surveyor-General of the State of California from August 1, 1884, to August 1, 1886" (Sacramento, CA: Sacramento State Office, 1886), http://www.slc.ca.gov/wp-content/uploads/2018/08/Willey _1884_1886.pdf, 15; California State Archives, "Land Grant Map MC 4:4–464, Guejito, George W. Hamley"; Rancho Guejito Vineyard, "Rancho Guejito Vineyard," https:// www.ranchoguejitovineyard.com/.

11. Mendell Lee Taylor, "The Western Services of Stephen Watts Kearny, 1815–1848," *New Mexico Historical Review* vol. 21, no. 3 (1946), https://digitalrepository.unm.edu/

nmhr/vol21/iss3/2, 183–84; Bryant, op. cit., 431–32; A Continent Divided, "Stephen Watts Kearny," *Browse-Biographies-US*, https://library.uta.edu/usmexicowar/item?bio_id =68&nation=US.

12. Tracy Family History, "The Bear Flag Revolt," http://www.thetracyfamilyhistory .net/C%202%20%20Bear%20Flag%20Revolt.htm.

13. Glenn J. Farris, "José Panto, *Capitan* of the Indian Pueblo of San Pascual, San Diego County," *Journal of California and Great Basin Anthropology*, vol. 16, no. 2 (1994), 149–61, https://escholarship.org/content/qt5ph0b0m3/qt5ph0b0m3_noSplash_f11e42 0563c8151b48db1bf492942697.pdf?t=krnqt6; Farris, "Captain Jose Panto and the San Pascual Indian Pueblo in San Diego County, 1835–1878," *San Diego Historical Society Quarterly*, vol. 43, no. 2 (Spring 1997), https://sandiegohistory.org/journal/1997/april/ panto/.

14. Smythe, op. cit., 173; William Heath Davis, *Sixty Years in California: A History of Events and Life in California* (San Francisco: A. J. Leary, 1889), 367.

15. San Fernando Valley Historical Society, "Andrés Pico," *Andrés Pico Adobe*, https: //sfvhs.com/andres-pico/; KCET, "The Life and Times of Pío Pico, Last Governor of Mexican California," *Food and Discovery-Lost LA*, https://www.kcet.org/shows/lost-la/ the-life-and-times-of-pio-pico-last-governor-of-mexican-california.

16. California Digital Newspaper Collection, "Elisor's Sale"; Charles W. Hughes, *Albert B. Smith and the Americanization of San Diego, 1830–1869* (Oceanside, CA: California Department of Parks and Recreation, San Diego Coast District, 2012), 30–39.

17. Naval History and Heritage Command, "Stockton, Robert F." *Photography-US People-S*, https://www.history.navy.mil/content/history/nhhc/our-collections/ photography/us-people/s/stockton-robert-f.html.

18. Lawrence E. Guillow, "Pandemonium in the Plaza: The First Los Angeles Riot, July 22, 1856," *Southern California Quarterly*, vol. 77, no. 3 (Fall 1995), https://inside.sfuhs .org/dept/history/US_History_reader/Chapter4/Guillowpandemonium.pdf, 184; Paul Spitzzeri, "The Los Angeles Jail and the 1860 Census," *Trembling on the Brink: Crime and Justice in Los Angeles, 1850–1875*, http://tremblingonthebrink.blogspot.com/2016/10/the -los-angeles-jail-and-1860-census.html.

Bibliography

Primary Sources:

Adams, John Quincy. Letter to Roger Sherman Baldwin. Baldwin Papers. Yale University Library.

Bayard, Samuel J. *A Sketch of the Life of Commodore Robert F. Stockton; with an Appendix Comprising His Correspondence with the Navy Department Respecting His Conquest of California.* New York: Derby & Jackson, 1856.

Bidwell, John. "Frémont in the Conquest of California." *The Museum of the City of San Francisco.* http://www.sfmuseum.org/hist6/fremont.html.

Bowman, Mary M. "Deposition of Archibald H. Gillespie Concerning Mission San Diego." *Annual Publication of the Historical Society of Southern California,* vol. 10, no. 3 (1917), 79–81. University of California Press on behalf of the Historical Society of Southern California. https://www.jstor.org/stable/41168748.

Bryant, Edwin. *What I Saw in California.* Lincoln: University of Nebraska Press, 1985.

California Digital Newspaper Collection. "Elisor's Sale." *San Diego Herald,* vol. 5, no. 5 (May 19, 1855), page 3, advertisements, column 1. https://cdnc.ucr.edu/?a=d &d=SDH18550519.2.10.1&srpos=3&e=------185-en--20--1--txt-txIN-hamley ----1855—.

California State Archives. "Land Grant Map MC 4:4–464, Guejito, George W. Hamley."

Colton, Rev. Walter, USN. *Three Years in California.* New York: A. S. Barnes & Company, 1850.

Dana, Richard Henry, Jr. *Two Years Before the Mast.* New York: Viking Penguin Inc., 1981.

Davis, William Heath. *Sixty Years in California: A History of Events and Life in California.* San Francisco: A. J. Leary, 1889.

Downey, Joseph T. *The Cruise of the Portsmouth, 1845–1847: A Sailor's View of the Naval Conquest of California,* ed. Howard Lamar. New Haven: Yale University Press, 1958.

Duvall, Robert Carson. "Log of the U.S. Frigate *Savannah* Kept by Robert Carson Duvall." *The Mexican War and California.* https://militarymuseum.org/History %20Mex%20War.html.

Emory, Lt. Col. W. H. *Notes of a Military Reconnoissance from Fort Leavenworth, in Missouri, to San Diego, in California.* Washington, DC: Wendell and Van Benthuysen, Printers, 1848.

Fournier, Alanson. "Logbook, 1846, February 28–1847, September 29." *Collections & Research*. https://research.mysticseaport.org/item/l031976/.

Haley, Nelson Cole. *Whale Hunt: The Narrative of a Voyage by Nelson Cole Haley, Harpooner in the Ship Charles W. Morgan, 1849–1853*. Mystic: Mystic Seaport Museum, Inc., 2002.

Hamley, George W. "Logbook, 1843, Aug. 17–1845, April." *Collections & Research*. https://research.mysticseaport.org/item/l031958/.

———. "Letter to H. D. Fitch, Oct. 5, 1847." BANC MSS C-B 55, folder 454. Berkeley: The Bancroft Library.

———. "Order in Favor of H. D. Fitch, Feb. 6, 1847." BANC MSS C-B 55, Folder 454. Berkeley, CA: The Bancroft Library.

Jackson, Donald, and Mary Lee Spence, eds. *The Expeditions of John Charles Frémont, Volume 1: Travels from 1838 to 1844*. Urbana: University of Illinois Press, 1970.

Library of Congress. Bosqui Eng. & Print. Co. *View of San Francisco, formerly Yerba Buena, in -7 before the discovery of gold*. [San Francisco?, 1884] Map. https://www.loc.gov/item/74693207/.

New Bedford Whaling Museum and Mystic Seaport Museum. "Stonington: 1843–1847." *American Crew List*. https://whalinghistory.org/?s=AC134881.

———. "*Magnolia*: 1845–1848." *American Voyage*. https://whalinghistory.org/?s=AV08768.

Robinson, Alfred. *Life in California: During a Residence of Several Years in That Territory*. New York: Wiley & Putnam, 1846.

Rowan, Stephen C. "Recollections of the Mexican War," vol. 14/3/46 (July 1888). https://www.usni.org/magazines/proceedings/1888/july/recollections-mexican-war.

Spence, Mary Lee, and Donald Jackson, eds. *The Expeditions of John Charles Frémont, Volume 2: The Bear Flag Revolt and the Court-Martial*. Urbana: University of Illinois Press, 1973.

Warner, Col. J. J. "Reminiscences of Early California from 1831 to 1846." *Annual Publications of the Historical Society of Southern California, 1907–1908*. Los Angeles: J. B. Walters, Printer, 1909.

Watson, Henry Bulls. "The Journals of Marine Second Lieutenant Henry Bulls Watson, 1845–1848." *Electronic Library Display*. https://www.marines.mil/News/Publications/MCPEL/Electronic-Library-Display/Article/899914/the-journals-of-marine-second-lieutenant-henry-bulls-watson-1845-1848/.

Williams, Thomas W. "Bill Sale 1/32 part Ship *Stonington*." VFM 1688: Twelve Bills of Sale [manuscript], 1824–1862. Mystic, CT: Mystic Seaport Museum.

SECONDARY SOURCES:

A Continent Divided. "Stephen Watts Kearny." *Browse-Biographies-US*. https://library.uta.edu/usmexicowar/item?bio_id=68&nation=US.

Bacich, Damian. "Native Americans of Southern California: The Kumeyaay." *The California Frontier Project*. https://www.californiafrontier.net/the-kumeyaay/#Kumeyaay_and_Missions.

Baker, Patricia. "The Bandini Family." *San Diego Historical Society Quarterly*, vol. 15, no. 1 (Winter 1969), https://sandiegohistory.org/journal/1969/january/part2-2/.

Bancroft, Hubert Howe. *History of California, Volume IV, 1840–1845*. San Francisco: A. L. Bancroft & Company, 1886.

———. *History of California, Volume V, 1846–1848*. San Francisco: The History Company, 1886.

Bandy, Marcy, and Maurice Bandy. *Saddleback Ancestors: Rancho Families of Orange County California*, rev. ed. Orange, CA: Orange County California Genealogical Society, 1998.

Barrows, H. D. "Memorial Sketch of Col. J. J. Warner." *Annual Publication of the Historical Society of Southern California*. Los Angeles: 1895.

Baughman, James P. *The Mallorys of Mystic: Six Generations in American Maritime Enterprise*. Middletown, CT: Wesleyan University Press, 1972.

Benjamin, Marcus. *John Bidwell, Pioneer: A Sketch of His Career*. Washington, DC: [s.n.], 1907. https://babel.hathitrust.org/cgi/pt?id=loc.ark:/13960/t1hh6t656&view=2up &seq=5.

Camp, Dick. "Archibald H. Gillespie, USMC: Presidential Secret Agent." *Leatherneck* (December 2013), 96, 12; *Marine Corps Gazette & Leatherneck Magazine of the Marines*, 12. https://mca-marines.org/wp-content/uploads/Archibald-Gillespie -San-Pasqual.pdf.

Campbell, W. B., and J. R. Moriarty. "The Struggle Over Secularization of the Missions on the Alta California Frontier." *San Diego Historical Society Quarterly*, vol. 15, no. 4 (Fall 1969). https://sandiegohistory.org/journal/1969/october/struggle/.

Center for Living History, Inc. "Captain Mervine." *Pictures*. http://www.cyane.org/ pictures.

Clayborn, Hannah. "A San Diego Landlord: Captain Henry Delano Fitch." *Hannah Clayborn's History of Healdsburg*. http://www.sonic.net/janosko/ourhealdsburg.com /history/fitch.htm.

Coffin, David. "Roll the Old Chariot." https://www.youtube.com/watch?v =49FWp7WLYKw&t=4s.

Colla, Phillip. "Aerial Photo of Kelp Forests at Cabrillo SMR, #30643." *Natural History Photography-Galleries*. http://www.oceanlight.com/spotlight.php?img=30643.

Connecticut General Assembly. "Jonathan Law." *The Governors of Connecticut*. https:// www.cga.ct.gov/hco/speakers/bios/Jon_Law_Gov.pdf.

Coons, Bruce. "A Brief History of Rancho Guejito." *Save Our Heritage Organisation*. http: //sohosandiego.org/reflections/2007-1/guejito_history.htm.

Coronado Historical Association and Coronado Museum. "A Timeline of Coronado History." *Coronado History*. https://coronadohistory.org/historic-coronado/a -timeline-of-coronado-history/.

C-SPAN. "La Plaza Mexican-American Cultural Center." *American History TV-American Artifacts*. https://www.c-span.org/video/?302512-1/la-plaza-mexican-american -cultural-center&event=302512&playEvent.

Curiosity Show. "Swinging the Lead: What Does That Mean, and Why?" https://www .youtube.com/watch?v=_73VunCxE1U.

The Day. "Kevin Crandall Describes Surviving a Lightning Strike." https://www.youtube
.com/watch?v=iZh0QAUuUIs.

del Castillo, Richard Griswold. "The U.S.–Mexican War in San Diego, 1846–1847."
San Diego Historical Society Quarterly, vol. 49, no. 1 (Winter 2003). https://
sandiegohistory.org/journal/2003/january/war-2/.

Denton, Sally. *Passion and Principle: John and Jessie Frémont, the Couple Whose Power,
Politics, and Love Shaped Nineteenth-Century America.* New York: Bloomsbury
USA, 2007.

Destroyer History Foundation. "RADM. LA VALLETTE." *Find a Ship-Selected
Ships G-L-USS La Vallette DD 448.* https://destroyerhistory.org/fletcherclass/ns
_lavallette/index.asp?r=44800&pid=44801.

DeVoto, Bernard. *The Year of Decision: 1846.* Boston: Houghton Mifflin Company, 1984.

DiveViz. "Point Loma." *Boat Dives and Trips.* https://chris-cheezem-799y.squarespace
.com/point-loma.

Driver, Les. "Carrillo's Flying Artillery: The Battle of San Pedro." *California Historical
Society Quarterly* (December 1969). https://www.militarymuseum.org/Cabbrillo
.pdf.

Duvall, Eric. "A Page from History: Bouncing along the Old La Playa Trail." *Point Loma
and OB Monthly.* https://www.pointloma-obmonthly.com/news/story/2021-07-18
/a-page-from-history-bouncing-along-the-old-la-playa-trail.

Eisenhower, John S. D. *So Far from God: The U.S. War with Mexico, 1846–1848.* Norman: University of Oklahoma Press, 1989.

Emett, Mike. "Fort Guijarros and the Battle of San Diego." *Clio: Your Guide to History.*
April 3, 2017. https://www.theclio.com/entry/35766.

Eyerly-Webb, Stephanie A., Rachele Solomon, Seong K. Lee, Eddy H. Carrillo, Dafney
L. Davare, Chauniqua Kiffin, and Andrew Rosenthal. "Lightning Burns and Electrical Trauma in a Couple Simultaneously Struck by Lightning." *NIH National
Library of Medicine-National Center for Biotechnology Information.* https://www.ncbi
.nlm.nih.gov/pmc/articles/PMC5965181/.

Farris, Glenn J. "Captain Jose Panto and the San Pascual Indian Pueblo in San Diego
County, 1835–1878." *San Diego Historical Society Quarterly*, vol. 43, no. 2 (Spring
1997). https://sandiegohistory.org/journal/1997/april/panto/.

———. José Panto, *Capitan* of the Indian Pueblo of San Pascual, San Diego County."
Journal of California and Great Basin Anthropology, vol. 16, no. 2 (1994), 149–61.
https://escholarship.org/content/qt5ph0b0m3/qt5ph0b0m3_noSplash_f11e42056
3c8151b48db1bf492942697.pdf?t=krnqt6.

Federal Judicial Center. "Richard Law." *Judges.* https://www.fjc.gov/history/judges/law
-richard.

Find a Grave. "Capt Alanson Fournier." https://www.findagrave.com/memorial/34554183
/alanson-fournier.

Forst, Jay G. "Coronado: A Beginning." *Coronado Journal*, vol. 75, no. 14 (Thursday, April
3, 1986). https://cdnc.ucr.edu/?a=d&d=CJ19860403&e=-------en--20--1--txt
-txIN-coronado+journal+april+3%2c+1986-------.

Foster, John M., Leonard Pitt, and Edna E. Kimbro. *Second Addendum Report: Archaeological and Historic Investigations at Campo de Cahuenga, CA-LAN-1945H.* Pacific Palisades, CA: Greenwood and Associates, 2000.

Georgia Historical Society. "John C. Frémont." *Learn-Explore Georgia History-Featured Historical Figures.* https://georgiahistory.com/education-outreach/online-exhibits /featured-historical-figures/john-charles-fremont/first-and-second-expeditions/.

GlobalSecurity.org. "Sailing Ship Armament." https://www.globalsecurity.org/military/ systems/ship/sail-armament.htm.

Granson, Hilary. "How to Control Fleas in Your Pet." *TexVetPets.org.* https://www .texvetpets.org/article/fleas-never-ending-itch/.

Greenberg, Amy S. *A Wicked War: Polk, Clay, Lincoln, and the 1846 U.S. Invasion of Mexico.* New York: Vintage Books, 2012.

Guardino, Peter. *The Dead March: A History of the Mexican-American War.* Cambridge: Harvard University Press, 2017.

Guillow, Lawrence E. "Pandemonium in the Plaza: The First Los Angeles Riot, July 22, 1856." *Southern California Quarterly*, vol. 77, no. 3 (Fall 1995). https://inside.sfuhs .org/dept/history/US_History_reader/Chapter4/Guillowpandemonium.pdf.

Gyory, Joanna, Arthur J. Mariano, and Edward H. Ryan. "The Gulf Stream." *Ocean Surface Currents-Atlantic.* https://oceancurrents.rsmas.miami.edu/atlantic/gulf-stream .html.

Hamilton, Harlan. *Lights & Legends: A Historical Guide to Lighthouses of Long Island Sound, Fishers Island Sound and Block Island Sound.* Stamford, CT: Westcott Cove Publishing Company, 1987.

Harlow, Neal. *California Conquered: War and Peace on the Pacific, 1846–1850.* Berkeley: University of California Press, 1982.

Heinz, Sharon, ed. *Saddleback Ancestors: Rancho Families of Orange County, California*, rev. ed. Orange, CA: Orange County California Genealogical Society, 1998. https:// occgs.com/projects/saddleback/saddleback.html.

History.com Editors. "Route 66 Decertified, Highway Signs Removed." *History-A&E Television Networks.* https://www.history.com/this-day-in-history/route-66-decertified.

Howe, Daniel Walker. *What Hath God Wrought: The Transformation of America, 1815–1848.* New York: Oxford University Press, 2007.

Hughes, Charles W. *Albert B. Smith and the Americanization of San Diego, 1830–1869.* Oceanside, CA: California Department of Parks and Recreation, San Diego Coast District, 2012.

Hunt, Rockwell D. "John Bidwell: A Prince Among Pioneers." *Annual Publication of the Historical Society of Southern California*, vol. 10, no. 3 (1917): 48–56. https://doi.org /10.2307/41168744.

Huntington Library, Art Museum, and Botanical Garden. "General Andrés Pico." *Photographs.* https://hdl.huntington.org/digital/collection/p15150coll2/id/8071.

Hussey, John Adam. "The Origin of the Gillespie Mission." *California Historical Society Quarterly.* https://www.militarymuseum.org/OriginGillespieMission.pdf.

Inskeep, Steve. *Imperfect Union: How Jessie and John Frémont Mapped the West, Invented Celebrity, and Helped Cause the Civil War.* New York: Penguin Press, 2020.

KCET. "The Life and Times of Pío Pico, Last Governor of Mexican California." *Food and Discovery-Lost LA.* https://www.kcet.org/shows/lost-la/the-life-and-times-of -pio-pico-last-governor-of-mexican-california.

Larkin, Rita, ed. "Historic Landmarks of San Diego County." *San Diego Historical Society Quarterly*, vol. 14, no. 3 (July 1968). https://sandiegohistory.org/journal/1968/july /landmarks/.

Leavitt, John F. *The Charles W. Morgan.* Mystic, CT: Mystic Seaport Museum, 1998.

Martha's Vineyard Museum. *Laura Jernegan: Girl on a Whaleship.* girlonawhaleship.org.

Masterson, Rosemary. "The Machado-Silvas Family." *San Diego Historical Society Quarterly*, vol. 15, no. 1 (Winter 1969). https://sandiegohistory.org/journal/1969/ january/part4-2/.

Merry, Robert W. *A Country of Vast Designs: James K. Polk, the Mexican War, and the Conquest of the American Continent.* New York: Simon & Schuster Paperbacks, 2009.

Miller, Ronald L. "A California Romance in Perspective." *San Diego Historical Society Quarterly*, vol. 19, no. 2 (Spring 1973). https://sandiegohistory.org/journal/1973/ april/fitch-2/.

Miller, Todd. "Point Loma Kelp Dive." https://www.youtube.com/watch?v =Z0QfTDVH4XE.

Mills, James R. *San Diego: Where California Began.* San Diego: The Journal of San Diego History, 1960. https://sandiegohistory.org/journal/1960/january/where-california -began/.

Monfort, Grace. "Few Celebrate Where Many Once Feted San Diego Hero Who Spiked Guns." *San Diego Sun*, 1938. http://albertbsmith.blogspot.com/.

Museums of History NSW. "Loading and Firing the Flintlock Musket." https://www .youtube.com/watch?v=lfGOLqxcbIg.

National Environmental Satellite, Data, and Information Service. "The Gulf Stream Seen through Sea Surface Temperature." https://www.nesdis.noaa.gov/news/the-gulf -stream-seen-through-sea-surface-temperature.

National Park Service. "Estudillo House, San Diego, California." *American Latino Heritage.* https://www.nps.gov/nr/travel/american_latino_heritage/estudillo_house .html.

———. "San Diego Mission Church (San Diego de Alcala.)" *Early History of the California Coast.* https://www.nps.gov/nr/travel/ca/ca3.htm#:~:text=The%20mission %20was%20founded%20in,fourth%20constructed%20at%20the%20site.

Naval History and Heritage Command. "*Congress IV* (Frigate.)" *Boats–Ships–Frigate: Ship History.* https://www.history.navy.mil/research/histories/ship-histories/danfs/c/ congress-iv.html.

———. "*Cyane II* (Sloop)." *DANFS-M.* https://www.history.navy.mil/research/histories/ ship-histories/danfs/c/cyane-sloop-ii.html.

———. "*Malek Adhel.*" *DANFS-M.* https://www.history.navy.mil/content/history/nhhc/ research/histories/ship-histories/danfs/m/malek-adhel.html.

———. "Stockton, Robert F." *Photography-US People-S.* https://www.history.navy.mil/ content/history/nhhc/our-collections/photography/us-people/s/stockton-robert-f .html.

———. "Uniforms of the U.S. Navy, 1830–1841." *Heritage—Uniforms*. https://www
.history.navy.mil/browse-by-topic/heritage/uniforms-and-personal-equipment/
uniforms-1830-1841.html.

New Bedford Whaling Museum. "Life Aboard." *Learn-Whaling History*. https://www
.whalingmuseum.org/learn/research-topics/whaling-history/life-aboard/.

———. "Whales and Hunting." *Learn-Whaling History*. https://www.whalingmuseum
.org/learn/research-topics/whaling-history/whales-and-hunting/.

———. "Whaling Crew List Database." *List View-168*. https://www.whalingmuseum
.org/online_exhibits/crewlist/listview.php?reverse=ASC&order_by=name&term=
&page=168.

Oceanwide Expeditions. "What to Expect When Crossing the Drake Passage." *Resources-Stories-Blog*. https://oceanwide-expeditions.com/blog/the-wild-drake-passage.

Off Grid with Doug & Stacy. "Lamb Birth from Start to Finish: Off-Grid Homesteading." https://www.youtube.com/watch?v=s5GTuLJgr0k.

Ogden, Adele. "Captain Henry Fitch, San Diego Merchant, 1825–1849." *San Diego
Historical Society Quarterly*, vol. 27, no. 4 (Fall 1981). https://sandiegohistory.org/
journal/1981/october/fitch/.

Oliver Hazard Perry Rhode Island. "ASK US ANY-
THING: Finding Water Depth! Soundings, Lead Lines, Fathoms, and More!"
https://www.youtube.com/watch?v=gCSQCuGnpYY.

Online Archive of California. "R. C. Duvall Journal and Log of U.S. Frigate
Savannah: And Other Material, 1845–1847." https://oac.cdlib.org/search?group
=Items;idT=UCb182960870.

Perkins, Arthur B. "Rancho San Francisco: A Study of a California Land Grant." *The
Historical Society of Southern California Quarterly* (June 1957). https://scvhistory
.com/scvhistory/perkins-rsf-1957.htm

Pourade, Richard F. *History of San Diego, Volume 3: The Silver Dons, 1833–1865*. San Diego
History Center, https://sandiegohistory.org/archives/books/dons/ch5/.

Rancho Carrillo Community. "Leo Carrillo." *More-History-Leo Carrillo*. https://www
.ranchocarrillo.com/history/leo-carrillo.

Rancho Guejito Vineyard. "Rancho Guejito Vineyard." https://www.ranchoguejitovineyard
.com/.

Rediker, Marcus. *The Amistad Rebellion: An Atlantic Odyssey of Slavery and Freedom*. New
York: Viking, 2012.

Roberts, David. *A Newer World: Kit Carson, John C. Frémont, and the Claiming of the American West*. New York: Simon & Schuster, 2000.

Rogers, Fred B. *Bear Flag Lieutenant: The Life Story of Henry L. Ford (1822–1860),
with Some Related and Contemporary Art of Alexander Edouart*. http://www
.militarymuseum.org/Ford.pdf.

Royce, Josiah. *California: From the Conquest in 1846 to the Second Vigilance Committee in
San Francisco*. Boston: Houghton Mifflin Company, 1914.

San Fernando Valley Historical Society. "Andrés Pico." *Andrés Pico Adobe*. https://sfvhs
.com/andres-pico/.

San Pasqual Battlefield State Historic Park. "The Battle of San Pasqual." *San Pasqual Battlefield State Historic Park: Virtual Battle Day Event 2020.* https://youtu.be/ijsOf1kmFVU.

Santelli, Gabrielle M. Neufeld. *Marines in the Mexican War.* Washington, DC: History and Museums Division Headquarters, US Marine Corps, 1991.

Savannah (ship, 1842). Wikimedia Commons. https://commons.wikimedia.org/wiki/Category:Savannah_(ship,_1842).

Sheringham Shantymen. "Pump Shanty." *Songs for Seafarers.* https://www.youtube.com/watch?v=oK6uruj2ab0.

Simon, Ken. *The Mark of Uncas.* SimonPure Media, 2002. https://www.youtube.com/watch?v=ohDSVulkCWY.

SJPL California Room Collections. "1850 Portrait of Major Samuel J. Hensley." *Historic Photograph Collection (SJPL California Room).* https://digitalcollections.sjlibrary.org/digital/collection/arbuckle/id/368.

Smith Official DNA & One Name Study. "Albert Benjamin Smith." https://www.smithsworldwide.org/tng/getperson.php?personID=I91998&tree=tree1.

Smythe, William E. *History of San Diego: 1542–1907.* San Diego: The History Company, 1907.

Social History Curators Group. "Tools of the Trade: The Cooper, Part 1: Dressing the Staves." https://www.youtube.com/watch?v=DJNzkojcqeg.

———. "Tools of the Trade: The Cooper, Part 2: Raising the Cask." https://www.youtube.com/watch?v=8mWX3tRvTcE.

———. "Tools of the Trade: The Cooper, Part 3: Chiming the Cask." https://www.youtube.com/watch?v=b3yLUWRWo3s&t=20s.

———. "Tools of the Trade: The Cooper, Part 4: Hooping." https://www.youtube.com/watch?v=PSih1yR_BSs&t=156s.

Spitzzeri, Paul. "The Los Angeles Jail and the 1860 Census." *Trembling on the Brink: Crime and Justice in Los Angeles, 1850–1875.* http://tremblingonthebrink.blogspot.com/2016/10/the-los-angeles-jail-and-1860-census.html.

Stevens, Robert White. *On the Stowage of Ships and Their Cargoes.* Plymouth, England: Stevens, 1858.

Taylor, Mendell Lee. "The Western Services of Stephen Watts Kearny, 1815–1848." *New Mexico Historical Review,* vol. 21, no. 3 (1946). https://digitalrepository.unm.edu/nmhr/vol21/iss3/2.

Thompson, Gerald. *Edward Beale & The American West.* Albuquerque: University of New Mexico Press, 1983.

Tracy Family History. "The Bear Flag Revolt." http://www.thetracyfamilyhistory.net/C%202%202%20%20Bear%20Flag%20Revolt.htm.

Traditional. "Haul Away Joe." United States Navy Band. https://www.youtube.com/watch?v=-emxN-PEKiA.

Traub, James. *John Quincy Adams: Militant Spirit.* New York: Basic Books, 2016.

US House of Representatives: History, Art & Architecture. "Richard Law." *People,* https://history.house.gov/People/Listing/L/LAW,-Richard-(L000127)/.

University of Southern California Libraries and California Historical Society. "Portrait of Don Miguel de Pedrorena." https://digitallibrary.usc.edu/asset-management /2A3BF1I77RR?FR_=1&W=1280&H=625.

Utah State Historical Society. "John Charles Fremont." *History to Go.* https://historytogo .utah.gov/fremont-john/.

Walker, Dale L. *Bear Flag Rising: The Conquest of California, 1846.* New York: Tom Doherty Associates, LLC, 1999.

Walsh, Victor. "The Machado Sisters: The Californianas of Old Town, San Diego." CA.GOV. https://www.parks.ca.gov/pages/663/files/MachadoSistersOfOldTown _ADA-Compliant_20191204.pdf.

Wander. "Travel to Talcahuano." *Destinations-Talcahuano.* https://www.wander.am/travel /talcahuano-82031.

Watson, Harry L. *Andrew Jackson vs. Henry Clay: Democracy and Development in Antebellum America.* Boston: Bedford/St. Martin's, 1998.

Webster, Ian. "$1 in 1846 ⊠ 2023 | Inflation Calculator." *Official Inflation Data, Alioth Finance.* https://www.officialdata.org/us/inflation/1846?amount=1.

Wellcome Collection. "Mahogany Medicine Chest, England, 1801–1900." *Science Museum, London. Attribution 4.0 International (CC BY 4.0).* https://wellcomecollection.org/ works/ysz9yw4d.

Wikimedia Commons contributors. "File:1857 U.S.C.S. Map of San Diego Bay, California -Geographicus - SanDiegoBay-uscs-1857.jpg," *Wikimedia Commons.* https: //commons.wikimedia.org/w/index.php?title=File:1857_U.S.C.S._Map_of_San _Diego_Bay,_California_-_Geographicus_-_SanDiegoBay-uscs-1857.jpg&oldid =745852967.

Wilentz, Sean. *The Rise of American Democracy: Jefferson to Lincoln.* New York: W. W. Norton & Company, 2005.

Willey, H. I. "Report of the Surveyor-General of the State of California from August 1, 1884, to August 1, 1886." Sacramento: Sacramento State Office, 1886. http://www .slc.ca.gov/wp-content/uploads/2018/08/Willey_1884_1886.pdf.

Winkle, Curtis. "A Short History of Oil: 1700–1870." *Trainings & Demos.* https://kimray .com/training/short-history-oil-1700-1870#:~:text=1846%3A%20Kerosene%20in %20Canada&text=This%20new%20discovery%20burned%20more,per%20gallon %20for%20whale%20oil.

Zane, Thomas L., ed. "Whalers Out of Mystic." *Collections & Research.* https://research .mysticseaport.org/info/ib69-3/.

Index

and, 250–51; leaving Hamley at San Blas, 244; lightning strike incident, 264–65; as master of the *Stonington*, 164; Maynard and, 147–48, 150–51, 160; Mayors and, 6; McDonnald and, 88; Merritt and, 48, 73–74; Milnor and, 60–61, 65–66, 144–45, 189–190, 211–12, 238–39, 255–56; Minor and, 108–9, 135, 136; post voyage, 288; readying ship for sea, 57; Rice and, 19–21, 216; at San Blas, 241–44; San Diego townsfolk passengers and, 57, 66–67; securing captured crew's belongings, 245; setting course for Monterey, 16–17; setting course for San Diego, 19; setting sail for Callao, 244; as temporary captain, 195, 209; Thompson and, 10–11, 143–44; updating passengers on progress, 222–24; Watson and, 218–19

Franciscan missions, 114

Frank, Joseph, 22–23, 122–23, 265, 272

Freeman, Jason, 118–19, 163–64, 192–93

Frémont, John C. "The Pathfinder": California assignment, 32, 39; Californio forces battling, 204; Castro confronting, 33–34; Gillespie

catching up with, 33; Hamley and, 198–99, 202; heading for Los Angeles, 38; post war, 288; at Rancho San Francisco, 200–202; Stockton and, 134, 201–2; at Sutter Buttes, 35

gale-force winds, 120, 222, 234, 249, 252, 260–62, 282

George Island, 261

Gillespie, Archibald H.: attacking Varela's men, 141; on board USS *Congress*, 129; Californio forces joining, 45; Frémont and, 33; joining forces with Kearny, 168; Larkins and, 33; at Los Angeles, 208; Mervine and, 72; Minor's report to, 130; organizing revolt, 45; Polk's mission for, 32; post war, 288; at San Pasqual Valley battle, 168; Stockton and, 46; Varela's assault on, 45

Gray, Andrew F. V., 170

Great Britain, 12

Grigsby, John, 36

Gulf of Alaska, 3

Gulf Stream, 281

Hamley, George W.: addressing the crew, 229–230; Anthony and, 25–26, 109; arrest in San Blas, 242; Carrillo and, 51; on crews' liberty ashore, 9; Duvall and, 92–93; at Ensenada,

137–38, 234; Fitch and, 43–44; Fournier and (*See* Hamley-Fournier exchange); Frémont and, 198–202; at Frémont's camp, 207; Hensley and, 154–55, 158; march to San Diego, 79; Mayors and, 5–6; Merritt and, 48–49, 51–52, 69, 83–85; Minor and, 116; monitoring *Stonington* transformation, 63; no longer in complete control of his ship, 69–70; order to clear storage area, 2; overseeing ship's maintenance, 109–10; Pedrorena and, 83; post arrest, 288–89; return as captain, 225; sailing skills, 24; at San Blas, 241–42; San Diego chief's request for protection by, 42–44; Simmons and, 99; welcoming *Magnolia* reinforcements, 98–99; whale sighting, 17

Hamley-Fournier exchange: on bilge levels, 235; on crew's return from liberty, 188–89; Ensenada excursion, 158–160; on food supplies, 104–5; on Fournier as temporary captain, 195; on granting crew liberty, 171–72, 236; on Hamley's return, 225–26; on Mayors' leaving, 6; on readying ship for hunting expedition, 135; on readying ship for sea, 231–32;

on rudder head issue, 15, 135–36, 142; at San Blas, 241; setting course for San Diego, 19; on ship's condition, 67–68; on ship's discharge from Navy service, 229; on Stockton's leaving San Diego, 134; on Stockton's orders, 146–47, 150; on taking on passengers, 236–37; on Thompson and Bedrake desertion, 9–10; on transformation to a naval warship, 59; updates on Hamley's assignment, 198–99; on US government commandeering the ship, 52–53

Harry, William, 62, 160–62, 173, 212–13, 229

Hensley, Samuel J., 154–55, 158, 162, 204–5

Holden, James, 50, 64, 85, 98, 119

Hopkins, George, 26, 192–93, 274–77, 279, 285

Ide, William, 35, 36

Indigenous people, 113–14

Islas Coronado. *See* Coronado Islands

Islas de Todos Santos, 137

Islas Marías archipelago, 241

Itata River, 252

Jackson, Andrew, 204

Frank and, 22–23, 122–23;
horseback riding, 180–86; on
hunting expedition, 105–7; at
liberty, 174, 176–79; lightning
strike incident, 263–65;
mainsail maintenance, 110;
McDonnald and, 21–22, 47,
88–91, 136–37, 174, 242–43,
266–270; resuming his duties,
271; on ship's discharge
from Navy service, 229–230;
signaling the troops, 216; as
stowaway, 19–21; transporting
sheep, 121–23
Rico, Francisco, 46
Rogers, Antone, 236, 241–42
rudder issues and repairs, 15–16,
135–36, 142–45, 146

San Blas, 236, 238, 241–44, 250
San Diego: Californio forces
siege on, 58–59, 113; citizens
of (*See* San Diego townsfolk);
Coronado Island, 102–3;
Coronado Islands, 115–16,
157, 164; customs collector
for, 50–51; False Bay, 28–29,
181–82; Fort Guijarros, 101,
104; Fort Stockton, 147–153;
harbor, 29; La Playa Trail to,
30; map of, 159; Merritt's
march to, 78–81; missions, 13;
navy reinforcements arrival,
99–101; plan to retake, 75–77;
Point Loma, 29, 70, 101,

180–86; Presidio Hill, 87, 95;
US occupation of, 38; *See also*
Fitch, Henry Delano
San Diego townsfolk: boarding
Stonington, 57–58; Fitch, Henry
Delano (*See* Fitch, Henry
Delano); Fournier addressing,
66–67; generosity/gratitude
of, 144, 177–79; Merritt
addressing, 74–75; Varela's
harassment campaign on,
87–88
San Fernando Valley, 204
San Francisco, 3–4, 7–9
San Gabriel River, 204–5
San José del Cabo, 235–36
San Pasqual Valley battle, 167–70
San Pedro, 64, 85–86, 92–94, 209,
215–16
San Ramon excursion, 154–56,
157–58
Santa Catalina Island, 19
Santa Cruz, 19
Santa Fé, 167–68, 170
Santa Ysabel, 168
secularization process, 114
Selden, Samuel, 168
sheep operation, 117–24
Simmons, Bezer, 99, 102–3
Sloat, John D., 37–38, 129
Slocum, Samuel, 258, 275
Smith, Albert, 75–77, 81, 289
"smoke out" the *Stonington*,
257–58
Sonoma, 35–36